Six Steps to Successful
Child Advocacy

For the children around the world who have been our inspiration,
the colleagues who have been our partners in creating change
for children, and our families who have provided steadfast support.

Six Steps to Successful Child Advocacy

Changing the World for Children

Amy Conley Wright

San Francisco State University

Kenneth J. Jaffe

International Child Resource Institute

Los Angeles | London | New Delhi
Singapore | Washington DC

Los Angeles | London | New Delhi
Singapore | Washington DC

FOR INFORMATION:

SAGE Publications, Inc.
2455 Teller Road
Thousand Oaks, California 91320
E-mail: order@sagepub.com

SAGE Publications Ltd.
1 Oliver's Yard
55 City Road
London EC1Y 1SP
United Kingdom

SAGE Publications India Pvt. Ltd.
B 1/I 1 Mohan Cooperative Industrial Area
Mathura Road, New Delhi 110 044
India

SAGE Publications Asia-Pacific Pte. Ltd.
3 Church Street
#10-04 Samsung Hub
Singapore 049483

Acquisitions Editor: Kassie Graves
Editorial Assistant: Elizabeth Luizzi
Production Editor: Brittany Bauhaus
Copy Editor: Beth Hammond
Typesetter: C&M Digitals (P) Ltd.
Proofreader: Scott Oney
Indexer: Marilyn Augst
Cover Designer: Candice Harman
Marketing Manager: Shari Countryman

Copyright © 2014 by SAGE Publications, Inc.

Printed in the United States of America

Library of Congress Cataloging-in-Publication Data

Wright, Amy Conley.
Six steps to successful child advocacy : changing the world for children / Amy Conley Wright, San Francisco State University, Kenneth J. Jaffe, International Child Resource Institute.

pages cm
Includes bibliographical references and index.

ISBN 978-1-4522-6094-5 (pbk. : alk. paper)
ISBN 978-1-4833-1216-3 (web pdf)
ISBN 978-1-4833-2323-7 (epub)

1. Children's rights. 2. Child welfare. 3. Children—Social conditions. 4. Children—Services for. I. Jaffe, Kenneth J. II. Title.

HQ789.W73 2013
362.70973—dc23   2013031337

This book is printed on acid-free paper.

13 14 15 16 17 10 9 8 7 6 5 4 3 2 1

Brief Contents

Detailed Contents

Acknowledgments

A book, like an advocacy project, benefits from the support of allies. We would like to express our appreciation to those who have supported the writing of this book.

Child advocates from around the world have contributed their wisdom and experience to enhancing the book. Our appreciation and admiration go to Alejandro Acosta Ayerbe, Caius Brandão, Margaret Brodkin, Maysoun Chehab, Radziah Daud, Dr. Jane Goodall, Maggie Kamau-Biruri, Datin Paduka Seri Rosmah Mansor, Vijaya Murthy, Kerstin Nash, Bonnie and Roger Neugebauer, Dr. Alan Pence, Liew Sau Pheng, Evelyn Quartey-Papafio, Deepak Raj Sapkota, Traci Siegel, and Dr. Sarah Taylor.

Ken Jaffe developed the six steps to successful child advocacy over the course of 30 years of training child advocates. This approach to advocacy has continued to develop based on feedback from their experiences. He has worked with grassroots organizations and national governments to try to change the world for children, including the Sonoma County California Child Care Planning Council, National Movement of Street Children in Brazil, Fundación Paniamor in Costa Rica, the National Child and Family Institute of Ecuador, National Association of Early Childhood Care and Education Malaysia, and many more. The joy of hearing about advocacy successes from those who have been trained provides encouragement for those of us in the field to continue our work.

Amy Conley Wright has been teaching a community service learning course on child advocacy for the past 3 years, in collaboration with the Children's Defense Fund California; Coleman Advocates for Children and Youth; Fight Crime, Invest in Kids; International Child Resource Institute; Parents for Public Schools; Parent Services Project; United Way of the Bay Area; and W. Haywood Burns Institute. The process of training undergraduate students to become child advocates for life has helped to inform the content of this book. Two examples of applied advocacy in the text are drawn from student work.

San Francisco State University provided Amy with a research and writing leave through the Presidential Award for Professional Development of Probationary Faculty. Thanks in particular to Dr. Rene Dahl for her ongoing support and for reviewing initial book materials. Erin O'Donohue and Dr. Sheldon Gen also provided valuable feedback on the book proposal. Amy also thanks James Midgley for mentoring on book development and referral to SAGE.

The International Child Resource Institute family has been supportive and encouraging of this book effort. Thanks in particular to Ambri Pukhraj, ICRI Operations and Programs Manager, for her assistance with contacting contributors and assisting with the book production process.

Our own families have also supported us as we developed the book. Ken is grateful to Ellen and their children, Michael and Laura. His children provide constant inspiration in his work and make him feel like the luckiest father in the world. Amy thanks her husband, Andrew, and parents, Megan and Donald, for their continual love and encouragement, and her newborn son, Henry, for being a reminder about the importance of child advocacy.

We appreciate the fine work of SAGE in bringing this book to publication. Kassie Graves, Senior Acquisitions Editor, expressed interest in the initial proposal and worked with us to improve the book project through gathering multidisciplinary reviews. Elizabeth Luizzi provided excellent help as Editorial Assistant. We are grateful to Beth Hammond for her careful work as Copy Editor and Brittany Bauhaus for oversight as Production Editor.

Amy Conley Wright
San Francisco State University

Kenneth J. Jaffe
International Child Resource Institute

Foreword

By Dr. Jane Goodall

Since 1986, I have spent roughly 300 days a year travelling around the world trying to raise awareness about some of the grim environmental issues facing our world today. They are many and interconnected. And they affect us all, especially the most vulnerable—young children. Some of the more obvious threats to our future are from deforestation (leading to soil erosion and often desertification as well as releasing CO^2 into the atmosphere); shrinking freshwater supplies; pollution of land, water, and air (through industrial, agricultural, and household emissions); depletion of fish stocks due to overfishing in increasingly polluted water; and increasing CO^2 emissions from our reckless burning of fossil fuels. CO^2 and methane contribute significantly to the so-called greenhouse gases that result in global warming and climate change. Methane is released as the permafrost melts. It is also produced in increasing quantities as a result of intensive farming of animals as more and more people eat more and more meat. And all of the above lead to the loss of biodiversity—the many life forms that have evolved into a complex and interrelated web of life that maintains the health of a given ecosystem. These factors have led to an environment in which the threats to human health, particularly children's health, seem to be accelerating.

Over and above all of this are the many social problems that threaten not only children's health but their very lives. Poverty leading to malnourishment and a weakened immune system; child abuse, often the result of dysfunctional families; alcohol and/or drug abuse by the parents; unwanted pregnancies; child trafficking whereby children are sold or abducted for slave labor, prostitution, or as child soldiers. Diseases caused, or possibly caused, by increased use of chemical pesticides and fertilizers and fungicides in industrial agriculture, urban gardening, and golf courses. Welfare systems that put children into foster homes where, only too often, they are neglected or abused. There are unacceptable levels of bullying in many schools, and many children are caught up in gang culture. Moreover, even in developed countries, early childhood education programs are so often among the first to suffer from cuts in government spending.

All of this means that thousands of children worldwide are deprived of a good start in life. This is a tragedy, as there is much evidence pointing to the tremendous value of positive experience in early childhood, especially during the first 2 years of life. Young children who grow up surrounded by stable loving relationships, learning by example, and through imaginative unstructured play, are more likely to be successful later in life.

I feel particularly strongly about this as a result of our long-term study of chimpanzees (over 50 years), our closest living relatives. Their DNA differs from ours by only just over one percent. The anatomy of the chimpanzee and human brain is almost the same—ours is just bigger—and chimpanzees are capable of many intellectual performances once thought unique to us. And there are similarities too in many aspects of behavior. Like us, chimpanzees kiss, embrace, pat one another in reassurance, beg for food or comfort with outstretched hand, swagger or shake the fist in threat, and are capable of brutality and violence on the one hand, compassion and true altruism on the other (as when a nonfamily member adopts an orphan).

Of particular relevance here are findings on the importance of early experience, especially the type of mothering and structure of the family, in shaping subsequent adult behavior. Thus, an infant with a good mother—affectionate, protective but not overprotective, tolerant but able to impose discipline, and above all supportive and willing to risk being beaten up by a more dominant individual in order to rescue the child if he or she gets into social difficulties—is more likely to be a confident and assertive adult and will probably rise to a relatively high social rank. The male can then potentially sire more offspring and the female will be a more successful mother. As far back as the mid-1960s, child psychiatrists John Bowlby and Rene Spitz were interested in this aspect of chimpanzee behavior since it supported their conclusions about the importance of early experience in shaping adult behavior in our own species.

This is why, when I began Jane Goodall's Roots & Shoots in 1991, I was anxious to involve young children. The program is now in more than 130 countries with members of all ages from preschool through university and beyond. And increasingly we are involving family members and communities.

I started Roots & Shoots (R&S) because as I traveled around the world, I met many young people—high school and college students especially—who seemed to have lost hope for the future. Some were apathetic, not seeming to care about anything except themselves. Some were depressed. Some were angry, even violent. When I talked with them, they told me that this was because we had compromised their future and there was nothing they could do about it.

Without doubt we have compromised their future. I look at small children and think how we have damaged the planet since I was their age, and I feel ashamed and angry. I often hear people quoting, "We have not inherited this planet from our parents, we have borrowed it from our children." But this is no longer true. We have not borrowed their future, we have *stolen* it.

But I do not believe it is too late to turn things around. The core message of Roots & Shoots is that every individual matters and makes a difference—every day. Each group choses three projects to make the world a better place: one for people, one for animals, and one for the environment. Running throughout Roots & Shoots is the theme of learning to live in harmony not only with each other—with different cultures, religions, and nations—but also with the natural world on which we depend for our survival.

Projects undertaken by R&S groups around the globe, by children of different ages in different situations, are many and varied. Let me give an example. In 2004, a Roots & Shoots group was started in the Sokoine primary school in the Kigoma region near the border of Gombe National Park in Tanzania. This school, though poor in terms of material possessions, has extensive land where many trees from the original forest still remain. Thanks to a far-sighted headmaster, the Roots & Shoots group began a project to learn about their forest, to protect the trees that were there, and to start a tree nursery with indigenous seedlings to restore areas where the original tree cover had been destroyed. Today the forest has recovered to a large extent—so much so that the school has been given a small grant for further work by an organization interested in carbon trading. Smita Dharsi, a teacher at a primary school in New Jersey, started a Roots & Shoots group there. She had moved to the United States as a child but had spent her early years in Kigoma and wanted to do something to help the children there. The members of her New Jersey Roots & Shoots group helped to raise money for the purchase of laptop computers for Roots & Shoots members of the Sokoine school. The two groups are now linked electronically and learn about and from each other.

Cross-cultural learning of this sort is very beneficial for fostering world citizens of the future who care about each other through understanding and have learned to take action to help each other. They learn that the problems suffered due to rural poverty in the developing world are very different from those suffered by children in deprived areas of the developed world.

I first met Ken Jaffe in 1997. When he told me about the International Child Resource Institute, it was immediately clear, to both of us, that some collaboration between our organizations would be beneficial since we both understand the importance of early childhood experience and we both believe in the importance of working not only with the child but with the family and the community. I was very impressed with the major success of Ken's program in different countries and the improvements in the lives of both child and family that could be demonstrated.

In the natural world, about which I know more, all life forms in a given ecosystem are interrelated, each depending on the others to create a healthy environment. The same is true in human societies. There can be little point in offering a child a marvelous early experience in school if the child must go back to a dysfunctional family. And working to improve things for one family is equally pointless if efforts are not also made to improve the situation if that family is part of a violent or depressed society. Yet no one organization can do everything.

This book provides a simple and clear step-by-step approach to helping people around the world make the lives of children healthier and happier everywhere. The authors and I share a passionate belief in the importance of forming collaborations between organizations working to improve conditions for youth. We must work with volunteers, parents, social workers, teachers, and community leaders to improve the condition of the entire community.

Preface

A CALL TO ADVOCACY

The present moment is one that demands advocacy on behalf of children. Children are facing major challenges around the world resulting from economic recession, globalization, war, and other issues. Since the global financial crisis of 2007–2008, economic problems have pushed more families into poverty and created a challenging future for youth seeking independence. In the name of fiscal austerity, budget cuts have sliced apart social safety nets intended to meet basic needs. These conditions have incited fears of a lost generation, with children exposed to a toxic mix of poverty, poorer quality services, and reduced opportunities.

The reality is that the world cannot afford a lost generation. Children's early experiences establish the foundation for their life courses and influence whether they will make contributions or become drains to their societies. During these years, as children are dependent on adults, they are especially vulnerable to risks such as poverty, poor nutrition, violence, and inadequate care. Because of their need for services such as education and health care in order to thrive, they are also disproportionally impacted by the actions or inactions of government.

Children need champions—people who care about them and are willing to fight on their behalf. Child advocates are people who speak up and speak out on behalf of children, whether it is an individual child, a group of children within a community, or a category of children affected by a social problem. Choosing to become a child advocate means making a passionate commitment to children and translating it into action. This book will prepare people willing to be champions for children to become skilled advocates acting on their behalf.

ABOUT THE AUTHORS

Six Steps to Successful Child Advocacy: Changing the World for Children emerged from the authors' recognition of the need for a comprehensive and methodical approach to child advocacy. Amy Conley Wright teaches an undergraduate course in child advocacy at San Francisco State University and conducts research on child advocacy. From more than 30 years of applied advocacy work and trainings, Ken Jaffe has distilled the process of child advocacy into a series of six steps that build on each other in a logical sequence. Combining their experience and expertise, this book emphasizes advocacy as a systematic process and cultivates the skills necessary to conduct each step of an advocacy plan.

Amy Conley Wright (MSW, PhD, University of California, Berkeley) is an Assistant Professor of Child and Adolescent Development at San Francisco State University. Her teaching, research, and practice experiences are in the areas of child advocacy, child and family policy, family support, and child maltreatment prevention, both domestically and internationally. From 2000 to 2001, she was the director of Romanian Children's Relief, where she managed three programs in hospitals and orphanages that promoted children's healthy development in institutional settings and transition to foster care. She has published a number of peer-reviewed articles in national and international journals, on the topics of birth parent peer support, child maltreatment prevention, child care as a social investment, and strategies for policy advocacy. With James Midgley, she is the coeditor of *Developmental Social Work: Investment Strategies and Professional Practice*, translated into Japanese, Korean, and Mandarin. Her current research focuses on policy advocacy by nonprofit organizations and advocacy by parents of children with special needs. She is a board member of the International Child Resource Institute, advisory board member of Romanian Children's Relief, and frequently provides consultation to community organizations.

Kenneth J. Jaffe (MA, University of California, Berkeley; JD, John F. Kennedy University College of Law) developed the six steps to successful child advocacy and has implemented them in more than 40 countries. He is the Executive Director of the International Child Resource Institute (ICRI), which he founded in 1981. ICRI is a nonprofit organization committed to improving the lives of children and families throughout the world through technical assistance and consultation, resource dissemination, and the establishment of model projects. ICRI has now worked in 57 countries on projects serving children and families. Ken currently oversees ICRI offices in Kenya, Ghana, Zimbabwe, Malaysia, India, Nepal, and Sweden and 10 project sites in the United States. He is the author of numerous articles on making change for children and coauthored the book *Straw Into Gold*, translated into Haitian Creole, Nepali, and the Ga dialect of Ghana. He has chaired numerous commissions and planning bodies worldwide, including the California Governor's Advisory Committee on Child Development, and was a founding member of the World Forum on Early Care and Education. He has improved more than 400 children's programs worldwide and has advised the governments of 15 countries on child and family policy. He has presented hundreds of seminars and keynotes to audiences of students, national leaders, and professionals worldwide and has lectured at universities around the world.

OVERVIEW OF THE BOOK

This book presents a series of six steps to achieve positive change for children. Along the way, the book identifies and cultivates key skills needed to carry out successful advocacy, including planning, research, and persuasive communication. Advocacy examples and words of wisdom from noted international child advocates are included throughout the book to illustrate concepts. Each chapter concludes with a suggested activity to aid readers in meeting their advocacy goals. Readers who complete each chapter activity will have an advocacy plan and tools for an advocacy campaign by the end of the book. The book is divided into three parts with a total of 10 chapters.

The first part of the book consists of three chapters that provide an overview of child advocacy and why individuals and organizations may choose to engage in advocacy. Chapter 1 offers an introduction to child advocacy, discusses why children are in special need of advocacy, and presents theoretical frameworks to guide the work of child advocacy. Chapter 2 describes the parameters of child advocacy and introduces key concepts like the levels of advocacy and the roles of allies, gatekeepers, and decision makers that are explored in depth throughout the book. Chapter 3 highlights the importance of formulating an advocacy plan and provides a detailed overview of the six steps approach.

The second part of the book lays out the six steps of successful child advocacy. Chapters 4 and 5 prepare readers to better understand their advocacy issues and conduct research for background and impact. Chapter 6 guides readers to prepare effective materials, using methods of persuasion and various mediums to spread their messages. Chapters 7 and 8 explain how to organize meetings that work with decision makers and the gatekeepers who may control access to them and how to conduct strategic follow-up with decision makers and fellow advocates. Chapter 9 describes methods to reinforce advocacy successes through recognition of key supporters and how to use monitoring and evaluation for accountability and learning from successes and failures.

The third part of the book consists of Chapter 10, which encourages readers to become lifelong advocates for children and develop partnerships with child advocacy organizations to advance a long-term advocacy agenda.

CHAPTER 1

Introduction

In rural Zimbabwe, young children are often raised by their siblings due to the death of their parents from the HIV/AIDS epidemic ravaging the country. These young children often miss out on the stimulation and care they need while their siblings supervise them rather than attend school. In 2007, the International Child Resource Institute (ICRI) was invited by the Women's University in Africa to build a child care center at a primary school site on their rural campus in Murambinda. At first, the child care center functioned in a tiny cottage overrun by rats, with more than 60 children napping on concrete floors without blankets. From these meager beginnings, ICRI child advocates worked with the community to design and build a child care center with bricks handcrafted out of the local adobe soil by village volunteers. Staff were carefully trained on developmentally appropriate care and education of young children, and the center was designed to stimulate all domains of children's development, using locally made materials and found objects. National media covered the grand opening, which helped to elevate respect for the preschool teachers and awareness of the center as a national model early childhood care and health program and training center for early childhood educators.

On the other side of the world, in Brazil, street children in the 1990s were routinely "disappeared" by off-duty police and soldiers employed by businessmen to clear them off the streets near their businesses and presumably kill them with total impunity from prosecution. The National Movement for the Street Children of Brazil (Movimiento) invited ICRI to collaborate on developing advocacy strategies and bringing international attention to this issue. Advocates collected stories from street children about their lives, finding that many were not orphans, but instead came from poor homes with parents who could not afford to care for them. An international letter-writing campaign was launched that intensified after the Candelária massacre, when a group of men including off-duty police officers opened fire on children sleeping in the courtyard of a church, killing eight of them and wounding many more. In response, Movimiento organized street children around the country and brought them to Brasilia (the capital of Brazil) to occupy the national capitol building while the legislators were out at lunch. The international and national attention from these events prompted a national educational campaign about street children and a number of prosecutions with a drop ever since in the number of disappearances.

1

Elsewhere in Latin America, the nation of Chile in the 1990s had an unacknowledged problem with various forms of child abuse, including sexual abuse. Initially, officials denied that sexual abuse existed in Chile, pointing to their tradition of Catholicism and refusing to admit that such a thing could happen in their country. ICRI was invited by the Ministry of Justice to conduct the first trainings of staff across the country at their programs for abused and neglected children. Training included detection and treatment of child sexual abuse for psychologists and methods for investigation and prosecution of perpetrators for judges and lawyers. After the first year of training, a scandal occurred when news broke of government officials' involvement with a child prostitution ring. National outrage prompted attention to child abuse and neglect, and the national government expanded the number of child abuse and neglect centers around the country. ICRI provided assistance to the national government in its effort to improve enforcement of their laws on child sexual abuse through prevention, treatment, and legal action. Teachers and program leaders were given information on the psychological impacts of child maltreatment and provided with intervention strategies to help children and their families.

Shifting to Nepal, a national law passed in 2000 mandated that children could no longer accompany their parents who were sent to prison. As a result, many children were living on the streets or under inadequate care, leaving them vulnerable and at great risk. During this period, there was a rapid increase in the development of group homes for the children of prisoners. The Central Child Welfare Board of the Nepali government asked ICRI to facilitate the establishment of a national coalition of organizations working with children of prisoners. These organizations were in competition for limited funds from the government and international donors, which created conflict. ICRI leadership organized a meeting to encourage 20 disparate children of prisoners groups to recognize that it was in their enlightened self-interest to join forces and share resources, such as fundraising efforts, staff training, and administrative support. While collaboration seemed doubtful on day one, by day four of the facilitation, the coalition had chosen a name (Network for Children, Prisoners, and Dependents) and committed to the terms of their collaboration. Since its development, the Network has received commendations from civil society groups and the government of Nepal; it has also received numerous grants for improvements to group home care, such as solar water heating, sanitation development, teacher training, and child psychology support services. Moreover, it serves as a model of networking that the country of Nepal had not seen before.

Another model of community collaboration is the grassroots, community based, youth-driven advocacy group Homies Organizing the Mission to Empower Youth (HOMEY), formerly fiscally and programmatically sponsored by ICRI. HOMEY emerged in the 1990s in response to gang violence in the diverse and densely populated Mission neighborhood in San Francisco, California. HOMEY's founders, former gang members themselves in many cases, wanted to prevent violence in their neighborhood and give youth alternatives to gang life. With financial support from the city of San Francisco and private foundations, HOMEY offers vocational training, microloans for small businesses, community advocacy, and peace-building strategies for youth and young adults. The *Homies* have been invited to most city youth-related commissions and boards, including efforts to reform juvenile justice. HOMEY also organizes and participates in community forums that defuse tensions between rival gangs. Their work has contributed to reducing violence and death among youth in the

Mission and increasing positive behaviors among youth such as school attendance and entrepreneurship.

These are just a few examples of successful advocacy on behalf of children and youth around the world. The themes they have in common and the steps taken to achieve these victories will be explored in this and subsequent chapters.

WHAT IS SUCCESSFUL CHILD ADVOCACY?

The word *advocacy* derives from the Latin "advocare," meaning "to call," and is related to "vocem," meaning "voice" ("Advocate," 2011). Advocacy, then, can be understood as using voice or acting as the voice of another. In relation to children, the importance of advocacy is particularly acute. Children generally cannot act as their own voice in important issues affecting them, such as policy development or matters of the court (see Box 1.1, The Silent Voice of the Child). Acting as the voice of children, advocacy often involves calling things as they are and identifying problems. It also involves calling on those who hold positions of authority in society to engage and involve them in solving problems for children. Child advocacy can be directed toward a problem that affects a single child or a cause that affects a group of children. This distinction is known as *case advocacy* versus *class* or *cause advocacy* (Kirst-Ashman & Hull, 2008).

BOX 1.1

The Silent Voice of the Child

**By Evelyn Quartey-Papafio, Officer in charge of the
National Nursery Teachers' Training Centre, Ghana Education Service (Ghana)**

If I have a voice, everyone will hear what I have to say.

If I have a voice, I would be treated with more respect.

Silent though I seem; I ask you to open your eyes.

Look, look again at the expression on my face.

Look, and look again.

My expression says, I am human, I have rights.

Treat me with respect, show me love, listen to me.

Let the joys of my heart flow naturally.

(Continued)

(Continued)

Whisper to me and I will listen to you.

My innocence quietly says,

Lead me on, that I may grow tall.

From the Experience of a Preschool Teacher:

"Teacher Rosemond yelled at me," 4-year-old Anita said as soon as she was picked up from the preschool.

"What happened?" her mum asked.

There was a brief silence, then Anita started another conversation about the fun she had with her friends at the playground. Later, all the family heard about the yelling, including Anita's father way off in his office, before he got home. Finally, Anita confessed the reason to Marian, her elder sister. "I refused to write '5' when Teacher Rosemond asked me to," she explained.

When Marian asked why, Anita sharply said Teacher Rosemond was not her teacher. She only substituted for her regular teacher, who was fond of all the children in the class. That evening, Anita wrote "5" on every piece of furniture, wall, and book cover in the house to demonstrate her ability to write "5."

A grandma called across the compound to Anita, "Stop playing in the mud and come up here." "You've spoilt the fun, Grandma," Anita murmured angrily, as she put her playthings away.

Anita has no voice, she just has to obey.

Who will speak for the child out there? Who will show the millions out there how to politely address the child or support his or her learning and development? Do adults respect the rights of the child? How patiently do adults listen to the children?

Successful child advocacy is simply those efforts that meet their intended goal of making positive change for children. As will be discussed later in this chapter, advocacy can take place on different levels; these include advocacy on behalf of a particular child, a group of children, or an issue affecting many children in the larger society. It is the premise of this book that the underlying methods of advocacy are basically the same for a range of goals. Often, the ultimate goal of advocacy is some type of policy change or the development of a critical mass that helps to implement that change. Policy change may involve a broad swath of activities that can include the passage of legislation, preventing passage of harmful legislation, establishing a new project, expanding an existing project, and other tangible outcomes.

Many methods are available in the successful child advocacy arsenal. These include legislative advocacy, legal advocacy, media advocacy, and organizational advocacy. *Legislative advocacy* is an effort to influence the passage of public policy. Efforts may be intended to secure the passage of favorable legislation or block unfavorable legislation. In some countries, such as the United States, there are restrictions on lobbying activities by nonprofit tax-exempt organizations. Another approach to making system-level change is *legal advocacy,* particularly class-action lawsuits on behalf of a group (or class) of people. In the United States, many changes to state or county-run child welfare systems have occurred due to successful class-action lawsuits. Advocates may turn to this option when they encounter difficulty making legislative change and can demonstrate that systems have not been held accountable for meeting promises to disempowered clients (Center for the Study of Social Policy, 1998). *Media campaigns* may complement legislative or legal advocacy or stand alone by helping to change public opinion on a certain matter. *Organizational advocacy* is a strategy to change practices for serving children and families, often from the inside by someone in a professional role in the organization.

WHY ARE CHILDREN IN SPECIAL NEED OF ADVOCACY?

Children are dependent on adults for their care (as discussed by Dr. Jane Goodall in the Preface), and this has meant historically that they have often been maltreated. Historian and psychotherapist Lloyd deMause (1995) noted,

> The history of childhood is a nightmare from which we have only recently begun to awaken. The further back in history one goes, the lower the level of child care, and the more likely children are to be killed, abandoned, beaten, terrorized, and sexually abused. (p. 1)

History is replete with examples of treatment of children that would be seen as sadistic in our own time, including the common practice of infanticide in the Ancient Greek and Roman empires; child sacrifice among the Aztec, Mayan, and Incan cultures; and mutilation such as castration of boys to preserve their high singing voices (the Castrati in 16th through 19th century Italy) and foot binding of girls in China until the 19th century (deMause, 1995; Grille, 2009). The view of children as people in their own right, rather than simply chattel of their fathers or masters, is of relatively recent origin.

Just as their age puts children into a class that often faces discrimination, children can also be part of other oppressed groups based on their race/ethnicity, caste, religion, social class, socioeconomic status, sexual orientation, and family structure as well as other elements of their background. Children who face particularly acute challenges include members of racial and ethnic groups like the Roma in Eastern Europe, Africans in Arab countries, Indigenous in Latin America and Australia, and African Americans and Latinos in the United States. These children are often subject to systems that seem to foster negative outcomes. For example, the Children's Defense Fund and American Civil Liberties Union have brought attention to what they call the Cradle to Prison Pipeline or School to Prison Pipeline, a systematic series of injustices and prejudice in the systems that serve poor children of color that seem to lead them inexorably toward school dropout and criminality from the time they are born or enter school (American Civil Liberties Union, 2008; Children's Defense Fund, 2007). These unjust systems are important targets for advocacy.

Many of the protections children enjoy today, particularly in the Western world, are products of the zeal of reformists during the Progressive Era, a term used by historians to describe the late 18th century and early 19th century in the United States and other Western countries. The child saving movement during the Progressive Era advocated for and achieved the development of social services systems serving children and youth. These included the child welfare system to investigate cases of child maltreatment and put children in substitute care. In the United States, the origin of child welfare services is often attributed to the advocacy of social worker Etta Wheeler on behalf of a maltreated child named Mary Ellen Wilson. Wheeler learned of Mary Ellen's severe maltreatment at the hands of her adoptive mother, and after initial attempts to spur intervention by New York City officials failed, she contacted the founder of the American Society of Prevention of Cruelty to Animals, Henry Bergh. They worked together to gain evidence of Mary Ellen's maltreatment and to bring a court case on her behalf, arguing that the child could experience irreparable harm if left in the home. Bergh used his social position and ties with the press to encourage coverage of the case by a *New York Times* reporter. The adoptive mother was charged with felonious assault, and Mary Ellen was removed from her custody, first to a group home and later to a new adoptive home with relatives of Etta Wheeler (Markel, 2009; Watkins, 1990). This story features many classic elements of child advocacy, including engaging allies, reaching out to the media, and blending micro and macro advocacy to create both individual and societal change. Other prominent child advocates of the Progressive Era include Mary Harris "Mother" Jones, who organized a children's march from Philadelphia to the New York home of then-President Theodore Roosevelt in protest of child labor (Smith, 1967), and Mary Church Terrell, who, in her role as the first president of the National Association of Colored Women and participant in the broader African American Women's Club Movement, established day nurseries, kindergartens, and orphanages for African American children (Roberts, 2004).

The notion of children's rights, as a guide and target for child advocacy, emerged slowly over the 20th century, culminating in the development of the United Nations Convention on the Rights of the Child. This document was preceded by earlier efforts to incorporate recognition of children's rights into international law. The short-lived League of Nations in 1924 passed the Geneva Declaration of the Rights of the Child with the stirring words that "mankind owes to the Child the best that it has to give" and setting forth the principle that children deserve to have their needs met, materially and spiritually (League of Nations, 1924, p. 1). The successor to the League of Nations, the United Nations, included in its 1948 Declaration of Human Rights the statement that "motherhood and childhood are entitled to special care and assistance" (United Nations, 1959b, Article 25). This was expanded in the 1959 United Nations Declaration on the Rights of the Child, which established principles such as nondiscrimination and special protection for children with disabilities, to promote the goal "that [the child] may have a happy childhood and enjoy for his own good and for the good of society . . . rights and freedoms" (United Nations, 1959a, p. 1). Yet these documents were more aspirational than impactful, since none were legally binding.

The U.N. Convention on the Rights of the Child (CRC) is an international legal instrument that recognizes that children have universal needs and that the obligation on the part of adults to meet these needs confers rights upon children. This document was ratified by the U.N. General Assembly in November 1989 and has since been ratified by every U.N. member nation with the exception of the United States and Somalia, making it the most ratified international human rights treaty in history (United Nations Children's Fund [UNICEF], 2006). Child advocacy organizations in the United States, such as the Campaign for U.S. Ratification of the CRC, have led efforts to build political will for ratification by the Senate, particularly since the beginning of the Obama administration. Opponents of ratification cite concerns of undermining United States law and parental rights (Cohen & DeBenedet, 2012). However, these concerns are unfounded since international treaties are legally barred from superseding U.S. law, and the CRC explicitly confirms that families are best able to raise children and should be supported by their countries (Morgan, 2009). Even in the United States, the CRC can provide a powerful set of goals for advocacy as well as lend legitimacy to advocacy efforts.

There are different categories of rights established by the CRC. These include the following: 1) general rights, such as the right to life, freedom of thought, religion, and expression; 2) protection rights, such as protection against abuse, neglect, and exploitation; 3) civil rights, such as the right to remain with or be reunited with one's family when that is in the child's best interests; 4) development and welfare rights, such as provision of a reasonable standard of living and access to education and health services; and 5) rights for children in special circumstances, such as children affected by armed conflict who have the right not to be conscripted into the armed forces (Muntarbhorn, 1992).

Using the Convention on the Rights of the Child as a guide for advocacy suggests using children's needs as a starting point and communicating the moral and ethical imperatives for adults to meet these needs. Community or institutional acceptance that adults are obligated to meet children's needs elevates the child's right to having those needs met to the level of entitlement or *de facto* rights (Children's Rights Education for Professionals, 2008). This is true whether or not the CRC is legally binding in a given jurisdiction. Considering the area of disability as one example of how the use of the CRC might look in practice, an advocate could take the issue of broadening access to local services for disabled children as an advocacy goal. This goal could be accomplished by passing ordinances that require handicap ramps, allow service dogs in all public buildings, and mandate every city staff member to be trained on access provision.

The Convention on the Rights of the Child also suggests that children deserve to participate in decisions that affect them. Article 12 states that children have the right to participate in decision-making processes that involve them and influence these decisions within their families, schools, and communities. Meaningful participation can take three forms: consultative processes that ask children to provide information to inform policy or services, participative initiatives that enable children to understand and apply democratic principles or have a direct hand in shaping policy or services, and promotion of self-advocacy that empowers children to develop their own goals and initiatives. While the first two may be led by adults, self-advocacy places adults in a supportive and advisory role and gives children primary responsibility (Lansdowne, 2001).

Youth voice is a broad approach to inclusion of young people in decisions that affect them. It goes far beyond advocacy to include participation in designing research, providing guidance to youth-serving organizations, and shaping the social and educational services they receive. A powerful form of youth voice is to involve consumers of services, such as child welfare, in reforming such services. For example, California Youth Connection (2013) trains and supports current and former youth in foster care to advocate with legislators, agency directors, and the media to promote policies and practices that will improve child welfare services. The HOMEY program mentioned earlier in this chapter has a yearly process of developing a youth-driven agenda for social change. Involving children and youth in decision making also offers significant benefits. They can improve proposed programs and policies by offering a perspective about possible effects on their target populations. They can also derive personal benefit through experiencing an opportunity for responsibility and autonomy that will prepare them for later adult roles (Beilenson, 1993).

Child and youth involvement in decision making is an ideal, but one that many societies are far from achieving. Children are typically silenced in decisions made on their behalf due to exclusion and marginalization. *Childism* (Young-Bruehl, 2012) or *adultism* (Bell, 1995) is a systematic form of prejudice against children and youth that regards them as inferior to adults and subjects them to adult control. This prejudice is reflected in personal interactions within families and communities, institutions such as schools, and political structures. Childism or adultism interacts with other forms of prejudice, like sexism and racism, potentially adding to the mistreatment and disrespect directed at children. While their developing and evolving capacities require adult guidance, children should also be empowered to the extent possible. Child advocacy by adults can give children and youth a voice, which they all too often lack, but adult allies must listen to children and involve them. It is important for child advocates to be reflective and conscious of this dynamic as they work on behalf of a relatively powerless group.

WHO CAN DO CHILD ADVOCACY?

Anyone may act as an advocate for children. An advocate for children may be a professional or volunteer, teacher or parent. Because of their status as a marginalized population, there are ethical reasons to advocate for children. These reasons are both personal and professional. In terms of personal reasons, adults bear responsibility toward the children in their lives, including the children of relatives, friends, and neighbors. But even beyond personal relationships, adults share responsibility for promoting the interests of the next generation. The professional code of ethics for a number of U.S. national associations, such as the National Association of Social Workers, the National Association for the Education of Young Children, and the American Counseling Associations, hold their members accountable for engaging in advocacy when they observe injustice and inequity affecting vulnerable populations such as children. For example, the National Association of Social Workers (2008) in the United States has a code of ethics that requires social workers to advocate for policies and services that meet basic human needs and promote social justice.

There are a number of professional organizations that employ people to act as the voice of children. These include child advocacy organizations that work on international, regional/state, and local levels to hold governments accountable for passing and implementing legislation responsive to children's needs. For example, the World Forum on Early Care and Education is creating a new cohort of global child advocates through the Global Leaders for Young Children Program (see Box 1.2 for a description). Lawyers and other members of the legal profession may also act as child advocates by representing the interests of an individual child in court proceedings or the interests of a group of children in a class action lawsuit. Some organizations combine policy advocacy on behalf of children with direct service delivery; the international organization Save the Children, for example, has advocacy offices focused on policy advocacy within the United Nations, the European Union, and the African Union and their member nations in addition to its direct service work in child protection and survival, emergency relief, education, and other areas. Child advocacy organizations may focus on a single advocacy topic; examples include End Child Prostitution, Child Pornography and Trafficking of Children for Sexual Purposes (ECPAT), an international organization headquartered in Thailand focused on child trafficking and exploitation; and Railway Children, an organization based in the United Kingdom that advocates for street children. Other advocacy organizations have a mission to address many issues that face children. Prominent organizations with a broad advocacy mission include Children's Defense Fund in the United States, Child Welfare League of Canada, and Families Australia, among many others. Professional staff members of these organizations have skills in research, communications, coalition building, and other advocacy actions to influence decision makers at the local, regional, national, and international levels. See Box 1.3 for the perspective a professional advocate working in the area of global health.

BOX 1.2

Building a Global Network of Children's Champions

By Bonnie and Roger Neugebauer, Founders,
World Forum on Early Care and Education (United States)

At the 2003 World Forum on Early Care and Education in Acapulco, Mexico, seasoned advocate Joan Lombardi was so inspired by her conversations with early childhood professionals from 65 nations that she suggested that the World Forum Foundation develop a training and mentoring initiative to mentor the next generation of champions for young children. Thus was launched Global Leaders for Young Children. Working with Lombardi, the World Forum hammered out this mission statement for Global Leaders:

> Global Leaders for Young Children is a World Forum Foundation project with the goal of improving life chances for young children by developing early childhood leaders who can become effective change agents and advocates for quality early childhood development in their home countries and regions. (World Forum Foundation, 2013)

In 2004, we put this mission into practice when the first cohort of Global Leaders met in Belfast for 3 days of training and inspiration. Since that date, 134 emerging leaders from 49 countries have graduated from the Global Leaders program and are participating in an ever-expanding global network of child advocates.

As an early partner in Global Leaders, the Boeing Company funded an evaluation conducted by the University of Wisconsin-Milwaukee. The final report, "An Evaluation of the World Forum Foundation's Global Leaders Program," validated the impact of the initiative, finding that the program helped participants advocate in new ways for young children, grow professionally, and become personally and professionally transformed by their experiences.

(Continued)

(Continued)

Over the years, a number of keys to success of the 2-year Global Leaders training programs have emerged:

- **Identifying emerging leaders**: In building the next generation of advocates, we are not looking for seasoned advocates nearing the ends of their careers, nor are we looking for novices—individuals totally new to the field. We are looking for emerging leaders—young professionals who have demonstrated potential to be committed, effective advocates.
- **Providing content and bonding**: Global Leaders participate in two face-to-face meetings. At these meetings, they are provided with tools and training on advocacy, leadership, and brain research. Just as importantly, they are given ample opportunities to develop energizing relationships that keep them connected with their peers for years as well as holding them each accountable to the team.
- **Conducting advocacy projects**: One of the most impactful aspects of the program is the advocacy projects where Global Leaders carry out a policy-related task in their countries. These projects provide an opportunity to put into practice the skills and knowledge they have learned.
- **Recruiting two leaders per country**: By having two emerging leaders from a country, they can work together as a team, supporting and inspiring each other.
- **Creating global and regional networks**: The program has evolved to establishing Global Leaders programs in various regions of the world. This gives the Global Leaders the opportunity to focus on issues and trends unique to their regions as well as connect with their peers around the world and put their regional issues into a global context.

Moving forward, Global Leaders for Young Children continues to evolve. Two innovations are being tested out. First, Global Leaders are being trained and encouraged to use social networking tools, both to enhance their advocacy projects and to strengthen their relationships with all other Global Leaders worldwide. Second, taking advantage of the growing Global Leaders cadre, we are recruiting graduates to serve as mentors for new Global Leaders. The expanding Global Leaders network promises to make a real difference nation by nation in improving the life chances of children.

BOX 1.3

Working as a Professional Advocate

By Traci Siegel, Senior Vice President, GMMB (United States)

I am fortunate that as a very young child I learned that the most important things in life are worth fighting for. As an adult, I'm grateful to have had the opportunity to turn that realization into my dream job: helping clients execute successful communications and advocacy campaigns aimed at improving health and development in the world's poorest countries.

(Continued)

(Continued)

I work at a strategic communications firm, GMMB, that specializes in supporting causes rather than promoting products. As we like to say, GMMB works to create real and lasting change in the world through our work with clients: in my case, in the area of global health. From working with countries to invest in young child nutrition, to executing high-octane campaigns that engage basketball stars and everyday people to Send a Net, Save a Life to help end malaria, to amplifying the need for greater access to vaccines and clean water among the world's poor, we use communications tools and strategies to broaden awareness and spur action to tackle some of the world's most devastating yet solvable problems.

At GMMB, we like to think of advocacy as "creating an environment in which people have the tools, information, and ability to change opinions, behavior, and policy." One of the main distinctions between advocacy and lobbying in our work is that while lobbying is direct, often one-to-one communications on a particular policy, advocacy can be much more broad. Many times, it is about creating a platform and building a movement that like-minded people of all walks of life can embrace and actively support in order to effect change in ways large and small.

Doing this kind of communications and advocacy work has afforded me some unforgettable opportunities. Seeing firsthand the impact on children's daily life of not having clean water to drink, safe spaces to play, nutritious foods to nurture their bodies and minds, or access to basic human rights like vaccines, sanitation, and education is what drives my colleagues and I to do this work.

To help in some small way to make a difference in people's lives through advocacy is a privilege that I get the chance to do every day—but *everyone* can have an impact by acting locally, and it all starts with just one small act.

Professional qualifications or employment are not necessary for acting on behalf of children. Parents are their children's first and most natural advocates. Parents must often provide a voice when their children's needs are not being met in terms of social services or education. Indeed, parents must often be the ones to initiate special testing or services when they have concerns about their children's development or learning abilities. There are also many ways that concerned citizens can work on behalf of children's issues. For example, there are volunteer roles that provide an opportunity to act as an advocate in the United States court system such as a guardian ad litem or court appointed special advocate. These are volunteers whom courts assign to represent the interests of children who are part of dependency court cases in the child welfare system. There are also informal ways that citizens can act on behalf of children: as voters who support initiatives and candidates that address children's issues, as residents who help to create safe and supportive neighborhoods, and as mentors who take an interest in a particular child and provide encouragement and caring.

Children and youth can also be empowered to be advocates. In this case, the role of the child advocate can be to help children find their own voices, to confront the injustices they face personally or recognize in their community or world. Authentic participation by children in decisions affecting their lives and communities allows them to initiate projects, make decisions, and be informed on issues. This stands in contrast to the use of children as decoration or tokens, where their involvement in a cause is manipulated by adults to achieve their own ends (Hart, 1992).

The common thread that connects those who engage in child advocacy is a passion to create change for a child or group of children. Motivation for child advocacy arises from the heart. While a person may feel the injustice of a situation, hand-wringing alone will not make changes for children. Becoming an advocate means channeling emotions toward productive efforts.

WHY DO WE ADVOCATE FOR CHILDREN?

Individuals and groups often come to advocacy by recognizing the need for change. The catalyst that inspires action may be an image, a circumstance, or a personal experience. For Eileen McHenry, Executive Director of Romanian Children's Relief, more than two decades of impassioned work on behalf of children in Romania's institutions began with the adoption of her daughter Juliana and the recognition of how she had been affected by early childhood care in poorly run orphanages. In the case of Tuga Tarle, former Prima Ballerina and Croatian cultural attaché to Australia, exposure to the suffering of children in her native Croatia prompted her to start Foundation Dora to offer services to children exposed to the trauma of war. Both women initially lacked professional training and experience in child advocacy or nonprofit administration. Inspiration to serve children led, and learning the necessary skills followed.

Inspiration for advocacy often comes from a heartfelt connection to a cause that one feels and perceives deeply. Among the multitude of injustices of the world, why does one particular issue tug at an advocate? What moves a person from a feeling of anger or sadness at a given situation to corrective action? Economists have theorized four major classifications, called *social motives* or *value orientations*, underpinning behaviors that benefit the self or others. Experiments based on game theory have established the reliability and consistency of these classifications. An individual would act in the following ways according to his or her social motive: 1) *competition* favors action promoting the greatest difference between gain to self and others, 2) *individualism* favors action that achieves the greatest gain for self, 3) *cooperation* favors action that creates gain for both self and others, and 4) *altruism* favors action that achieves the greatest gain for others (Sattler & Kerr, 1991). While there may be other, more complex reasons for involvement, child advocates are often motivated by cooperation or altruism. Cooperation may guide the actions of an advocate when he or she is working with other parents to make changes to policies within a school. Not only will one's own children benefit, but so will other children within the school. Altruism may underlie an advocate's behaviors when no direct benefit will accrue to the advocate or his or her family, such as helping to build a school for children in an area devastated by a tsunami. Both motivations are consonant with the role of child advocate.

One person at her kitchen table can start a movement that changes the world. After the death of her child caused by a repeat drunk driver, Candy Lightner channeled her anger into advocacy efforts to increase public awareness of the dangers of drunk driving. The organization she founded, Mothers Against Drunk Driving (MADD), is today one of the most well-regarded nonprofit organizations in the United States and has been instrumental in passing state legislation addressing drunk driving. Similarly, the parents of Lorenzo Odone sought a cure for the rare disease afflicting their son (Adrenoleukodystrophy [ALD]), as told in the film Lorenzo's Oil. In response to the disinterest of pharmaceutical companies, they conducted their own research until they identified a dietary treatment involving modified oil and found a chemist to produce it. Their efforts have led to greater attention to the disease and research on this treatment approach.

While reading this book, consider what drives your motivation and how to sustain it. Motivation is like a fire that can burn out, if not tended. What is the source of your fire for child advocacy? Is it a heart-wrenching image of children suffering from deprivation, an event like a hurricane that suddenly pushes families into homelessness, or a child you care about not having her needs met by an unresponsive system? The activity at the end of this chapter provides questions intended to guide self-reflection. While going through the process of identifying your cause and learning through this book how to set goals and create the change you hope you achieve, find ways to sustain motivation despite the setbacks that are bound to happen (see Chapter 10 for more discussion on sustaining motivation).

Practices that promote a balanced life and good health can also be applied to sustaining motivation. These include self-care through adequate rest and exercise, recognizing what can and cannot be controlled, understanding one's own limitations in terms of time and energy, and having a spiritual perspective as well as a sense of humor (Malikow, 2007). The "watchwords of advocacy" in Chapter 2 also provide suggestions and mantras to help advocates keep perspective and stay motivated. An important way to keep going in advocacy work is to find strength in numbers and join with others to achieve your efforts. A discussion of how to find partners for your advocacy efforts and a description of national and international advocacy organizations is discussed in Chapters 2 and 10.

WHAT ARE THE FRAMEWORKS FOR CHILD ADVOCACY?

Theoretical and legal frameworks can help child advocates develop appropriate aims for their advocacy efforts. What do children need and deserve, in terms of their fundamental rights as human beings, as well as their special status as developing beings who are dependent on their families, communities, and societies to provide special care and protection? Insights on the relationship between a child's development and community and other factors are provided by Bronfenbrenner's Ecological Model, the Maslow Hierarchy of Needs, and resilience theory as set forth by Rutter and others. Theories are important because they guide what to look for and how to make sense of information. These theories are drawn from fields such as psychology and provide ways of understanding human needs, behavior, and development. They are well-established theories that have been tested and supported by research and provide guidance on planning child advocacy efforts that can provide children with what they need to thrive and meet their full potential. No one theory explains children's development, so a combination of theories is useful to shed light on different aspects of development and how these interact with the social environment. Each of the three theories will be described in turn in the following paragraphs.

Ecological Model

Children do not exist in isolation but rather in an interconnected network of relationships and environments that begin with those closest to the child and extend to the national and even international level. The Ecological Model (Bronfenbrenner, 1979) is a useful way to think about children and their environments. The child is at the center of this model and is surrounded by concentric systems (see Box 1.4). The first is called the *Microsystem* and is formed by the child's immediate environments like the family, peers, neighborhood, school, child care centers, and religious community. Interconnections between these environments, such as the connection between a neighborhood and school, form the next layer, called the *Mesosystem*. Environments in which children do not participate directly, but which nonetheless influence them in one of their Microsystems, make up the *Exosystem*; an example would be the parent's employer. The *Macrosystem* is the outermost system made up of the child's society and subculture. The model also includes the *Chronosystem*, or the pattern of events and changes to environments over time. When these environments mirror each other with similar expectations, goals, and values and have sufficient resources to support children, this can create a promotive environment for child development; conversely, when environments have conflicting messages and insufficient resources, they can be inhibitive of children's development. In terms of the latter, imagine the challenges for a child when the school holds her responsible for completing hours of nightly homework, but she must care for younger siblings and do household chores after school. Children are more likely to experience inhibitive environments when they are subject to prejudice, racism, discrimination, and oppression due to social position and class (Coll et al., 1996).

There are three key principles for understanding the Ecological Model. First, development occurs in increasingly complex reciprocal interactions between the individual and the environment; this means that children encounter a greater number of and more complex environments as they grown older. Consider the different social experiences of an infant, who may only spend time within the home, child care, and medical facilities, compared with a teenager, whose social world can include school, employment, extracurricular activities, friends' homes, and many other settings. Second, development is the product of characteristics of the person, the environment, and the nature of the outcome under examination. This highlights the uniqueness of each individual and how his or her qualities such as temperament interact with his or her relationships and social environments and how that ultimately results in outcomes; for example, a shy and reserved child will interact differently with a teacher than an outgoing one, and this influences the child's relationship and related outcomes, such as grades. Third, proximal (close) processes are generally more influential than distal (far) influences. This means children are most influenced by their closest relationships and environments, such as families and schools, and less by more abstract influences such as political structures and societal attitudes. However, these distal forces can be experienced by children within their closest environments, such as when a family is dependent on cash aid from the government, suggesting the interconnectedness of each level (Bronfenbrenner, 1979).

BOX 1.4

Applying Bronfenbrenner's Ecological Model

Develop an ecological model for a child you know to explore the potential need for advocacy in this child's life. Fill in the blanks with the most important social relationships and environments for this child (e.g., family, school, child care) and identify whether there are any problems, considering the concept of promotive and inhibitive environments.

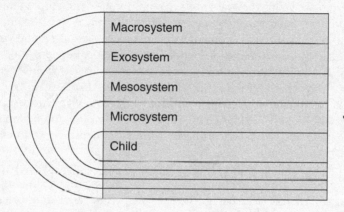

In terms of advocacy, the Bronfenbrenner Ecological Model has three major implications. First, to improve the lives of children, it is often necessary to influence the chain of environments, institutions, and systems that directly impact them. This means that advocates must take these environments into consideration when assessing children's needs and seeking opportunities for bettering children's lives. Moreover, an advocate may be benefiting children when addressing causes not directly related to children, such as neighborhood safety or employee work-life balance. While the term *child advocacy* is most commonly used, efforts to benefit children are likely to go beyond an individual child to include advocacy on behalf of families, schools, or communities. The need to target the relationships and systems in a child's life is not always obvious.

An example of child advocacy efforts on behalf of street children in Brazil highlights this point. The mayor of Brazil's capital, Brasilia, learned that many children on the street were there not because they were orphaned but because of difficult economic conditions or abuse. His office conducted assessments in some of the city's poorest neighborhoods and saw that many of the families could not afford to properly care for their children. Recognizing the need to address this root cause of children living on the street, the city of Brasilia launched an effort to work with local businesses and industry to find ways to develop jobs and training programs. The focus population was mothers who were trained in different fields so that they could become gainfully employed and their children could return home again. Services were also offered to families to help them locate their children and to support the family after reunification. This example illustrates the importance of working with communities and understanding their needs in order to develop appropriate solutions to problems.

A second important implication to draw from the Ecological Model is that children are embedded within relationships. Meaningful change for children comes when advocates can become allies with important figures in children's lives like their parents, teachers, child care providers, religious leaders, and others. Uniting on behalf of children can be a catalyst for achieving greater and more sustainable change. This kind of bottom-up change that comes from activating the grass roots in communities and tapping into desires to promote the common good can be contrasted with top-down, professional-led models of advocacy that target particular problem behaviors among children and youth often based on an agenda set by governments or foundations (Lerner & Benson, 2003).

Third, the Ecological Model provides several target areas for advocacy efforts. Child advocates may direct their efforts at the Microsystem level to advocate for change on behalf of a particular child. This is called *micro advocacy*, also known as *case advocacy*. The needs for advocacy within these settings change as children develop; for example, an infant with special needs may need advocacy primarily within the medical system whereas advocacy within the school system may also be needed as the child grows older (Alper, Schloss, & Schloss, 1995). Operating at the Mesosystem level, advocates may operate within local environments like schools and communities to make change on behalf of a group of children. This is called *mezzo advocacy*. At the Exosystem level, advocates can promote change for social services for children, youth, and families, such as the juvenile justice or child welfare systems. Macrosystem advocacy efforts aim to shift societal beliefs and may take the form of public service announcements related to harmful practices, such as drug use among teenagers. Creating change at the Exosystem and Macrosystem levels is *macro advocacy*. Each of these forms of advocacy is explained in greater detail in Chapter 2, "Parameters of Advocacy."

Hierarchy of Needs

Just as there are a multitude of targets for child advocacy, from the child to each of the child's major relationships and environments, so too are there numerous types of changes for which to advocate. The Maslow Hierarchy of Needs provides a helpful lens for considering what children need. Frequently envisioned as a pyramid, the Maslow (1943) Hierarchy of Needs is based on the premise that basic human needs must be at least somewhat satisfied for higher, more advanced needs to emerge. The base is constituted of *physiological needs* for food, water, and other forms of basic sustenance such as shelter and clothing. *Safety needs* come next, including freedom from physical threats and security that may come from a job and other stable routines. If physiological and safety needs are met, the *love needs* arise for both giving and receiving love. The next highest level is made up of the *esteem needs*; this takes the form of desire for achievement and reputation or prestige. The four needs previously described make up the deficiency needs that, while unsatisfied, cause an individual feelings of anxiety. The pyramid is capped with the *need for self-actualization*, also described as the growth need, which consists of an individual expressing his full potential and making the most of his talents. Since each level of needs must be achieved to reach the next, this highlights the importance of advocacy across the spectrum from basic to self-actualization needs.

Advocacy can address needs at any level of the Maslow hierarchy. On the most basic level, advocacy can involve ensuring that children's survival needs for food, clothing, and shelter are met. Addressing safety needs may entail protecting children in a war zone or simply a dangerous neighborhood. Providing children with love and belonging may take the form of supporting families or finding suitable alternative placements for children when their families are unable to care for them. Recognizing and supporting children's need for identity and self-esteem may include providing opportunities for education and recreation. On the theme of self-actualization, advocacy for children can mean holding society accountable for caring for its youngest members and promoting peace in the world.

Resilience Theory and Risk and Protective Factors

Advocates often work on behalf of children facing difficult life circumstances. Resilience is defined as "positive adaptation despite experiences of significant adversity or trauma" (Luthar & Cicchetti, 2000, p. 857). Resilience is a process or phenomenon that people go through, not a stable trait that certain people possess, bringing attention to how individuals deal with risk through coping mechanisms, subconscious tendencies, and personal agency (Rutter, 2006). As circumstances change, risk alters and the likelihood of experiencing negative outcomes changes. These moments can be turning points in a child's developmental trajectory. The concept of resilience captures these individual differences in how people respond to challenges (Rutter, 1987).

Aspects and experiences present within a child, family, or community can increase or decrease the likelihood that a child will experience a negative outcome. *Risk factors* or mechanisms, also called vulnerability factors, exacerbate the likelihood of experiencing a negative outcome when facing a particular adversity (Luthar & Cichetti, 2000). Having a difficult temperament, for example, can increase a child's risk of experiencing a negative outcome such as school failure due to the greater likelihood of experiencing more discordant interactions. The cumulative effect of risk factors is key—the number of risk factors may be more significant than having any one risk factor (Rutter, 1987). *Protective factors* work inversely by reducing the likelihood of experiencing a negative outcome and also offer greater benefit when multiple factors are present. A positive relationship with at least one adult is a powerful protective factor. Engaging in advocacy on behalf of self or others can also be a protective factor that promotes resilience. A child facing adversity may experience the impetus to help themselves through advocacy, which can act as a psychological buffer and connect the child to the community (Grover, 2005). This is all the more reason to involve children in advocacy projects that benefit themselves, their communities, and other children.

Resilience theory and risk and protective factors research suggest that appropriate targets of advocacy are policies and programs that promote positive outcomes for children by strengthening protective factors. Evidence that children experiencing multiple risk factors are likely to experience negative outcomes that are difficult to remediate (Luthar & Cichetti, 2000) provides a strong rationale for preventative programs that seek to increase the number of protective factors in children's lives. Common protective factors for children at the individual level include social and problem-solving skills, positive attitude, and low childhood stress. Interpersonal and social factors that can be protective include attachment to parents, high level of commitment to school, and involvement in activities. Supportive environmental factors include opportunities for education, employment, and other prosocial activities; caring relationships with adults; and social support from nonfamily members (Jenson & Fraser, 2010). These protective factors can be incorporated as goals as part of micro advocacy on behalf of an individual child, mezzo advocacy on behalf of a group of children or community, and macro advocacy related to a social problem.

This book will prepare you to begin your advocacy project, conduct the necessary six steps to achieve success, and sustain your success by positioning you for further advocacy efforts that build on your initial achievements. The next chapter begins the process by describing the parameters of advocacy.

Activity: Exploring Your Motivations to Be an Advocate

It can be helpful to maintain a reflective journal related to your advocacy work, to record your efforts and reflect on what did and did not work (see Chapter 10 for a discussion of reflective journaling). Begin your reflection by taking some time to consider these questions to clarify your motivations to be an advocate.

1. What is the source of your fire for child advocacy? It may be helpful to close your eyes and imagine the image, story, news, or other source that first sparked your interest in child advocacy.

2. What is the goal for your advocacy work? Is it something you can achieve in the short term, or is it a long-term goal?

3. What is the context for your advocacy work—the local, regional (state or province), national, or international level?

4. What types of challenges are you likely to encounter? What can you control about your advocacy work, and what will you have to let go of?

5. How will you persist in efforts toward your goal, despite inevitable challenges? What inspiration will keep you going?

6. Do you prefer working alone or as part of a team? Where can you find others to collaborate on your advocacy goal?

7. What are your methods for self-care to avoid burnout?

REFERENCES

Advocate. (2011, March). In *Oxford English Dictionary [OED] Online*. Oxford University Press. Retrieved from http://0-www.oed.com.opac.sfsu.edu/view/Entry/3022

Alper, S., Schloss, P., & Schloss, C. (1995). Families of children with disabilities in elementary and middle school: Advocacy models and strategies. *Exceptional Children, 62*(3), 261–270.

American Civil Liberties Union (2008). *School-to-prison pipeline: Factsheet*. Retrieved from http://www .aclu.org/racial-justice/school-prison-pipeline-fact-sheet-pdf

Beilenson, J. (1993). Looking for young people, listening for youth voice. *Social Policy, 24*(1), 8–13.

Bell, J. (1995). *Understanding adultism: A key to developing positive youth-adult relationships*. Retrieved from http://www.freechild.org/bell.htm

Bronfenbrenner, U. (1979). *The ecology of human development: Experiments by nature and design*. Cambridge, MA: Harvard University Press.

California Youth Connection (2013). *CYC's youth leadership*. Retrieved from http://www.calyouthconn .org/youth-leadership

Center for the Study of Social Policy (1998, January). *New roles for old adversaries: The challenge of using litigation to achieve system reform*. Retrieved from http://www.cssp.org/uploadFiles/New_ Roles_for_Old_Adversaries.pdf

Children's Defense Fund (2007). *America's Cradle to Prison Pipeline^SM*. Retrieved from http://www .childrensdefense.org/child-research-data-publications/data/cradle-prison-pipeline-report- 2007-full-lowres.pdf

Children's Rights Education for Professionals (2008). *The relationships between rights and needs*. Retrieved from http://labspace.open.ac.uk/mod/oucontent/view.php?id=425702& section=1.2.3

Cohen, L. J., & DeBenedet, A. T. (2012, January 24). Why is the U.S. against children's rights? *Time Magazine*. Retrieved from http://ideas.time.com/2012/01/24/why-is-the-us-against-childrens-rights/

Coll, C. G., Crnic, K., Lamberty, G., Wasik, B. H., Jenkins, R., Garcia, H. V., & McAdoo, H. P. (1996). An integrative model for the study of developmental competencies in minority children. *Child Development, 67*(5), 1891–1914.

deMause, L. (1995). *The history of childhood. The Master Work Series*. Dunmore, PA: Jason Aronson.

Grille, R. (2009). *Parenting for a peaceful world*. Gabriola Island, BC: New Society Publishers.

Grover, S. (2005). Advocacy by children as a causal factor in promoting resilience. *Childhood, 12*(4), 527–538.

Hart, R. A. (1992). *Children's participation: From tokenism to citizenship*. Florence, Italy: UNICEF International Child Development Centre. Retrieved from http://www.unicef-irc.org/publications/ pdf/childrens_participation.pdf

Jenson, J. M., & Fraser, M. W. (2010). A risk and resilience framework for child, youth, and family policy. In J. M. Jenson & M. W. Fraser (Eds.), *Social policy for children and families: A risk and resilience perspective* (pp. 5–24). Thousand Oaks, CA: SAGE.

Kirst-Ashman, K. K., & Hull, G. H., Jr. (2008). *Brooks/Cole empowerment series: Generalist practice with organizations and communities*. Belmont, CA: Brooks/Cole Cengage Learning.

Lansdowne, G. (2001). *Promoting children's participation in democratic decision-making*. Florence, Italy: UNICEF Inocenti Research Centre. Retrieved from http://www.unicef-irc.org/publications/pdf/ insight6.pdf

League of Nations (1924). *Geneva Declaration of the Rights of the Child of 1924*. Retrieved from http:// www.un-documents.net/gdrc1924.htm

Lerner, R. M., & Benson, P. L. (2003). *Developmental assets and asset-building communities: Implications for research, policy, and practice*. New York, NY: Springer.

Luthar, S. S., & Cicchetti, D. (2000). The construct of resilience: Implications for interventions and social policies. *Development and Psychopathology, 12*(4), 857–885.

Malikow, M. (2007, Spring). Staying motivated and avoiding burnout. *Kappa Delta Pi Record, 43*(3), 117–121.

Markel, H. (2009, December 14). Case shined first light on abuse of children. *New York Times*, p. D6. Retrieved from http://www.nytimes.com/2009/12/15/health/15abus.html?_r=0

Maslow, A. H. (1943). A theory of human motivation. *Psychological Review, 1943*(50), 370–396.

Morgan, H. (2009). A child's rights: As the Convention on the Rights of the Child celebrates 20 years as international law, advocates call for U.S. ratification. *Children's Voice*. Retrieved from http://www.cwla.org/voice/ND09child.html

Muntarbhorn, V. (1992). The Convention on the Rights of the Child: Reaching the unreached? *Bulletin of Human Rights, 91*(2), 67–70.

National Association of Social Workers (2008). *Code of ethics of the National Association of Social Workers.* Retrieved from http://www.socialworkers.org/pubs/code/code.asp

Roberts, D. E. (2004). Black club women and child welfare: Lessons for modern reform. *Florida State University Law Review, 32*, 957–972.

Rutter, M. (1987). Psychosocial resilience and protective mechanisms. *American Journal of Orthopsychiatry, 57*(3), 316–331.

Rutter, M. (2006). Implications of resilience concepts for scientific understanding. *Annals of the New York Academy of Sciences, 1094*(1), 1–12.

Sattler, D. N., & Kerr, N. L. (1991). Might versus morality explored: Motivational and cognitive bases for social motives. *Journal of Personality and Social Psychology, 60*, 756–765.

Smith, R. E. (1967). The March of the Mill Children. *The Social Service Review, 41*(3), 298–303.

United Nations (1959a). *Declaration of the rights of the child.* Retrieved from http://www1.umn.edu/humanrts/instree/k1drc.htm

United Nations (1959b). *The universal declaration of human rights.* Retrieved from http://www.un.org/en/documents/udhr/

United Nations Children's Fund [UNICEF] (2006). *Convention on the Rights of the Child: Frequently asked questions.* Retrieved from http://www.unicef.org/crc/index_30229.html

Watkins, S. A. (1990). The Mary Ellen myth: Correcting child welfare history. *Social Work, 35*(6), 500–503.

World Forum Foundation (2013). *Global Leaders for Young Children.* Retrieved from http://www.worldforumfoundation.org/working-groups/global-leaders-for-young-children/

Young-Bruehl, E. (2012). *Childism: Confronting prejudice against children.* New Haven, CT: Yale University Press.

C H A P T E R   2

Parameters of Advocacy

Before you start planning your advocacy campaign, it is helpful to understand the parameters of advocacy. These are the conditions that structure the work of advocacy. First is developing your advocacy plan and understanding the level of change you wish you create. This may be change at the micro level for an individual child; the mezzo level for a group or community; or the macro level for policy change at a state, national, or international level. Then there are the collaborators and allies who can help you with your work. There are also those with power over your cause, the gatekeepers and decision makers. The context of your advocacy work, which includes the historical time frame and political climate, also has bearing on your potential for success. It can be helpful to develop a mission statement to provide focus to your advocacy work. But first, it is important to prepare for your advocacy efforts by learning the watchwords that should guide advocates on their journeys.

THE WATCHWORDS OF ADVOCACY

In order to launch into the world of advocacy, it is important to understand the underpinnings of the world of the child advocate and to dive in or become part of that world. There are certain *watchwords* that both define child advocates and empower them to most effectively function. These statements encapsulate the key catchphrases or axioms utilized on a regular basis to keep advocates grounded and moving forward toward their goals.

The most important single phrase to be held in mind during the entire advocacy process is *I will not take no for an answer.* This phrase is often used by advocates during moments of great stress where they see that the decision maker or gatekeeper with whom they wish to work either does not understand the principles of their particular advocacy effort or is not able to provide them with the answers that they seek. Even if the decision maker or gatekeeper may disagree with them or not provide them with support initially, advocates must believe that if given the right information, they will come around to support the advocacy effort due to education and persuasion. By not taking "no" for an answer, advocates are always ready to proceed to the "yes" that they seek.

The second key watchword is that advocates *must always keep their ego in check.* If advocates are ego driven, it will be difficult for them to face the number of negative responses or "nos" that they receive. Potentially successful advocates must decide early to maintain the mindset that decision makers or gatekeepers are not saying "no" to them personally but rather do not fully grasp the information the advocates have provided to them. Therefore, advocates must maintain control of their ego response. Advocates unable to do so may walk away from the project if they receive more "nos" then "yeses."

This leads us to the next watchword, *there will always be more "nos" then "yeses" in an effective advocacy campaign.* Since many advocates describe their efforts as "getting to a yes" to improve conditions for children and families, they fight an ongoing battle to reach unanimity with all of those in the line of decision making. Yet there will always be more individuals who are not able to provide the necessary support, funding, energy, collaboration, or final decision making than those who will. It is important to keep in mind that with each step of the decision-making process, you may receive an initial negative response, but you will ultimately be able to provide decision makers with the necessary information and resources so that they can make a decision in your favor.

Aside from keeping one's ego in check, the effective advocate must also *work within a comfortable emotional range* that allows the advocate to be most productive. This has to do with the role of passion and emotion in advocacy work. There is a need for balance, whereby advocates are careful, beyond reproach, and provide good information but also show a level of passion, thoughtfulness, and introspection that helps to inform the decision maker or gatekeeper. Here is an example of what not to do: a woman who wished to become involved with a major international child advocacy campaign focusing on street children and youth came to meet with one of the authors. She expressed a great desire to right the wrongs that had been carried out by governments, businesspeople, and others against street children. As she continued to talk about her desire to become involved in the effort, she burst into tears and was virtually inconsolable. It became clear to the author that she would not be a good candidate for the leadership team of the advocacy effort. While it may be self-evident why the individual was not chosen, it should be clarified that it is certainly effective to combine intellect and emotion when carrying out an effective advocacy effort. However, when emotional energy leads, rationality does not always follow. One can combine the head and the heart in an effective manner in order to maintain a strong commitment to reach the desired goal. But if individuals are so emotionally wrought on an issue that they cannot maintain a level of balance and composure, it makes them far less effective and can often damage the overall effort within the campaign.

Another important watchword is to *tell the whole story.* This means that an advocate must endeavor to tell the truth at all times and be forthright with information. To do this, you must deeply know not only your own advocacy effort but also the positions of your opponents and help the gatekeeper and the decision maker understand what the opposition will say about your effort and how they can overcome resistance from the opposition. This is not to say that an advocate cannot state that the opposition is utilizing tactics that may be inappropriate under the circumstances. It is simply to say that the advocate will always be best served and supported by the truth.

A cautionary tale on this topic is the fate of a remarkable man who worked tirelessly in the State of California to improve conditions for foster children and children with special needs over many years. He fought a one-man crusade inspired by difficulties of some of his own family members. For more than 20 years, this gentleman worked the corridors of the California State Legislature, attempting to improve legislation and develop better oversight, licensure, and greater support services for vulnerable children in the state's foster care system. However, one evening when the advocate was very tired after a long day of advocacy, he made the mistake of not telling the full story to a key legislator whose vote would be necessary to get his group's legislation passed by a finance committee. When the legislator found out that this individual had not told him the full story and did not prepare him for opposition from others, he did what most decision makers and gatekeepers will do. He quietly froze the advocate out and made clear to his staff that he would not entertain meetings with the advocate from that time forward. Word spread in the legislature and several other key committee members also excluded this gentleman. The result was that the advocate became less effective for a period of 4 or 5 years until he built up his reputation for veracity once again.

Related to being truthful, another watchword is *always do what you say you will do.* Gatekeepers and decision makers who may support or oppose advocacy campaigns at the micro, mezzo, or macro level will expect and should be provided with clear follow-up in a timely manner. As an advocate, you can develop long-term relationships that will stand you in good stead for continuing to make change for children. The authors, in assembling this book, have called upon many colleagues to offer illuminating contributions to each chapter of the book. This happened only because relationships have been built around the world with key individuals with whom they have developed trust, with an understanding that the authors will not steer them wrong.

Finally, there are two additional pieces of advice to keep in mind for your advocacy campaign. *The advocate must be a good planner* from the outset of the advocacy project. The planning process will help to develop goals and objectives and link them to a plan with all activities listed. Part of this planning process entails determining who will carry out each activity in the plan, identifying how long each activity may take, and estimating how much the advocacy effort will cost in nonpersonnel and personnel costs. In addition, planning also involves defining milestones or indicators of progress and evaluating the overall advocacy effort. Planning your advocacy effort and suggestions of tools to use will be discussed in Chapter 3. Another watchword is that *the advocate must know when to speak and when to listen.* Observe body language and listen carefully during your interactions with gatekeepers and decision makers. This will help you to understand when a decision maker is cleverly clearing the room and escorting your people out before informing you about a decision on your issue. See Step 4, Chapter 7, for ways to avoid this.

TYPES OF ADVOCACY: MICRO, MEZZO, AND MACRO

As you consider the goal of your advocacy efforts, it is important first to consider the level of change that you seek. Child advocacy takes place in different settings for different purposes. Some advocates become interested in creating social change for children when they witness an injustice experienced by a particular child. Others become impassioned by a community problem affecting a group of children. Still others become passionate about a social issue that may affect large populations of children on a regional, national, or international level. These different levels of advocacy can be connected, and one type of advocacy may lead to another.

For example, an advocate may work on behalf of a particular child only to find that other children are also encountering the same problems in a community, spurring an effort to create community-level change. Likewise, an advocate may develop a passionate interest in a topic like child maltreatment that may lead her to become an advocate for a particular child in the foster care system. The six steps method introduced in Chapter 3 and elaborated on for the rest of the book may be applied to advocacy at any of these levels.

Advocacy for a particular child may be called *case* advocacy or *micro* (small) advocacy. Parents or other family members often become involved as advocates for their own children, particularly on behalf of children with special needs (see Box 2.1 for an example). A parent may seek appropriate accommodation for a child's special needs; for example, in the United States, there is a federally protected process for requesting assessments and learning adaptations known as an Individualized Education Plan. Professionals who work with children, such as teachers, may advocate for a particular child to ensure his or her needs are met. A community member may also become an advocate for a particular child on an informal or formal basis. Examples of this are guardians ad litem or court-appointed special advocates (CASAs), who are community members that volunteer to advocate on behalf of a child in the child welfare system, including talking with the child and representing the child's best interests in court (Court Appointed Special Advocates for Children, 2013). Children and youth may also become advocates for themselves, a process known as *self-advocacy*. Self-advocacy was a significant part of the child advocacy project in Brazil described in Box 2.3. Advocacy on behalf of a particular child may take place within institutions that serve children, such as schools and social services programs. Another venue for micro advocacy is the court system, either for advocacy on behalf of a child who is a dependent of the state in foster care or for litigation to protect children's rights. Micro advocacy may become mezzo or macro advocacy as people who advocate for individual children begin to address systemic problems. An example of this occurred in Malaysia when a group of parents of children with autism attending an integrated school, led by the school's director, developed a media campaign that featured typically developing and special needs children interviewed together about their friendships. Their work led to new efforts at integration of special needs children into the Malaysian public school system.

BOX 2.1

An Example of Micro Advocacy: July 22 Is Fragile X Awareness Day

By Sarah Taylor, Parent and Assistant Professor, Department of
Social Work, California State University, East Bay (United States)

When my son, Quinn, was 7 months old, I began to suspect something was wrong. He did not babble, could not sit up, and just felt different from other babies of the same age. The pediatrician assured me that my child was fine, perhaps just a little delayed.

At every subsequent checkup, I reiterated my concerns but was always told there were no major problems. When my son was 15 months old, we went to a birthday party where another parent who was a pediatric physical therapist saw that he could not eat any solid food, could not pull up to stand, did not speak, and did not interact at all with the other children. After the party, this parent expressed her concern, which gave me the confidence to insist that my son be referred for a developmental evaluation.

The developmental pediatrician confirmed that Quinn had global developmental delays. She referred us to a neurologist, but the neurologist did not feel that my son had a disability. She ordered an MRI since his head was large, but other than that, she agreed with the pediatrician that my son was only mildly delayed. To placate us, she ordered a $2,000 chromosomal array test and a few other metabolic tests.

After the tests came back negative, we were referred to a geneticist. At the geneticist's office, we met a young resident who immediately suggested that our son, then almost 2 years old, might have Fragile X Syndrome (FXS). We were surprised by this since the neurologist did not order that test for our son, but we agreed to have him tested. He received a positive diagnosis about 2 weeks later. This simple blood test cost just $300. Our pediatrician could have ordered the test when I first expressed concerns, which would have saved us months of anxiety, medical expenses, hours spent filling out paperwork, and numerous medical appointments. My son also could have begun treatments specifically for FXS sooner.

Had we not persisted in trying to learn what was wrong, we might still be unclear as to why his development is delayed. He is now 6 years old, and though he is happy and doing well, there are many challenges. His vocabulary is limited to concrete needs in the present, primarily expressed in two-word phrases such as "want cookie." We are still working on potty training. He gets very easily overstimulated, and when that happens, he bites, pulls hair, and kicks because he cannot express his feelings any other way.

Now that we have a diagnosis, we can share resources and support with other families affected by FXS all over the world via social media. Researchers are developing social, behavioral, and medical treatments for FXS. Without this diagnosis, we would not have access to this supportive community or the potentially life-changing treatments that will become available within the next decade.

We continue to advocate for FXS awareness and encourage other parents that regardless of the disabilities their children may have, to listen to their intuition when they feel something is wrong. July 22 is Fragile X Awareness Day. To learn more about FXS, see: http://www.fragilex.org

When the target of advocacy is a group or community, this is known as *mezzo* (meaning middle) advocacy (see Box 2.2 for an example). A group of individuals may come together in a community to create change. When the focus is on empowering communities to speak for themselves, this is known as *community organizing*. A community organizer works with communities to identify their concerns and build their power to demand change from the existing power structure (Alinsky, 1989). President Barak Obama was formerly a professional community organizer in Chicago, Illinois. Particularly in the United States, many communities have groups that do organizing of residents, achieving neighborhood and municipal victories (Dreier, 2007). A common focus of change for community organizing is children's issues. Families in a neighborhood may come together to organize for local school reform. Community members may also come together to create safe playgrounds for children or social opportunities to promote youth development.

BOX 2.2

An Example of Mezzo Advocacy, Involving Preschoolers in Community Change

By Kerstin Nash, Pre-kindergarten (Pre-K) teacher (United States)

I work in a preschool in Northern California. There are 21 Pre-K students and three teachers in my classroom. Our school's philosophy is that children learn through play and that by observing the child's interests, we as educators can provide a curriculum that expands their world knowledge. Children learn through doing, and if given real world opportunities, these will cement their current knowledge and expand their schemas.

One morning a student arrived complaining about the crosswalk near the school. The cars wouldn't stop for his mother and himself at the crosswalk. He said the paint was all chipped. So we took a class trip to the crosswalk. The paint was faded and barely visible.

We made this a teachable experience. The next day the class walked downtown to city hall. We located the city clerk in charge of road conditions and repair. We verbally complained about the crosswalk. She said she would look into it. Then we went back to school and brainstormed other solutions for the current crosswalk situation. The children drew pictures and we wrote down their words. They had great solutions for repairing the crosswalk. These include flashing lights, lit up signs, and even a gate to stop cars from going through the crosswalk.

The next week we walked back to city hall, and this time we brought all our pictures with the written suggestions and a batch of oatmeal cookies. We learned the crosswalk gets painted every year and that 6 months before it was not painted because there was local construction. It was not due to be painted for 6 more months. The clerk said she would put in a work order.

Two weeks later, a truck and a crew were at the crosswalk. We all went out and watched them paint the lines. It was very exciting, and the children had their first hands-on experience of being advocates for change.

At the *macro* level, advocates seek to address a social problem affecting a potentially large group of children (macro means large). This may be at a state, national, or even international level (see Box 2.3 for an example). Advocates may be interested in addressing a social injustice through *systems change*, or fundamentally transforming institutions and policies. Two common approaches to advocacy at the macro level are influencing public policy and initiating a class action lawsuit for change through case law. The goal of policy advocacy is to adopt, modify, or reject a particular policy proposal often by building public support on an issue or applying pressure to decision makers (Gen & Wright, 2013). Specific advocacy approaches include *programmatic (or issue) advocacy*, taking a position on a current or proposed public policy; *legislative advocacy*, or lobbying of legislators; *political campaign activity* to support or oppose political candidates; *demonstrations,* rallying public support around an issue or policy; *boycotts*, to encourage or discourage business with a targeted entity; *litigation*, or using legal action to advance a cause (Hopkins, 1992); and *grassroots advocacy*, or engaging individual citizens in an advocacy effort (McCarthy & Castelli, 2002). Class action lawsuits can also achieve broad change by bringing a lawsuit on behalf of a *class* (e.g., children in foster care) due to systematic problems and rights violations. The potential benefits include sparking and sustaining institutional change, requiring officials to acknowledge problems, and promoting accountability for change. However, there can be drawbacks, such as creating additional burdens on overworked systems or encouraging a sense of failure and demoralization among staff (Center for the Study of Social Policy, 1998). An example that resulted in real change was the Wilder case, a lawsuit alleging that the New York City child welfare system's dependence on religious social service (primarily Catholic and Jewish) organizations resulted in systemic discrimination against minority children not of their religion. The case took 26 years before it was resolved, ultimately resulting in changing the system to become more secular and appointing a watchdog panel to provide oversight to social services (Bernstein, 2011).

BOX 2.3

An Example of Macro Advocacy,
ICRI Brazil Project and the Plight of Street Children

By Caius Brandão, Former Brazil Project Coordinator,
International Child Resource Institute (ICRI) (Brazil)

At the decline of the military dictatorship in the 1980s, Brazilian society came to grips with the situation of poverty and violence to which many of its children had fallen victim. According to the Brazilian Institute for Social and Economic Analyses (IBASE), during the period of 1984 to 1989, almost 2,000 children and teenagers were killed. Later on, Brazil's Attorney General Office reported a drastic increase in the numbers of such deaths: 5,644 children between the ages of 5 and 17 were victims of violent deaths in the period between 1988 and 1991. Brazilian child advocacy groups denounced the death squads freely operating in many Brazilian states. Police officers were frequently accused of murdering destitute minors, and businessmen were alleged to contract professional killers in what was described as cleaning the streets. The National Movement of Street Boys and Girls (MNMMR) and Amnesty International estimated that over 90% of such crimes went unpunished. The lack of political will to effectively tackle widespread violence against the children of the poor in Brazil

(Continued)

(Continued)

and to prosecute their assailants was one of the key reasons for the daily murders of children and adolescents in that country.

For this reason, in 1993, ICRI started its Brazil Project to orchestrate an effort of the international community to pressure the Brazilian government to put a halt to the impunity for these crimes. The project organized comprehensive research material on the situation of Brazilian street children and made them available to the media, foundations, nongovernmental organizations, and scholars; staged candlelight vigils and street demonstrations in front of the Brazilian Consulate in San Francisco, CA; and launched a letter-writing campaign addressed to then-president of Brazil, Fernando Henrique Cardoso. Hundreds of human rights groups around the world were invited to form a strong network against the impunity of death squad members in Brazil. In 1994, ICRI's awareness campaign was endorsed by national and international organizations, including Amnesty International, Brazil Action Solidarity Network, Global Exchange, and the Rainforest Action Network.

In October of 1995, the ICRI Brazil Project, in conjunction with Global Exchange, organized the U.S. delegation to attend the MNMMR's Fourth National Meeting of Street Boys and Girls. Approximately 850 young activists and 100 educators from every corner of Brazil gathered in Brasília-Federal District to demand immediate protection for children living on the streets. Several other countries were represented by delegations of youth and adults, including Canada, Spain, England, France, the Netherlands, Argentina, Peru, Bolivia, Colombia, and the United States. The U.S. delegation organized by ICRI and Global Exchange was formed by students, researchers, youth activists, and child advocates from different regions of the country.

Looking back on those years, the enormous progress the Brazilian society has made to uphold the fundamental rights of their children has become evident. Indeed, the credit belongs to Brazilians themselves, who were able to galvanize a nationwide movement to improve the lives of their youngsters. Notwithstanding, the international community played a crucial role in providing financial resources and political support to their plight. However modest its contribution might have been, ICRI is very proud to have been part of this history.

Whether you are interested in promoting change for a particular child at the micro level, a group of children at the mezzo level, or a category of children at the macro level, an important consideration is what you as an advocate hope to achieve. An appropriate target for advocacy on behalf of children is the implementation of high-quality services on their behalf. Advocates need to know what works for children and families related to the outcome or social problem that they hope to address. Social interventions with strong research findings supporting the efficacy of the approach are known as *evidence-based programs*. This designation means that a program has been shown to be effective through high-quality research and has been recognized by government or research institutions as meeting a standard of evidence for effectiveness (Cooney, Huser, Small, & O'Connor, 2007). One way this type of designation may be achieved is through a *systematic review*. A systematic review is conducted by researchers to identify, synthesize, and evaluate the research on a particular topic. The Campbell Collaborative is a source of systematic reviews in the areas of social welfare, education, and criminal justice programs available for free online.

Specifically related to evidence-based programs for children, families, and communities, The Promising Practices Network, operated by the Rand Corporation, uses two standards for assessing programs. Proven practices are those programs that have been evaluated with a strong research design that includes a sizable comparison group, including studies where individuals have been randomly assigned to the treatment or the comparison. Evaluations have shown that the program is effective with at least one statistically significant substantial effect size of 20% or greater change in the target outcome. Promising practices have also been evaluated with a research design that includes a comparison group, but the comparison group may be smaller or the study may have some other weakness like not controlling factors statistically that may differentiate the treatment and comparison groups. The effect may also be smaller with a minimum of 1% change in the target outcome. Examples of proven practices across a range of children and family outcome areas are included in Box 2.4.

BOX 2.4

Examples of Evidence-Based Programs

Outcome Area	Program Name	Program Description
Healthy and safe children	The Incredible Years	The Incredible Years is a parenting training program targeted at families of children birth to 12 years exhibiting or at risk for conduct problems. The program teaches age-appropriate parenting skills, designed to improve children's social, emotional, and academic competence.
Children ready for school	Chicago Parent-Child Centers	The Chicago Parent-Child Centers are comprehensive early childhood and family support programs that serve children in low-income communities. Parents are involved in the preschool as classroom volunteers, and they also receive home visits and referrals to community resources.
Children succeeding in school	Big Brothers, Big Sisters	Big Brothers, Big Sisters matches children ages 6 to 18 who meet certain at-risk criteria with volunteer mentors in their communities or school sites, who spend 3 to 5 hours with them each week for a minimum of a year and build supportive relationships.

(Continued)

(Continued)		
Outcome Area	**Program Name**	**Program Description**
Strong families	Nurse-Family Partnership	Nurse-Family Partnership provides regular home visits by nurses to first-time mothers who are also low-income, unmarried, or under 19, from pregnancy until the child's second birthday. These interactions focus on improving maternal health, parenting skills, and planning for the future.

Source: Promising Practices Network (2013). *Programs that work.* Retrieved from http://www.promisingpractices.net/programs_outcome.asp

REACHING OUT TO ALLIES: BUILDING A COALITION

While some advocacy can be done on your own, your campaign may benefit by building a coalition of like-minded individuals who share your vision for creating social change for children. A *coalition* is a temporary alliance of individuals, organizations, or nation-states acting in concert toward a mutual goal. The reason to work together with others is to demonstrate greater support for a desired social change and pool talent and resources. The policy studies literature on interest groups suggests that coalitions can be powerful actors in promoting policy change, particularly when coalitions have resources, status, and sizable memberships (Baumgartner & Leech, 1998). In particular, *Advocacy Coalition Framework* theory highlights the roles of coalitions of actors such as interest group leaders, researchers, legislators, and journalists in coming together around shared policy beliefs and working together to pursue their common policy objectives (Sabatier & Jenkins-Smith, 1999).

A helpful place to start in terms of identifying allies for achieving your advocacy objective is to review the groups or organizations that may also be working on your topic. You can conduct an Internet search for the subject of your advocacy interest to identify like-minded groups. If you find an established organization that is working on your advocacy issue, consider volunteering or even working for the organization. This is a great way to build your own skills, knowledge, and social network while making change on your advocacy issue. If you don't find an established organization, social media is another place to check for informal groups. Facebook Causes and Twitter hash tags (#) identify interest groups. Meetup and Yahoo Groups are also ways to find or create communities through the Internet. You could join or start a group through any of these means and plan offline meetings for your advocacy campaign.

Here are some suggestions for starting your own group if you do not find an established organization or group to join. Outreach is the first step to develop a group. Your outreach plan should match the level of change that you are seeking: micro, mezzo, or macro. For micro change, you may seek specific allies to help you advocate for a particular child, such as others who care about the child, like teachers, relatives, and community members.

Alternatively, you can also seek out other micro-level advocates looking after the interests of other children to swap information and advice. For the mezzo level, seeking to make change for a group or neighborhood, it may make sense to reach out to a particular group, like parents of children with special needs, or seek out community members via a local venues, like a church or park, to bring people together. At the macro level, for change at a regional, state, national, or even international level, the Internet may be the most useful tool to bring people together virtually over physical distance. At the mezzo and macro levels, consider making a flyer to invite people to come together in person or on the Internet to discuss the advocacy goal.

At that first meeting with potential fellow advocates, it is helpful to have an agenda that covers a few basic things. First, make time to get to know the people who have come to the meeting. Ask people to share their motivations and potential contributions. It is also helpful to start forming a group identity. Three ways to do this at your initial meeting are to come up with a group name, mission, and ground rules. If you will be seeking change at the mezzo or macro levels, it is helpful to develop a group name that is linked with your neighborhood, region, state, or nation. When you begin to look for those who have influence over your cause (see section later in this chapter, Influencing Outcomes: Gatekeepers and Decision Makers), this kind of name will signal that you are a constituency that deserves attention, particularly from elected officials who need to support voters in their districts. Developing a mission can help coalesce the purpose of your group. A mission can simply be a sentence or short statement about the aims of your group. See the activity at the end of this chapter for suggestions on developing a mission statement. Finally, ground rules are helpful to establish at the outset so that there is agreement about how a group will run. Encourage the group to set their own ground rules to start building cohesion and mutual agreement. Ask people what has worked well in their past experience of working with groups. You might supply a couple of common ground rules and ask for feedback about whether they are appropriate for your group or could be adjusted. Common ground rules include the following: 1) listening actively and respecting others when they are talking, 2) respectfully challenging ideas by asking one another questions but refraining from personal attacks, and 3) being conscious of body language and nonverbal responses since these can be as disrespectful as words (Gorski, 1995).

Be aware that advocacy groups, like any team, go through stages. The most popular stage model of team development is Tuckman's model of forming, storming, norming, performing, and adjourning (Tuckman, 1965; Tuckman & Jensen, 1977). In stage one, the team is *forming* as members get to know each other, agree upon a goal, and start planning for the task ahead. People tend to be on good behavior and are cautious about inciting conflict. This changes in stage two, *storming*, as conflicting ideas surface about the chosen task and the team has discussions about leadership and procedures. While potentially uncomfortable, storming holds an important purpose as tensions are worked out and roles are established. This sets the groundwork for stage three, *norming*, as the team settles on one plan and team members dedicate themselves to a shared goal. All the potential created in previous stages can be realized in stage four, *performing*, as the team engages in the task at hand. The team has strategies in place to handle challenges that may arise, like conflict. These first four stages may repeat on a team, particularly if there are changes in leadership that return the group to the storming stage. Once the intended goal has been met, the fifth and final stage is *adjourning* as the group dissolves. This is a time of looking back on the accomplishments of the team and expressing appreciation for contributions (this relates to Chapter 9, "Step 6—Reinforcing Successful Advocacy Outcomes").

As a method to give structure to the forming and storming stages of team development, the GRPI model of team development has been developed (Beckhard, 1972; Raue, Tang, Weiland, & Wenzlik, 2013). This acronym stands for Goals, Roles, Processes, and Interactions. *Goals* are the agreed-upon purpose of the group; this is something you can make explicit by developing a mission statement collaboratively. *Roles* are responsibilities and tasks that align with the goals; these should be communicated among the group so that members can support each other. *Processes* are decisions about how work will be done, including handling communications, conflict, and decision making. *Interactions* have to do with the tone and behaviors of the team members; treating each other with respect can promote cohesion and help the group achieve its goals while negative behaviors can be harmful and ultimately cause the group to deteriorate. Proactively deciding on goals, roles, processes, and interpersonal relationships can give clarity to the group's tasks and avoid conflict. Conversely, a lack of clarity around one of these factors can cascade into problems related to another; for example, lack of clarity around goals can create confusion in terms of roles.

While there can be many roles on a team, there are certain necessary leadership tasks related to managing team development and dynamics. The leader has the job of overseeing the process of developing goals and monitoring activities to ensure their relevance to achieving the goals. There is a management part to play in terms of overseeing the various roles associated with the project and making sure that they are identified and filled and responsible parties are held accountable. As the team develops procedures, the leader assesses these procedures and encourages the team to refine them as needed. In terms of interactions, the leader establishes a climate conducive to constructive working relationships and addresses conflicts before they can become damaging to the team. Leadership roles can be fluid and shared, yet clarity is needed so that someone is charged with keeping the team on track. It can be helpful to engage your advocacy group in an activity to build teamwork and assess each member's leadership styles to understand how each member's strengths can be utilized. A popular activity is the Leadership Compass (Trimble, 2007). This activity asks participants to review working style profiles and select the one that is closest to their style. Then the group discusses the positives and negatives of different styles, identifies potential for conflict, and considers how they can balance out each other's strengths and weaknesses. Check the references for a link to a complete description of this activity.

INFLUENCING OUTCOMES: GATEKEEPERS AND DECISION MAKERS

Just as you need allies to develop your advocacy project, you also need to win over key figures who have power over your advocacy issue. Perhaps the most crucial lesson for a new child advocate is learning the complex nature of decision making that is the key to winning at your advocacy effort. Most would-be advocates think that the vast majority of their attention will go to the decision maker responsible for the ultimate agreement, legislation, or policy decision needed to achieve their advocacy goals. In fact, in most cases, there is someone or some group who will stand in the way of, or in a line of procession up to, the decision maker who will make that ultimate decision. While these individuals may not use this term themselves, we define a *gatekeeper* as someone through whom you must pass in order to gain access to the ultimate decision maker related to your issue. Decision makers are usually easier for advocates to identify. A *decision maker* is the individual or individuals who can be of help in meeting your advocacy goals. A decision maker can be an elected or appointed official, a key figure who influences other decision makers, a public figure who can help bring your message to a larger group, or simply an individual without whom you cannot get the decisions you need made. See Box 2.5 for a description of what gatekeepers control and what decision makers control. Gatekeepers and decision makers may become calculated supporters who work with you out of self-interest or champions who become convinced of the merits of your work. In this section, we will describe and provide examples of the nuances and necessities of gaining the attention, interest, and agreement of both gatekeepers and decision makers.

BOX 2.5

What Gatekeepers Control and What Decision Makers Control

Gatekeepers control . . .

- Accessing decision makers
- Providing advice on how to approach the decision maker
- Setting the tone and agenda of the meeting with the decision maker
- Ensuring completion of promised follow-up by decision makers
- Promoting inside advocacy on behalf of the advocacy group
- Sharing tips about other potential allies

Decision makers control . . .

- Being an advocate for a cause within an inner circle
- Acting as spokesperson for an issue
- Authoring or cosponsoring legislation
- Voting on advocates' supported legislation
- Winning over other votes
- Assuring the right experts are included in legislative hearings
- Accessing higher or other levels of decision makers

Gatekeepers play a unique role and are found around the world. It will be up to you as an advocate to determine whom the gatekeeper may be for a certain decision maker and how you gain access to that person. The gatekeeper is what is often referred to as a bureaucrat. One example is a legislative aide to a national or local government official. Some gatekeepers are involved in governance as members of city, county, state, or national staffs.

This gatekeeper role is seen in such diverse titles as staffer to a city planning commission, assistant to a minister of a government agency, head or member of an advisory body who informs the decision maker regarding trends and needs in a particular field, legislative or administrative counsel to a decision maker, the funding officer who controls access to the decision-making board of a foundation, and many more. Many gatekeepers in government keep their jobs even if the person they advise or protect has been defeated in an election and replaced by another elected or appointed official whom they will now be charged with supporting. Gatekeepers gain power through their role and must be treated with special care. They walk a sensitive line and need allies just like you to do their jobs best.

In each case, the gatekeeper has the role of opening the door either a crack or very wide to allow you to pass through to the decision maker. This role may take various forms. The gatekeeper may be obstructive by maintaining ongoing control and keeping you from passing through to the decision maker due to a feeling that you will contribute nothing to the decision maker. Alternatively, the gatekeeper may join with you out of the notion that you will add something to the decision maker's or their own status and assist you in preparing the right materials and developing an understanding of how best to approach a particular decision maker to achieve change. In some cases, gatekeepers can solve challenges or problems related to access to certain supports or services without the necessity of having to go to the decision maker for final approval. For example, staff to planning commissions and departments may be able to interpret statutes and provide advice for changing the size or configuration of a child care center. If effectively engaged, gatekeepers will understand that providing you with access will bring them distinction, positive feedback, or new opportunities for their decision maker. As advocates for children and families, we must understand the motivations of the gatekeeper. Here are some guidelines to keep in mind for understanding and working with gatekeepers:

- Every gatekeeper wants to feel appreciated and recognized above all by his superior(s).

- Every gatekeeper is interested in putting his decision maker in the best light at all times.

- Every gatekeeper wants his decision maker to constantly believe that he is doing the right thing for that decision maker.

- No gatekeeper wants to be left feeling as though he is unsure of the background, honesty, or soundness of a proposal brought by the advocate.

Developing a positive, interactive, friendly, and mutually supportive relationship with a gatekeeper will do wonders in moving your advocacy plan forward. By approaching the gatekeeper slowly as a potential friend and ally, you will have the best chances of success. Partnerships often start with an assessment by the advocate of whether or not he or she shares any common ground with the gatekeeper. With the advent of Google and people search mechanisms, the advocate is only a click away from gaining information on gatekeepers who have been at their jobs for more than a year or two. You may notice in their resume where they grew up, what schools they attended, what interests they may have, or whether they have served other decision makers previously and use this information to engage in a positive dialogue and establish rapport. Always treat the gatekeeper with respect. Follow the same guidelines when meeting with the gatekeeper as you do with the decision maker (see Chapter 7, "Step 4—Making Meetings That Work," for more detail). Demonstrate your respect by showing value and responding promptly to the gatekeeper's opinions, ideas, and need for follow-up. The ideal outcome is when the gatekeeper decides to accompany you to the meeting with the decision maker and can act as a gentle (inside) advocate in order to move your agenda forward. Since there is a symbiotic relationship between the gatekeeper and decision maker, it is important that the decision maker understand that you have developed a relationship with the gatekeeper and the gatekeeper has seen fit to move you to the next level, through either a meeting or a direct conversation with the decision maker. Maintain your relationship with the gatekeeper through warm thanks and continued check-ins from your advocacy group.

An example of the role of an effective gatekeeper to a decision maker is provided by the following example. Barry Brokaw was a longtime legislative aide to some of the most important people in the California State Assembly and Senate. During his long relationship with then-assembly member Dan Boatwright, the chair of the Assembly Ways and Means Committee (the group responsible for all Assembly legislative funding matters), he was able to provide access to the assembly member when advocacy groups or individuals were able to present a strong case as to why it was necessary. For example, in the development of a piece of legislation to fund child abuse prevention and family stress centers, a group of advocates from the Childcare Council of Contra Costa County met with Barry Brokaw. After the advocates demonstrated support from several thousand voters in assembly member Boatwright's district, Barry was able to guide the group to persuade the assembly member to author the legislation that was sought. Without the gatekeeper's steering and clear guidance regarding what materials the decision maker would need, the advocates would never have been able to accomplish the following: 1) gain Mr. Boatwright's agreement to be the primary author of the legislation, 2) become the expert witnesses Mr. Boatwright needed because of his lack of understanding of children's issues, 3) work with such a tenacious assembly member who hated to lose and voted in favor of his own legislation, 4) work with an author who was able to gain the governor's signature on the legislation at a time of fiscal austerity, and 5) enact family stress center legislation that led the way to many other initiatives to reduce child abuse and improve counseling of at-risk parents. As this example illustrates, a gatekeeper is an individual who takes on a series of complex and often subtle roles in relation to his or her decision maker.

Another example of a gatekeeper who becomes a champion for a group of advocates is the former chief aide to the then-governor of California. A group of advocates had previously worked with the aide, Percy Pinkney, on children's issues in San Francisco. Percy met the advocates to give them a tour of the governor's offices, and as they walked, he asked questions and showed interest in the advocates' issue. Without prior warning, he steered the advocates directly into the governor's inner office, saying, "Governor, I've brought in some people whom I think you should talk to." Out of his strong interest in the topic, this gatekeeper took bold action on behalf of the advocates in a short period of time.

Good decision makers remain open, available, accessible, thoughtful, and welcoming of those who can assist in best doing their job and meeting the objectives of their own work. Sadly, because of the clash between the skills necessary for such a job and the type of person that such a job attracts, decision makers do not always possess the aforementioned skills. As a result, an effective advocate must show tremendous tolerance, people skills, and focus in order to gain the trust and understanding of the decision maker as related to your advocacy issue. In the long run, the relationships you build with the decision makers will help you create the change for children and families that you are seeking. Many top decision makers may know little or nothing about conditions for children or families but, because of the nature of their role and position, hold power over your advocacy goal. For example, a decision maker may be the editor of a national newspaper or the director of an Internet site that will give prominence to your issue. A decision maker may be a powerful legislator who has the connections to get your desired legislation passed. A decision maker may be a government minister of women, children, and social welfare in a country that is trying to serve special needs children in a comprehensive manner for the first time. The decision maker's tasks can be many and varied.

Look for the decision maker who can help you reach your goal, possibly by championing your effort to a broader population, providing a chance to receive funding for your cause, making necessary introductions to key organizations, or spearheading the development of new legislation for children and families. It is far easier to gain the involvement of a decision maker in countries where the decision maker is running for elective office or is appointed by someone who will see his or her work more favorably when that decision maker is supporting children's issues. For example, the best choice for a legislator to support new policy development may be one with little knowledge of child and family issues but who is in the ideal position to help your legislation be passed.

Returning to the previous example, the decision maker was an individual with tremendous power to support or defeat proposed legislation that would fund major areas of children and family services. Assembly member Dan Boatwright, longtime Chair of the Assembly Ways and Means Committee of California and a fiscal conservative, often encouraged his colleagues to vote against, and himself voted against, legislation with fiscal requirements. As a result, a majority of legislation with attached funds over several years failed at the state level. However, the Childcare Council of Contra Costa County developed an advocacy strategy asking Boatwright to become the primary author of their legislation. This group was well aware that Boatwright hated to lose and would never seek defeat of a piece of legislation for which he was the primary author. They approached him within three months of a major election that was hotly contested in his district. When the Childcare Council sought a meeting with him, they accurately claimed that they represented nearly 20,000 votes within the assemblyman's district. This type of clout was such that Boatwright saw that there was no alternative but to agree to be the primary author and move the bill forward without much further ado. This decision maker proved instrumental in getting a new Family Stress Center established through funding from the California legislature, one of the few funded pieces of legislation passed on behalf of children that year. In the words of Saul Alinsky (1989), "No politician can sit on a hot issue if you make it hot enough" (p. xxiv).

TIMING AND STRATEGIC CONSIDERATIONS

In addition to the people involved in your advocacy work, the context in which you are doing your advocacy also contributes greatly to the likelihood of success or failure. This is true at the micro, mezzo, and macro levels but particularly holds at the macro level when you are trying to make big change. The arc of policy change can be on the scale of decades for some issues (Sabatier & Jenkins-Smith, 1999) until public opinion and political opportunity align so that change on an issue is possible. Each political environment, from a local city council to national parliaments, presents a different set of challenges and opportunities. In Chapter 4, "Step 1—Knowing Your Issue," you will begin to develop an understanding of the setting for your advocacy campaign, including analyzing the problem, policy context, and stakeholders.

Historic moments hold different potential for the likelihood of successfully creating social change. These moments may be predictable, unpredictable, or planned (Tadros, 2009). A predictable moment, as previously mentioned, can be during the time of an election. Politicians may be more receptive to children's causes at such times for the positive public image such sponsorship can confer. As the example in this chapter illustrated, if you can prove that your cause is supported by constituents, you can use the time leading up to a campaign to your advantage. Sometimes opportunities for change are created by unpredictable events, such as natural disasters (e.g., hurricanes, tsunamis), human accidents (e.g., nuclear power plant meltdowns, levy breaches), or other crises (e.g., acts of terrorism, school shootings). These types of events have been described as *trigger events* (Moyer, 2001) or *focusing events* (Birkland, 1997) that bring strong attention to a social issue and spur the public's demand for political change. For example, after the Port Arthur massacre, when a shooter went on a rampage at a tourist attraction and killed 35 people and wounded 18 with a semi-automatic assault weapon, the Australian public demanded and the parliament delivered major gun reform (Alpers, 2012). Advocates can turn tragedies into opportunities to prevent future disasters by acting swiftly to encourage constructive change. A planned moment for change can come as a result of deliberate activities designed to promote public awareness of an issue. Examples include organizing a conference around a social issue, encouraging media coverage through celebrity endorsement, and organizing rallies and protests.

The theory of multiple streams (Kingdon, 1984) suggests that a *policy window* can open and change can occur when three streams of events converge so that a particular issue rises to the top of policy makers' agendas. One is the *problem stream*, which represents how a problem is brought to public attention (e.g., through research from advocacy organizations, public pressure from constituents, or a focusing event) and defined (through framing, as discussed in Chapter 4), as well as its perceived importance. Even when a problem is perceived as important, it can be trumped by other issues seen as more pressing or budgetary concerns in times of economic problems. Another is the *policy stream*, which indicates the slate of possible solutions proposed for the problem. Solutions in the policy stream are apt to be more appealing when they resonate with the public's views, are compatible with the society's values, and are seen as technically feasible and reasonable in cost. The third is the *political stream*, which describes the political atmosphere such as the current political leadership, political mood (e.g., fiscally conservative), and the activities of advocacy and opposition groups. Even with a serious problem and clear solutions, advocates may beat their heads against the wall in the wrong political climate, getting nowhere with unreceptive politicians and necessitating a review and modification of their efforts.

Multiple streams theory suggests that advocates can deliberately influence the process for social change. You can deliberately build strategies into your advocacy projects to influence these different streams. For example, advocates can engage in public education to promote awareness of a problem or mobilize citizens through protests to build political will for change. They can also conduct research and develop proposals for addressing social problems and circulate these to decision makers and the public (Coffman, 2007). A starting place can be to develop a time line of events that have influence on awareness of your issue by identifying major events like the passage of new legislation or a high-profile legal case. Use this time line to develop your understanding of the historical context as well as plan for what may happen in the future, for example, with political changes due to elections (Gordon, 2002).

Ultimately, awareness about timing and context can help you develop an advocacy campaign that is realistic and feasible. Particularly for macro advocacy, prepare for gradual change. Most policy change is incremental, not fundamental, meaning that change occurs through little tweaks over time rather than sweeping changes. Having considered the parameters of advocacy in this chapter, including types of advocacy, key figures, and timing, the next chapter will prepare you to start planning your advocacy effort and introduce you to the six steps of successful child advocacy.

Activity: Developing a Mission Statement for Your Advocacy Project

This is an activity that you can do as an individual or as part of a group. If you are doing this in a group setting, prepare by bringing block paper and markers so that you can take notes that are visible to the members.

- Ask people to brainstorm words that capture your purpose. Ask for action verbs as well as nouns and adjectives.
- Write these on a board or large piece of paper to honor everyone's contribution.
- Review the main ideas that have emerged.
- Develop a succinct sentence or two that encapsulates the group's main ideas.

REFERENCES

Alinsky, S. (1989). *Rules for radicals: A practical primer for realistic radicals.* New York, NY: Vintage Press.

Alpers, P. (2012, December 17). Gun control: Change is possible—and fast. *CNN Opinion.* Retrieved from http://www.cnn.com/2012/12/16/opinion/australia-gun-laws

Baumgartner, F. R., & Leech, B. L. (1998). *Basic interests: The importance of groups in politics and in political science.* Princeton, NJ: Princeton University Press.

Beckhard, R. (1972). Optimizing team building effort. *Journal of Contemporary Business, 1*(3), 23–32.

Bernstein, N. (2011). *The lost children of Wilder: The epic struggle to change foster care.* New York, NY: Vintage Books.

Birkland, T. (1997). *After disaster: Agenda setting, public policy, and focusing events.* Washington, DC: Georgetown University Press.

Center for the Study of Social Policy (1998). *New roles for old adversaries: The challenge of using litigation to achieve system reform.* Retrieved from http://www.cssp.org/publications/child-welfare/top-five/new-roles-for-old-adversaries-the-challenge-of-using-litigation-to-achieve-system-reform.pdf

Coffman, J. (2007, Spring). Evaluation based on theories of the policy process. *The Evaluation Exchange, 13*(1&2). Retrieved from http://www.hfrp.org/evaluation/the-evaluation-exchange/issue-archive/advocacy-and-policy-change/evaluation-based-on-theories-of-the-policy-process

Cooney, S. M., Huser, M., Small, S., & O'Connor, C. (2007, October). Evidence-based programs: An overview. *What works, Wisconsin—Research to practice series, 6.* Retrieved from http://www.uwex.edu/ces/flp/families/whatworks_06.pdf

Court Appointed Special Advocates for Children (2013). *What does it mean to be a CASA volunteer?* Retrieved from http://www.casaforchildren.org/site/c.mtJSJ7MPIsE/b.6350721/k.112A/What_Does_It_Mean_To_Be_a_CASA_Volunteer.htm

Dreier, P. (2007). Community organizing for what? Progressive politics and movement building in America. In M. Orr (Ed.), *Transforming the city: Community organizing and the challenge of political change* (pp. 218–251). Lawrence, KS: University Press of Kansas.

Gen, S., & Wright, A. C. (2013). Policy advocacy organizations: A framework linking theory and practice. *Journal of Policy Practice, 12*(3), 163–193.

Gordon, G. (2002). *Practical action in advocacy.* Retrieved from http://tilz.tearfund.org/webdocs/Tilz/Roots/English/Advocacy%20toolkit/Advocacy%20toolkit_E_FULL%20DOC_Part%20C.pdf

Gorski, P. C. (1995). *Guide for setting ground rules.* Retrieved from http://www.edchange.org/multicultural/activities/groundrules.html

Hopkins, B. R. (1992). *Charity, advocacy and the law.* New York, NY: Wiley.

Kingdon, J. W. (1984). *Agendas, alternatives and public policies.* New York, NY: Longman.

McCarthy, J. D., & Castelli, J. (2002). The necessity for studying organizational advocacy comparatively. In P. Flynn & V. A. Hodgkinson (Eds.), *Measuring the impact of the nonprofit sector* (pp. 103–121). New York, NY: Plenum.

Moyer, B. (2001). *Doing democracy: The MAP model for organizing social movements.* Gabriola Island, BC: New Society.

Promising Practices Network (2013). *Programs that work.* Retrieved from http://www.promisingpractices.net/programs_outcome.asp

Raue, S., Tang, S., Weiland, C., & Wenzlik, C. (2013). *The GRPI model—an approach to team development.* Retrieved from http://www.systemic-excellence-group.com/sites/default/files/raue_tang_weiland_wenzlik_2013_the_grpi_model_an_approach_for_team_development.pdf

Sabatier, P. A., & Jenkins-Smith, H. C. (1999). The Advocacy Coalition Framework: An assessment. In P. A. Sabatier (Ed.), *Theories of the Policy Process* (pp. 117–166). Boulder, CO: Westview Press.

Tadros, N., & People's Advocacy (2009). Crafting your advocacy strategy. *UNICEF Wiki.* Retrieved from http://www.advocate-for-children.org/doku.php?id=advocacy:crafting_advocacy_strategy:crafting_your_advocacty_strategy&rev=1257278345

Trimble, N. (2007). *Leadership compass.* Retrieved from http://encorps.nationalserviceresources.org/resources/documents/LeadershipCompass.pdf

Tuckman, B. W. (1965). Developmental sequence in small groups. *Psychological Bulletin, 63*(6), 249–272.

Tuckman, B. W., & Jensen, M. A. C. (1977, December). Stages of small-group development revisited. *Group & Organization Studies, 2*(4), 419–427.

Planning Your Project With the Six Steps to Successful Child Advocacy

The reasons to plan for advocacy are addressed in this chapter, including assessing the need for resources and ensuring that plans are realistic. Strategies for planning are introduced, including Gantt charts, theory of change, and logic models. A *planning blueprint* is offered as a tool for systematically defining an advocacy plan with goals, objectives, activities, responsible parties, deadlines, milestones, costs, and evaluation. Each of the six steps to successful child advocacy is briefly described in preparation for later chapters where each step is elaborated. This discussion highlights where readers will begin the six steps (with child advocacy goals) and where they will finish (hopefully having accomplished substantive change on behalf of children). The contribution of each of the six steps toward reaching the goal is described. A discussion of fundraising for advocacy uses the six steps approach to outline a plan for soliciting funding from various sources. A case study of the Malaysian Child Resource Institute and other advocacy groups in Kuala Lumpur, Malaysia, gives a brief overview of how a national movement for children's rights and well-being was developed, pointing out how their plan incorporated each of the six steps and utilized the planning blueprint. An activity encourages readers to outline their own plan for advocacy, combining the use of a planning blueprint with the six steps to successful child advocacy approach.

DEVELOPING YOUR ADVOCACY PLAN

Why plan for an advocacy effort? Imagine yourself leaving for a road trip. Before your departure, it makes sense to figure out the purpose of the travel and the destination. This would be the equivalent of determining the mission and the vision of an advocacy campaign. You would have the condition of your car checked and determine who is coming and who is driving. In the same way, it is helpful to make an internal assessment of your resources, identify allies, and establish leadership for advocacy. It would also be prudent to check the weather and road conditions. Similarly, it is wise in an advocacy campaign to be aware of external factors that may promote or inhibit your advocacy goals, such as public opinion or political events. Then it comes down to making specific plans for your trip, such as the routes you will take, the reservations you will need, and how much money you will need to spend. Here is where you get down to the action planning stage of advocacy to determine major strategies, specific plans, and budgets. Of course on a road trip, as with an advocacy campaign, things may come up and plans may need to change. Yet the initial planning that you have done will help you determine the best course of action while remaining flexible.

Advocacy planning is part of a larger tradition of project management. While human history is replete with examples of major projects that have required systematic planning, such as architectural wonders like the pyramids of Egypt, the modern era of project management has its roots in early 20th century notions of scientific management. Frederick Winslow Taylor (1914), considered the father of scientific management, proposed a process of analyzing workflows to minimize waste and inefficiency. This was during an era of increasing systematization in industrial production, particularly manufacturing. The production of cars in an assembly line, for example, was generally designed to follow structural approaches to good planning. Fully assembling a car requires systematically planning where workers would be needed to intersect with the vehicle as it travels along an assembly line. A well-designed plan uses minimal resources and eliminates waste.

An early planning instrument, still in wide usage today, is the *Gantt chart*. Designed by Henry L. Gantt around 1910, a Gantt chart lays out tasks against a time frame. The left column of a Gantt chart lists the activities or tasks associated with a project while time frames are arrayed along the top of the chart. Bars are used to represent each task and the time (start, duration, and end time) associated with it. The person responsible for the activity is noted using initials. This provides information on which activities are associated with a project, how long they will take, and which activities will overlap, all at a glance (Wilson, 2003). See Box 3.1 for an example of a Gantt chart used for an advocacy project involving children and youth in setting community advocacy priorities.

BOX 3.1

Example of a Gantt Chart Used for an Advocacy Campaign

Responsible Person	Activities and Tasks	June	July	August
GOAL: Plan and implement public exhibition of child and youth ideas for community advocacy				
JK, RC	Brainstorm options for public exhibition with youth and children			
JK	Identify location, timing, and external groups to involve/invite			

(Continued)

(Continued)				
Responsible Person	**Activities and Tasks**	**June**	**July**	**August**
JK, RC, BT	Involve all stakeholders in regular meetings			
JK	Organize a public exhibition at a community center			
JK, BT	Debrief with groups about results of exhibition—follow up on any leads			

A more recent innovation that can be used for mapping out an advocacy plan is *theory of change* planning. The theory of change approach was initially developed by Carol Weiss (1995) of the Aspen Institute Community Change Roundtable in response to the challenges presented by evaluating community change efforts. Efforts to create widespread change in a community are often complex, and those organizing such efforts often fail to clearly conceptualize the intermediary steps to change and the assumptions that underlie their plans (Anderson, 2004). A theory of change planning effort involves setting the goal of a change effort and then mapping backwards to identify the steps needed to get there. These steps are often represented as a graphic that lays out the causal chain from interventions to short-term outcomes to the ultimate goal. See Box 3.2 for potential components of a theory of change for policy advocacy. Part of the purpose of a theory of change process is to bring to light the assumptions that connect the pieces of this chain. Those involved are asked to articulate why they think certain interventions may lead to short-term outcomes and how these short-term outcomes will ultimately result in reaching the desired goal. When assumptions are based on research, or best practices for a particular type of services, the overall theory of change may hold more promise and validity. *Indicators* are also included, meaning specific and measurable targets for each short-term outcome that can be assessed using data and evaluation (Anderson, n.d.). Engaging in this type of planning at the beginning can help to avoid pitfalls, such as engaging in an effort that is unlikely to meet its target due to flawed assumptions or conditions outside of the planners' control (Forti, 2012). While the theory of change approach is helpful as a conceptual tool for planning, logic models are operational in purpose and include more detail to support designing, planning, managing, and evaluating a project (Knowlton & Phillips, 2009).

Advocacy organizations and their supporters are increasingly using logic models to map out the process of a given advocacy effort. A *logic model* is a visual aid that diagrams the connections between resources, activities, and intended outcomes (W. K. Kellogg Foundation, 2004). Logic models describing advocacy efforts typically highlight resources such as well-trained staff, connections to decision makers, and sufficient funding; activities such as media outreach, lobbying, and constituent education; and results such as getting favorable legislation passed and implemented, blocking unfavorable legislation, and improving conditions for the advocacy effort's target population; and the connections between resources, activities, and results (Gen & Wright, 2013). Developing your own logic model for your advocacy project will help you now for planning your work, on an ongoing basis for monitoring your project, and later for guiding your evaluation efforts. See Chapter 9, "Step 6—Reinforcing Successful Advocacy Outcomes," for a discussion of monitoring and evaluation of advocacy using logic models.

BOX 3.2

Theory of Change for Policy Advocacy

Inputs/ Competencies (necessary conditions)	Activities (things to do, actions)	Proximal Outcomes (indirect and near-term)	Distal Outcomes (indirect and long-term)	Impacts
• Sense of agency in the political process • People and relationships • Specialized knowledge and skills • Material resources	• Coalition building (e.g., networking and relationship building) • Engaging and mobilizing the public (e.g., community organizing, voter registration, rallies, protests, and contacting legislators) • Engaging decision makers (e.g., relationship building, education, and lobbying) • Information campaigning (e.g., research, policy analysis, framing messages, media advocacy) • Reform efforts (e.g., pilots, demonstrations, and litigation) • Defensive activities (to defeat undesirable policies) • Policy monitoring (as policies are implemented)	• Promoting a democratic environment through transparency, accountability, and participation of civil society • Changes in public views, including changes in beliefs and attitudes and development of a base of support • Changes in decision makers' views by getting on a political agenda or shifting political will	• Policy adoption (for improved policy or blocking unwanted policy) • Implementation change (for improved implementation and enforcement of policies)	• Desired changes for target population • Desired changes in services and systems • People-centered policy making

Source: Adapted from Gen, S., & Wright, A. C. (2013). Policy advocacy organizations: A framework linking theory and practice. *Journal of Policy Practice, 12*(3), 163–193.

Prior to engaging in an advocacy effort, it is necessary to ensure that one is prepared with the necessary resources, also called inputs, of the advocacy effort. The level of resources relates to the scope of the project. For example, financial resources are often necessary to carry out a larger advocacy effort, but the amount of money to make a small, local change is different from the amount needed to make a national or international change. Many successful advocacy efforts have required little or no funding (but many volunteer hours). Certain qualities and skills are also necessary antecedents to engaging in advocacy. The ability to demonstrate leadership in terms of envisioning an advocacy plan, engaging partners, and carrying out the plan is crucial to success. Likewise, various skills may be needed during the advocacy project. This book will help with the development of useful advocacy skills, including planning, research, and persuasive communication. A final resource or input that is useful to advocacy is relationships with others also interested in making a change. These relationships can be leveraged to organize collective action, one of the types of activities that can be used to reach an advocacy goal.

Changes resulting from child advocacy efforts may be short or intermediate term (also known as *proximal*) or long-term (also known as *distal*), as can be seen from Box 3.2. Proximal changes typically cluster around efforts to build relationships and provide education. Examples of proximal outcomes in terms of relationship building would include getting a group of decision makers, such as a county board of supervisors, to make a commitment to a particular issue, building a constituency who actively support a cause, or making an influential long-term ally. Proximal educational outcomes for an advocacy effort could be to inform a segment of the public on a particular issue or create broad-based awareness among voters. Achieving a major outcome like policy change often comes from the seeds of smaller outcomes.

Theory of change models and logic models illustrate the value of planning an advocacy effort. They can help advocates set the bar at the beginning of an effort by identifying what they consider successful outcomes and benchmarks along the way. Then, working backwards, advocates can identify which activities are likely to lead to successful outcomes and what resources are needed to engage in those activities. Laying out the steps of an advocacy effort can provide a game plan that offers direction and motivation to an advocate or group of advocates. The planning blueprint described next complements the development of a theory of change or logic model by allowing for further elaboration of the plan to meet identified goals.

A tool to plan your advocacy effort, known as the *planning blueprint*, is provided in Box 3.3. (see p. 46). This tool has elements of both the theory of change and logic model approaches, including the idea of *backward mapping*, from your goal to the necessary objectives and actions to achieve it. It also has an element of time like the Gantt chart. The tool allows the advocacy team to move from initial concept to realistic plan by working as a team on a concise (preferably one- to three-page) planning document. It was developed by the International Child Resource Institute in the 1980s for advocacy and program planning purposes based on an earlier version utilized by the Public Management Institute in San Francisco. The following are the components of the planning blueprint:

A. *Goals or Outcomes*: Goals are the outcome of all efforts to make change or improvements. Think about the desired net impact or effect of all of the work to be accomplished to change conditions for a specific child or family or children and families in a community, a region, a nation, or the world. Using *goalese*, write these statements as though the change has already taken place.

B. *Objectives*: Each objective should clearly answer four questions. The first question is *who* will do the work? The second question is *what* will the work be comprised of? The third question is *how many* children and families will be impacted by the work to be accomplished on each objective? The fourth question is *when* will the work be accomplished? Incorporating each of these four elements allows you to develop *SMART* objectives, an acronym that stands for specific, measurable, attainable, relevant, and time-bound.

C. *Activities*: Activities should be targeted to effectively meet each objective. A list of many activities may be necessary in order to accomplish one objective. In order to determine all of the activities necessary to reach each objective, an advocacy team can brainstorm all of the activities that it may take in order to meet the objective to successfully reach the goal.

D. *Who*: This column asks the question who will complete each activity and requires that you designate an individual or individuals to be responsible for each activity. Designating an individual to accomplish each activity allows for the first major reality check for the planning effort. If you note that only your initials are beside every or most activities listed and you are aware that no one human being could accomplish this number of activities within a reasonable period of time, you must adjust activities, eliminate some, or delegate to team members.

E. *Time*: Having established the responsible person, it is now necessary to estimate the amount of time that each activity will take. For example, if you are attempting to develop and carry out an activity that requires recruitment of volunteers and you have established who will recruit those volunteers, you must also ascribe an estimated amount of time for volunteer recruitment. While the estimate may not be completely accurate, it is helpful to establish realistic time lines for each activity.

F. *Performance Measures/Indicators*: A *performance measure* is an output or indicator that signals whether an activity has been accomplished. It simply notes whether an objective, such as recruiting volunteers, has been met. Monitor these outputs to keep track of the activities that have been accomplished. See Chapter 9, "Step 6— Reinforcing Successful Advocacy Outcomes," for more information on monitoring outputs.

G. *Budget*: If your advocacy effort requires expenditures, the next column notes costs. This can be split into two columns, for personnel and nonpersonnel costs. Personnel costs are payments for those who are carrying out work. If a volunteer conducts the work, you will not need to enter anything into the budget column unless you will value the staff time at a certain rate per hour. If you are working with a nonprofit organization or research institute, there may be indirect administrative costs, generally a fixed percentage of the costs associated with their services (e.g., 20%). Nonpersonnel costs are all other costs, including supplies. After assessing the cost of each activity, a subtotal is added at the bottom of the column.

H. *Evaluation*: Every good advocacy plan must have a method to evaluate the success of the project after it is established. There are different strategies for evaluation of an advocacy effort. An *internal evaluation* involves meeting regularly (at least quarterly) to review the logic model and planning blueprint and make any changes to the activity plans necessary in order to keep the project on track. *External evaluation* is conducted by an outside evaluator who can help advocates understand how they can conduct their work more efficiently and effectively. This can involve a *formative evaluation*, which takes place while an advocacy project is currently under way to inform improvements. At the end of an advocacy campaign, a *summative evaluation* may be conducted, which helps identify lessons learned that may be applied for future efforts. Sources of external evaluation include university evaluation classes or consultants when funding is available. See Chapter 9 for more information on evaluating advocacy projects.

BOX 3.3

Format of Planning Blueprint

Goals (Outcomes)	Objectives	Activities	Who	Time	Performance Measures (Milestones)	Cost	Evaluation
States what will have happened if all steps are accomplished. Frequently used words in writing a goal are "increased," "improved," or "enhanced."	Provides a measure of the outcome. Answers the question: "*Who* will do *what* for *how many* by *when*?"	Describes the specific steps to be accomplished toward meeting the objectives.	Indicates the person or persons responsible for implementing each of the activities.	States the specific dates or period of time in which each activity will be accomplished.	Describes outputs that will show that each activity has been achieved.	Assesses the cost of each activity. Used to help develop the overall budget. Identify both non-personnel and personnel costs.	Answers the question: "Have the activities that have been carried out met their performance measures, which have gone to meet the objectives and desired outcomes?"

Subtotal Cost (nonpersonnel) = $_____ + Subtotal Cost (personnel) = $_____ + Administrative Overhead = $_____ = Grand Total $_____

An example of a completed planning blueprint is included in Box 3.5, which accompanies the case study at the conclusion of the chapter. The case study describes an advocacy campaign that used the six steps of successful child advocacy to reach its goals. These steps are described in the next section.

INTRODUCING THE SIX STEPS TO SUCCESSFUL CHILD ADVOCACY

The six steps discussed throughout this book are the product of more than 20 years of refinement by trial and error. They have been influenced by the latest planning techniques gathered from around the world. Through a process of learning and adjusting, these steps have been reviewed, refined, and reworked as child advocacy has changed. The following is a brief overview of the six steps, each of which is later elaborated in its own chapter, that will launch the advocate into the core work of transforming the lives of children.

Step 1: Knowing Your Issue

Simply deciding to conduct advocacy will not make one an advocate. It is necessary to go far beyond simple statements of wanting to "save the world for children" by first learning to understand and frame the issue or issues that are at the core of your potential advocacy effort. This framing takes the form of understanding how you can make your issue clear and understandable so that decision makers or gatekeepers will understand your issue in a manner that helps them support your desired change or lead you in the right direction. Knowing the issue means being able to effectively, briefly, and directly tell the world about your advocacy issue and help the necessary gatekeepers and decision makers to understand and speak of your issue as though it were their own. The purpose of this step is to learn about your topic so that you can present it in a way that ensures that your issue is *yes-able* to those within the decision-making chain of the advocacy effort. The concept of a yes-able decision means that decision makers will understand what they must do in order to assist you through their positions, knowledge, or decision-making capability to reach your goal. As an advocate, you must know not only who will support your proposed solutions but also what the opposition might say and how their arguments may be counteracted.

Step 2: Research for Background and Impact

Step 2 follows from Step 1 by requiring that you conduct research on your issue. This step provides you with a systematic approach to information gathering to support the development of summary sheets to educate not only the gatekeepers and decision makers but also your own constituency. You may use secondary research to gather existing information or primary research where little or no objective information exists. Examples of secondary research already available on your topic might include demographic data, polling data, and research studies. Examples of primary research that you could conduct yourself might include surveys, interviews, and focus groups. The research you will conduct in Step 2 will form the backbone of your advocacy effort by providing evidence for your suggested solutions.

Step 3: Preparing Effective Materials

After you have fully framed your issue and conducted the research for background and impact that supports your advocacy position, you will need to share your information with key decision makers, often through their gatekeepers, as well as your allies or team members. It is useful to develop techniques for sharing the information in a manner customized for the decision makers who can best utilize it. Unless they are completely fascinated by an idea or subject area, decision makers are unlikely to review more than one page of material. Since that is the case, this step involves the development of a summary sheet that presents an issue succinctly for someone with a relatively short attention span and a need to move on to other things in a rapid-fire manner. The summary sheet is used when moving to Step 4, making meetings that work.

Step 4: Making Meetings That Work

In order to successfully utilize the materials that you have gathered through effective research and write-ups, you will need to make a series of strategic meetings that will be the key to accomplishing your advocacy plan. Some may support you because they agree with your issue, and some will do it because their support of your advocacy campaign offers some personal advantage. These meetings may be with those who control access to decision makers, known as gatekeepers, or may be with decision makers themselves. The challenge can be to gain meetings with those who are not under any obligation to meet with you. This step will allow you to explore not only how meetings are made but also what to say, what not to say, whom to bring, whom to leave at home, and most important, how to follow up after a meeting experience, known as *memorializing the meeting*. In this step, the advocate will begin to see how good research, presentation skills, active listening, reading the room, and using intuition about the decision maker will lead you to the desired goal.

Step 5: Conducting Strategic Follow-Up

Step 5 calls for strategic and appropriate follow-up with decision makers and engaging your supporters so that they are prepared for the necessary advocacy activities along the way. This step entails understanding all the decision-making steps needed to reach your advocacy goals as well as remaining connected to decision makers, so that you can supply needed follow-up, and allies, so that you can keep them updated on the advocacy project as it progresses. You must follow up with *us* (your team) and *them* (the decision makers and gatekeepers) at the same time. Social media is a helpful tool for maintaining these connections and sharing information in a timely and accessible manner. Follow-up is what will, in the end, most directly lead to achieving your advocacy goals.

Step 6: Reinforcing Successful Advocacy Outcomes

If you have reached Step 6, it means that you have been at least partially, if not fully, successful in your advocacy endeavor. Step 6 is specifically designed to ensure that you will be able to continue your work by building on your previous successes and forming lasting bonds with gatekeepers, decision makers, and your own advocacy collaborators in order to gain more successful advocacy results in the future. The most important feature of maintaining positive relationships with gatekeepers and decision makers is to know how they wish to be thanked. Most elected officials want to be thanked in the most public way possible. Speaking of a decision maker in flattering terms in a media article will earn the advocate the decision maker's goodwill toward future advocacy efforts. Some decision makers want to be thanked quietly so that few others may know of the assistance that they have provided you and your team. It is imperative that the advocate discern how best to recognize the decision maker to gain the greatest chance for future positive results while not harming the generally fragile relationship that has been established.

These six steps will be thoroughly reviewed and explained in the chapters to follow. In real life, the six steps may occur in a different order or may loop between stages with some repetition of steps. For example, it may be necessary to conduct Step 2, research for background and impact, before developing a clear understanding on how to frame an issue as part of Step 1, understanding your issue. Or a meeting with a decision maker as part of Step 4 may require that you conduct more research (Step 2) or create new materials (Step 3). Be aware that the realities of an advocacy campaign can be messy and require the advocate to think and react quickly, modifying his or her plans in response to changing realities. The next section provides some insights into finding funding for your advocacy work using the six steps approach to guide your efforts.

APPLYING THE SIX STEPS TO FUNDRAISING FOR ADVOCACY

For the planning stage of many advocacy projects, fundraising to assist in the advocacy effort, and in certain cases to fund new programs for children, is an essential component. The six steps approach provides a strategy to raise the necessary material support for your advocacy project. Each step of the process is summarized to help you gain awareness on how to implement fundraising as part of a successful advocacy agenda.

Step 1 of a fundraising plan is *knowing your issue*. Just as in advocacy planning, knowledgeable fund development specialists will define their issues to appeal to a wide variety of funders who may be able to provide support. A well-defined issue will allow the advocate to look beyond the obvious funding sources and provide the greatest chances of receiving support from the broadest possible audience. Knowing the issue and defining it clearly will help to set the advocate on the right course to fund development success.

Step 2 of a fund development plan is to *conduct research for background and impact*. In this case, conduct research on potential funding opportunities that might support your advocacy solutions for children and families. There are certain key reference books and locales around the world that can assist the would-be advocate in raising funds. For example, the Foundation Center (headquartered in New York, with locations throughout the United States) provides a treasure trove of information and resources for grant seekers. The Foundation Center website offers advocates an opportunity to purchase various levels of access to information from the Foundation Center Directory. Thousands of funders are listed and can be accessed through conducting keyword searches. Information on funders includes the names of organizations the foundation has funded in the past and the amount, useful information to have when targeting a particular funder. Keyword searches can include the names of countries or regions in which a potential funder may provide funding. Summaries are available for funders of certain subject areas, some of which may be of interest to child advocates. An advocate seeking funding for a campaign related to child protection, for example, may find funders interested in this topic. Begin your search by casting the nets broadly and continue to refine your search terms as you find potential funders that may fit with your topic. The hub-and-spoke approach described in Chapter 4, "Step 1—Knowing Your Issue," can give you some ideas for search terms broadly related to your advocacy topic.

Other useful research can be gathered on donations by corporations from sources such as government or private agencies. As part of a movement for corporate social responsibility, many for-profit institutions give back to their communities through direct giving programs, sponsorship programs, matching gifts programs, in-kind donations of goods, and volunteer programs that allow employees to serve the community during work hours. Corporations are often interested in partnering with child advocates so that they can receive tax write-offs and other benefits from the countries in which they are located. Corporate giving can also provide positive publicity, another reason why a company may be willing to provide donations to child and family issues. Local chambers of commerce, which exist around the world, often provide useful information on who is a large employer in your community. Local service organizations or clubs comprised of business owners, such as Rotary Clubs and Lions Clubs, may also provide funding to well-developed advocacy efforts.

The *preparation of effective materials* is the critical third step to success in fund development. These materials differ from the ones normally presented by advocates but have certain overarching similarities. For example, while a summary sheet may be all that is necessary to gain a foothold with a gatekeeper or decision maker, much more is required in order to gain that level of partnership with a funder. Start by developing a list of all potential funders, including foundations, corporations, individual donors, and government agencies. This list should include the following information:

- the name of the potential funder,
- the grant range or giving range (if known),
- the major subject areas funded by that donor (if known),
- the process for submitting a proposal or gaining a meeting with the potential funder, and
- all of the decision-making steps through which you must shepherd the proposal.

Once you have established your potential audiences and before you prepare a proposal, you should attempt to make contact with the funder. An initial conversation may provide insights on what the funder is looking for, which can help you tailor your proposal, though it can be difficult to set up such contacts as funding becomes more competitive and sought after. Follow the guidelines established by the funder and provide the types of information the funder will require. A typical proposal, or *letter of intent* (LOI) as the initial contact with a funder is generally known, will include several components. First, provide a history and background of the advocates or advocacy effort, including describing the reason for such an advocacy effort. Second, document the need addressed by the advocacy effort supported by research or background information on the issues being advocated for (or against). Third, clearly state the goals, objectives, and activity plan, including who will accomplish each activity, how long it will take, and how much it will cost. This is the section where you place your budget for the funding requested. Also specify which indicators will be used to determine progress and how the overall project will be evaluated. Draw this information from your planning blueprint described earlier in this chapter. The fourth and final piece of an effective proposal will include an outcomes section that describes what will happen if the advocacy is successful and what will happen if it is not. In your discussion, emphasize how the funding will help the advocacy project achieve success.

Step 4 in the process of securing funding is *making meetings that work*. There are specific ways to make meetings work with various types of funders. The strategy will vary depending on whether you are seeking funding from individual donors, foundations, companies or corporations, or government sources. Individual donors are often the most willing to support advocacy efforts. The process of gaining support is less formal than with the other sources but should still include providing the donor with a description of your advocacy plan and frequent updates. Many advocates have received wonderful support from individuals or small affinity groups after publicizing the need to make change related to children and families. Letters to the editor in a local paper can be one way to raise your profile and bring donors to you. An example of this type of financing occurred in Solano County, California, after state budget cuts threatened the closure of an emergency shelter for maltreated children. Out of desperation, staff and supporters of the shelter decided to develop a nonprofit to continue the program and wrote letters to the editors of several local papers describing the situation. A resident of the county, from a very wealthy family, called one of the newspapers and asked to be connected to the advocacy group. She ultimately paid the full bill for the shelter's operating costs for several years.

With foundations, a meeting can often be made either in person or on the telephone with a funding officer. However, this is not accomplished without doing sufficient prework to establish a letter of intent and using that initial contact to gain a meeting. It has become more and more difficult over the past several years to gain a meeting with a foundation funder. However, if that potential funder has an interest in your advocacy subject, the meeting is much easier to procure. Following your research in Step 2, it is helpful to identify members of your advocacy team who have had previous dealings with potential funders. Setting up meetings with foundations includes the components of Step 4, making meetings that work, including knowing the decision maker, providing a letter of intent, bringing people to the meeting whom the decision maker knows and with whom he or she feels comfortable, and being able to develop a dialogue (not a monologue) with the decision maker. By the time you complete your meeting with a foundation funder, you should have gained greater knowledge of the requirements of submitting a full proposal, the time line for such a process, and the process for follow-up in the decision-making effort.

Companies or corporations may be best approached through your allies who have close contacts with company leadership. While some companies have corporate foundations but also provide direct corporate donations, these should be handled differently. Corporate foundations should be treated like other foundations while company donations require a different approach. Corporations, unlike foundations, are not in the business of giving out funding. As a result, one must appeal among other things to the ability for the company to receive a tax write-off in various countries. These tax advantages help many companies to reduce their indebtedness and to balance the amount that they might give to the government with a donated amount that will help their communities. The company must understand that those they fund will assist them in being seen in a better light in their own community, country, and the world. A company that is trying to develop a new line of children's products that are safe and environmentally friendly, for example, would be well-served by linking with a group advocating for better conditions for children and families. It should be noted that most forms of advocacy are tax deductible whereas directly lobbying politicians is not. Even where tax deductions are not available as an incentive, supporting a company by helping it to improve its image can also provide an advocate with a chance at receiving funding to support an advocacy project.

Government funding must be approached in a similar manner to the others. While government representatives, like other funders, may insist that they are completely neutral, they are influenced by the same expertise, sincerity, honesty, and ability to write good proposals that influence other potential donors. The key to receiving government funds is to know early enough which Requests for Proposals (RFPs) will be distributed, how long you have to talk to government officials before submitting your proposal (since the time for questions is short and specified), and how you can link your approach to match the guidelines of the government's request. Custom tailor your materials to the needs of each different funding decision maker.

As with your advocacy effort, you must *conduct strategic follow-up* with the potential funder in Step 5. Follow-up can include providing supporting materials to the funder as requested. You can also keep the funder appraised of your progress through updates, which may occur informally through social media and formally through progress reports. As described by Maggie Kamau-Biruri, ICRI Africa founder and highly successful fundraiser, a way to gain ongoing fiscal support is through *friendraising* (see Box 3.4 for a description of friendraising). Maggie makes the experience for the decision maker so positive and supportive that she makes friends for life of her funders. This type of follow-up, conducted with honesty and integrity, makes the difference.

BOX 3.4

Advocacy Through Friendraising

By Maggie Kamau-Biruri, ICRI Africa Founder and Director Emeritus (Kenya)

Raising money for children and families is increasingly challenging, especially in this age of financial crisis and the ever greater competition for funding from a limited pool of donors. Advocates for children and families should think of other ways to raise funds for their causes. Relationship fundraising or *friendraising* is one way that could help promote your advocacy efforts. Friendraising entails building a unique relationship between the donor and your work. It involves cultivation of a deeper relationship that makes the donor feel more connected to your cause beyond monetary investments. Successful friendraising leads to the donor becoming your advocate and creates opportunities for reaching out to others in his or her circles.

How to Do Friendraising:

There is no formula for friendraising, but here are some key principles that should be applied:

Personalized outreach—When you begin cultivating a donor, make the conversation as organic as possible, avoiding formality and use of jargon. If the donor was introduced to you by a mutual friend, colleague, or acquaintance, bring this up and try to find common ground to break the ice. Discuss your advocacy work, personalizing it and showing why this work is important to you.

Consistent follow-up—Continue the conversation by e-mail or phone. Send a picture or story showing how your work is helping children and families. Avoid overloading donors with information by gauging their level of interest and using your judgment on what level of engagement would be most comfortable to the donor. If the donor can be visited easily, ask for a face-to-face meeting or arrange for the donor to visit your program to see for him- or herself the good work that you are doing.

The ask—The best case scenario would be if the donor asks you to submit a request—this happens many times where you do not even need to ask. However, if this does not happen, you MUST ask. Depending on how your relationship has evolved, make a case for the donor to invest in your cause, highlighting how this gift will kick-start a new, much-needed initiative or build on a successful project that might be coming to an end. You could also ask the donor to provide a matching fund gift—a gift that will keep giving. All these kinds of requests place donors at the center of your advocacy work, providing them with ownership for the cause.

Continued stewardship—Once donors have given financial gifts, continue to engage them in your work, recognize them, invite them to special events, and even ask them to be speakers to both beneficiaries and other donors. Show them that you value them beyond their money and that they, too, are now advocates for children and families. Social media tools such as Facebook, Twitter, and LinkedIn provide helpful methods for friendraising cultivation and stewardship.

How do you know that you have successfully friendraised? Here are some signs:

- If the donor asks for a request before you do the ask
- If the donor gives you more than you asked for
- If the donor apologizes for having given you less than you had asked for and makes arrangements for future funding without your solicitation
- If the donor is the one reaching out to you, asking you to join her or him to reach out to others
- If the donor is giving to your cause when it is clearly outside his or her focus area
- If the donor comes together with others to form a donor group for your cause to discuss how best to ensure that your work goes on

Engender goodwill and continued support by *reinforcing successful outcomes*, in the sixth and final step. Unlike public officials and elected decision makers, who appreciate positive attention associated with supporting an advocacy campaign, funders often prefer to be acknowledged quietly instead. This is particularly true with certain individual donors or foundations or other funders who want to maintain a low profile so as not to receive a flood of unwanted proposals. Other funders may welcome being mentioned in your promotional materials, such as websites and brochures. This can be worked out in conversation with the funder.

Sometimes, despite the best efforts and intentions, a fundraising effort may initially be unsuccessful. ICRI and a local child care council developed a funding proposal in one county to hire a children's advocate to work on projects such as expanding child care options and improving quality of existing programs. After an arduous process of meeting with the prospective funders, the funding request was denied. While this might have been the darkest moment for the advocacy team, it in fact led to a deeper level of understanding and the development of a better proposal. The advocates requested a conversation with the funding officer to review why the project was not funded. The call to the funding officer stated, "We like to learn from our mistakes and would very much appreciate gaining a better understanding of the decision-making process and why the proposal was not approved." The funding officer prefaced the meeting by stating, "Please don't take this as gospel because I am only the funding officer and only advise the board, which decides on your proposal, but if I were you, I would have written it in this way." As the advocate wrote furiously, the program officer outlined several points while continuing to disclaim, "Please don't take this as gospel." As a result of the meeting, ICRI wrote a proposal along the precise lines modestly suggested by the funding officer. After the proposal was resubmitted, it received full funding that continued for a 10-year period. As this example illustrates, even losses in the advocacy and funding arena can be dealt with so that a successful advocate can maintain the resolve to achieve the desired outcome for children and families.

Case Study: The Six Steps in Action, Malaysian Child Resource Institute and Other Advocacy Groups in Malaysia

For several years, International Child Resource Institute (ICRI) offered trainings on child advocacy to the Malaysian government and various child and family organizations working in the country. These trainings utilized the planning blueprint to help these groups develop clear goals, objectives, and action plans in order to enable their work. In 1997, a major breakthrough took place when the Malaysian government initiated development of the first national plan for the children of Malaysia. ICRI was invited to lead a national child advocacy workshop, bringing together nongovernmental organizations (NGOs) serving children and government ministries responsible for children's issues. UNICEF, the Malaysian Child Resource Institute, and the government's National Ministry of Planning were the cosponsors of the effort.

There were serious questions about whether a meeting of the minds could take place among these stakeholders that would result in the development of a major national plan. The government officials and NGO leaders broke into groups to create planning blueprints for various aspects of children's issues in the country. Through their collaborative work, the workshop became the catalyst for the creation of the first national plan for children. The use of the planning blueprint enabled a common language that led to greater understanding between government officials and NGO leaders.

This collaboration began to narrow and focus on the issues (Step 1) in common for the stakeholders. Those issues included the desire for integration of special needs children in educational programs, expansion and quality improvement for early childhood programs, reform of primary and secondary school education, prevention and treatment for maltreated children, and improved services for maternal and child health. The group then divided into interest areas and conducted research for background and impact (Step 2) by gathering data on the prevalence of issues like disabilities among children, various forms of child maltreatment, and poor health outcomes. Each of the interest groups prepared summary sheets and other materials (Step 3) that described their issues and how the various issues interrelated. The fact that these groups had been part of a national planning effort with the government assisted them greatly in making meetings that worked (Step 4) with key gatekeepers, such as advisers to government officials, and decision makers, such as the Minister of Women, Community, and Development. They then conducted follow-up and built strong constituencies around each of the issues (Step 5). The campaign took several years to reach full momentum during which time the advocates became members of important boards and commissions and continued to work closely with government officials in promoting their parts of the national plan. The national plan was ultimately fully enacted with evaluation and monitoring, and most advocates involved felt that the work was responsible for significant change in the betterment of conditions for the children of Malaysia. One concrete change is the Permata Negara initiative, started in 2007, which has established hundreds of high-quality early childhood programs for low-income families. The decision makers received broad publicity, and the advocates publicly thanked them for their work (Step 6). One example of public recognition came during the country's first international conference on early childhood education in 2009. The Prime Minister and First Lady were recognized for their leadership on behalf of children's issues. See Chapter 7, Boxes 7.1 and 7.2, for perspectives from advocates and a decision maker on this advocacy effort.

Activity: Outlining Your Advocacy Plan

Begin to outline your own advocacy plan, combining the use of a planning blueprint (see Box 3.5) with the six steps to successful child advocacy approach. Sketch out your initial ideas for an advocacy goal and how you might put that goal in concrete terms by developing objectives. Consider what activities would be necessary to achieve those results and who might be able to partner with you on these activities. What is a reasonable time frame for conducting these activities, and how would you know through observable milestones that the objectives had been achieved? Will you need funding to carry out your activities, and if so, how could you find possible funding sources using the strategies described in the previous section? What are your thoughts on how to evaluate whether your project has reached its goal? These initial ideas will be modified and refined as the rest of the book carries you through a detailed discussion of each of the six steps.

BOX 3.5

Example of Completed Planning Blueprint

Goals (Outcomes)	Objectives	Activities	Who	Time	Performance Measures (Milestones)	Cost	Evaluation
A fully developed and implemented national plan for the children of Malaysia.	The Malaysian government and NGOs will develop a plan for joint work to provide care, education, health, and development for Malaysia's most vulnerable children within two years of project inception.	1) Identify and analyze issues (Step 1) 2) Conduct background research and prepare for national advocacy meeting (Steps 2–3) 3) Gain agreement from key decision makers on final plan (Step 4) 4) Work with stakeholders to roll out new programs for children following national plan (Step 5) 5) Conduct major national thank-you effort for gatekeepers, decision makers, national NGOs, and government leadership (Step 6)	1) Meetings among issue groups (name each group) 2) Consultant hired to do research and develop materials 3) Lead advocates of issues groups 4) Consultant hired to do strategic planning 5) Public relations firm	1) 3 months (January–March) 2) 6 months (April–August) 3) 3 months (September–November) 4) 1 year (December–December) 5) 1 month (January)	1–2) Development of a summary sheet outlining issues, research, and proposed solutions 3) Gatekeepers and decision makers agree to work on campaign 4) National plan rollout event is held with the Prime Minister and First Lady 5) Gala at national conference on early childhood with formal thank-you to the Prime Minister and First Lady	1) Refreshments for issue group meetings 2) Personnel costs for consultant 3) Personnel costs for lead advocate travel expenses 4) Personnel costs for consultant 5) Pro bono assistance from public relations firm	1) Internal evaluation with quarterly meetings of project staff to review and adjust the planning blueprint 2) Assessment of community awareness of new programs with in-person and telephone surveys 3) Assessment of consumer satisfaction for new programs with focus groups of parents 4) External evaluation annually with final report on outcomes of new programs, with reference to the project logic model

Subtotal Cost (nonpersonnel) = $_____ + Subtotal Cost (personnel) = $_____ + Administrative Overhead = $_____ =

Grand Total $_____

REFERENCES

Anderson, A. A. (2004, October). *Theory of change as a tool for strategic planning: A report on early experiences.* Washington, DC: The Aspen Institute Roundtable on Community Change. Retrieved from http://www.theoryofchange.org/pdf/tocII_final4.pdf

Anderson, A. A. (n.d.). *The community builder's approach to theory of change: A practical guide to theory development.* New York, NY: The Aspen Institute Roundtable on Community Change. Retrieved from http://www.aspeninstitute.org/sites/default/files/content/docs/rcc/rcccommbuildersapproach .pdf

Forti, M. (2012, May). Six theory of change pitfalls to avoid. *Stanford Social Innovation Review.* Retrieved from http://www.ssireview.org/blog/entry/six_theory_of_change_pitfalls_to_avoid

Gen, S., & Wright, A. C. (2013). Policy advocacy organizations: A framework linking theory and practice. *Journal of Policy Practice, 12*(3), 163–193.

Knowlton, L. W., & Phillips, C. C. (2009). *The logic model guidebook: Better strategies for great results.* Los Angeles, CA: SAGE.

Taylor, F. W. (1914). *The principles of scientific management.* New York, NY: Harper.

Weiss, C. H. (1995). Nothing as practical as good theory: Exploring theory-based evaluation for comprehensive community initiatives for children and families (pp. 65–92). In J. P. Connell, A. C. Kubisch, L. B. Schorr, & C. H. Weiss (Eds.), *New approaches to evaluating community initiatives: Concepts, methods, and contexts.* Washington, DC: Aspen Institute.

Wilson, J. M. (2003). Gantt charts: A centenary appreciation. *European Journal of Operational Research, 149*(2), 430–437.

W. K. Kellogg Foundation (2004). *Logic model development guide.* Retrieved from: http://www.exinfm .com/training/pdfiles/logicModel.pdf

CHAPTER 4

Step 1—Knowing Your Issue

An advocate must be clear on precisely which outcome he or she desires and in what form. This chapter discusses how to formulate the issue in such a way that it is clear and understandable to someone who has little or no background in the field. The first step is to identify the issue of concern as well as the population most affected. Once the issue is identified, it is important to analyze the issue for stakeholders. Several problem analysis tools are introduced, including the hub-and-spoke approach to defining an issue, which entails identifying the full breadth and scope of the issue as well as enumerating all the other issues it touches. There is also a description of analyzing the policy context, which can be influential for micro, mezzo, or macro advocacy. The discussion of analyzing the issue and policy context leads to an explanation of framing and how to package an issue in a way that educates the decision maker and others as to the issues at hand and the consequences related to those issues. Readers are encouraged to investigate evidence-based programs in their advocacy area and to incorporate such approaches in their advocacy goals. The concepts of identifying, analyzing, and framing an issue to raise national awareness on child maltreatment are illustrated in a case study from Fundación Paniamor, a nonprofit organization in Costa Rica. The chapter concludes with an activity to analyze an advocacy issue based on the hub-and-spoke approach.

IDENTIFYING THE ISSUE

You may come to your path as a child advocate and this book with a clear advocacy issue in mind. Or you may be deeply concerned about the well-being of children and motivated to do something about it but unsure where to start. In either case, it is appropriate to do a *needs assessment* to identify and assess the needs to target with your advocacy. A needs assessment is a process to identify what must change to address disparities between the current situation and the desired one, to prioritize these needs, and to choose which ones to address. Kaufman, one of the early originators of needs assessment, and his colleagues (1993) identify three levels of needs assessment: needs at the societal level, needs at an organizational level, and needs of individuals and small groups. They recommend the following basic procedure:

1. Identify your ideal vision of this issue and its impacts on individuals and society.

2. Determine the current status of the issue and its impacts on individuals and society.

3. Consider the gap between the ideal vision and the current status of the issue.

4. Create a realistic overarching goal or mission.

5. Break down the overarching goal into objectives for each gap that you address.

6. Present your list of identified needs to allies, champions, and other stakeholders.

7. Decide on various methods to address the needs and determine advantages and disadvantages for each method (Kaufman, Rojas, & Mayer, 1993).

First, decide if your concerns are at a micro, mezzo, or macro level (defined in Chapter 2). If you already have individuals, organizations, or communities with which you plan to collaborate on advocacy, invite them to a brainstorming session to collectively develop your advocacy goal. Envision the ideal scenario and discuss how this compares with the current reality. As discussed in Chapter 3, as part of developing your planning blueprint, a goal is written as though you have already accomplished the desired change. Identify the beneficiary of change (a single child at the micro level, a group or community at the mezzo level, a category of children affected by a social issue at the macro level) and specify the new condition for the beneficiaries. For example, here are three goals at the micro, mezzo, and macro levels:

• Micro: A child with special needs is able to participate in an afterschool program.

• Mezzo: Children in a community have a safe and appropriate place to play.

• Macro: Youth in state juvenile detention facilities receive education and rehabilitative services.

Now consider the current state of the issues you care about and the gap from the current status to the ideal. What would be the major things that would have to change to realize this vision? List everything you know about the issue; these may be facts, inference, or speculation (Nagy, 2013). A fact is something objectively known to be true. Inference is a logical deduction based on evidence. Speculation comes from thinking about a subject and forming an opinion based on incomplete evidence. See Box 4.1 for examples of possible facts, inference, and speculation about the goals identified above. What are the gaps between what you know and need to know, and what are the hunches that need investigation? List all the things that you need to know. These will become your research questions for "Step 2—Research for Background and Impact" (Chapter 5).

BOX 4.1

Examples of Facts, Inference, and Speculation About Goals at Different Advocacy Levels

Advocacy Level	Advocacy Goal	What Do You Know?
Micro	A child with special needs is able to participate in an afterschool program	• Fact: An assessment by the school district found that the afterschool program lacks accessible entrances and restrooms. • Inference: Because they have never had any special needs children, the staff probably have not received specialized training on appropriate accommodations for children with special needs. • Speculation: Staff and children may have negative attitudes and stereotypes about the abilities of special needs children.
Mezzo	Children in a community have a safe and appropriate place to play	• Fact: A site visit showed that the local park has equipment for older children but lacks a play space for younger children. • Inference: Because it was built 40 years ago, the playground equipment probably does not meet current safety standards. • Speculation: Since it is run-down, the park may attract illegal activity.
Macro	Youth in state juvenile detention facilities receive education and rehabilitative services	• Fact: A class action lawsuit found that youth in a state juvenile detention facility were not receiving sufficient access to education and rehabilitative services. • Inference: Because youth who enter juvenile detention facilities may already be facing academic challenges that put them at risk for school failure, intensive tutoring and other services may be needed. • Speculation: Investment in services may pay off in lower rates of reincarceration.

Move from your goal and identification of gaps to developing a problem statement. Use what you know about the problem to briefly and succinctly describe the general problem that your advocacy will address in one to two sentences. For an individual child, you could describe the child's situation or condition that you are trying to ameliorate.

For mezzo or macro advocacy, sketch out the basics about the social problem or concern. Describe the current status of the issue and the desired change, identifying the *who, what, when, where,* and *how* of the issue. As you learn more about the issue in Chapter 5, "Step 2—Research for Background and Impact," you may choose to revise the problem statement. Here are examples of problem statements based on the previously stated goals:

- Micro: The afterschool program at a particular elementary school is not equipped to serve children with special needs. A child who has recently enrolled at the school would benefit from socialization and academic enrichment activities with peers in the afterschool program with appropriate accommodations.

- Mezzo: A community has few safe, public spaces for children to play, and its existing parks are poorly kept with inadequate play structures. Children and families in the community would enjoy recreating and socializing in parks that included facilities for children of various ages that were well maintained.

- Macro: A state is under pressure to reform its juvenile justice system after negative media coverage and class action lawsuits alleging lack of appropriate services. Youth in the facility would be more likely to experience positive outcomes postdischarge if they receive academic and social services.

After defining the problem, make a decision about whether this is the problem you want to attempt to solve through advocacy. It is possible you have identified more than one problem and need to prioritize to select your focus. Consider the following criteria as you decide on the focus of your advocacy efforts: 1) Is the issue important to you and to others and meaningful in terms of its impacts on those most affected? 2) Is it feasible for you (and your allies/supporters) to make a significant impact on this issue, given your time and resources? 3) Are there others who are better positioned to address this issue who might take on responsibility or become allies? 4) What are the potential negative consequences, if any, if your advocacy goal is achieved? (Nagy, 2013). Once you have defined your advocacy problem and decided to make it the focus of your advocacy effort, it is time to analyze the issue in greater detail.

ANALYZING THE ISSUE

Albert Einstein is said to have commented, "If I were given 1 hour to save the planet, I would spend 59 minutes defining the problem and 1 minute resolving it." This speaks to the importance of analyzing an issue before deciding on a course of action. By jumping into solution mode too quickly, you risk misunderstanding the situation and misdirecting your efforts, wasting time and resources. This section offers several approaches to forming a deeper understanding of your issue (see Box 4.2 for an overview of the planning tools and why you would use them). In this step, develop hypotheses that can be checked in "Step 2—Research for Background and Impact" (Chapter 5).

BOX 4.2

An Overview of Tools for Analyzing Your Issue

Planning Tool	Description	Purpose
The hub-and-spoke approach	Identification of a central issue and all interrelated secondary issues	Provides a way of articulating secondary issues, which may be additional ways of framing your issue to appeal to different potential allies, supporters, and funders
But why?	Method to get to the root cause of a problem	Explores multiple facets of a problem to generate a range of solutions
Problem tree	Diagram for outlining the causes and consequences related to an issue	Informs advocacy tools by identifying the causes of an issue and consequences if solutions are not pursued
Force field analysis	List of forces, in order of significance, that may promote or impede a possible change	Enables advocates to build on forces in favor of change and address barriers that may hold back change

The Hub-and-Spoke Approach

The *hub-and-spoke approach* is a way to understand the central problem and all of the related issues connected to it. Picture an old-fashioned wagon wheel (see Box 4.3 for a diagram). There is a central hub of the wheel and spokes that radiate out from the hub. It is crucial for advocates to understand the irreducible core of what it is that they want to change, symbolized by the hub of the wheel. For any social problem that may be the focus of your advocacy, there are a variety of ancillary issues that are related and can be used to explain to others the different angles of an issue, symbolized by the spokes. The hub gives the depth of the issue, and the spokes give the alternate angles for explaining it. For example, lack of employer-provided child care not only creates stress for families but can also lead to reduced worker productivity and greater turnover. You can develop your hub-and-spoke model of your advocacy issue by developing hypotheses based on your current knowledge and then completing research (Chapter 5, Step 2) to learn as much information about your issue as possible and verify and add to your model. See the end of the chapter for an activity that will ask you to develop an initial hub-and-spoke model of your advocacy issue. Use a "yes, and" approach to build your hub-and-spoke model. Ask yourself:

- "What is the central problem?"
- "Yes, and what other issues connect to that problem?"
- "Yes, and what else connects those issues?"

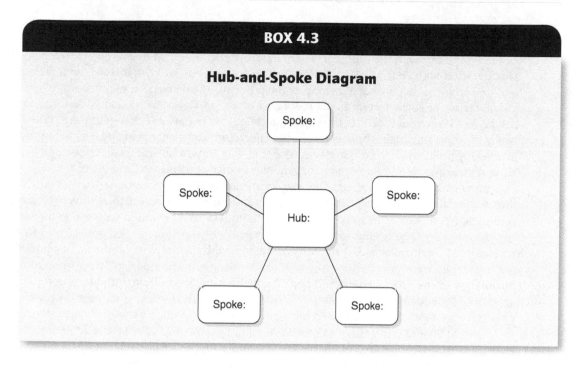

BOX 4.3

Hub-and-Spoke Diagram

The hub-and-spoke approach can be illustrated using the example of a campaign to promote inclusion of special needs children in educational settings initiated by child advocates in Malaysia (mentioned in Chapter 2). The hub or core of the issue addressed by these advocates was an argument about rights—that special needs children have a right to education like everyone else. Many related spoke issues shoot off from this hub. Inclusion in educational settings means integrating special needs children in other facets of a school, such as sports and extracurricular activities. It also means eliminating barriers that might keep children from attending or participating in school, such as lack of wheelchairs or other specialized equipment. Real inclusion also requires a change in attitudes about how teachers, administrators, and even other children within the school perceive individuals with special needs. Using the hub-and-spoke approach could help an advocate in Malaysia thoroughly explain an issue and appeal to different potential allies, supporters, and funders. For example, the British Council, an organization that promotes education and cultural opportunities, has a program to bring British special needs educators to other countries to train other educators on methods for involving special needs children in sports. An advocate can encourage schools to take advantage of this opportunity as part of an advocacy plan.

But Why?

Just as the question "yes, and?" is central to the hub-and-spoke approach, *"but why?"* is another questioning approach that seeks to get at the heart of an issue. This approach is also called the *5 Whys* and is used in industry (Serrat, 2009). The conversation will be richer, with the potential for more insightful solutions, if you can involve people with direct knowledge of the issue. Start with the problem statement. Now ask, "Why did this happen? Follow up that question with "but why?" and other probing questions. For each answer, continue to ask "but why?" until you reach the root of the problem. The discussion might identify individual factors or social factors as the root cause of the problem. For individual factors, you might decide on a solution that promotes education and behavioral change through developing effective materials. For social factors, a mezzo or macro change may be called for by addressing political or economic issues. The "but why?" approach offers an opportunity to explore multiple facets of a problem to generate a range of solutions (Lopez, 2013).

For the Malaysia special needs advocacy campaign previously mentioned, a "but why?" analysis would start with a problem statement and then probe into deeper layers of the issue. Begin by considering a problem statement: Prior to 2006, children with special needs in Malaysia were largely educated in separate schools or separate special education classrooms within regular schools. A majority of children with special needs could be integrated into regular educational classrooms with accommodations and support, offering numerous advantages to the special needs and typically developing children, including greater integration of individuals with disabilities in society. Start with the first question: Why were children educated in separate classrooms and schools? Depending on who is participating and their knowledge and experience, there might be a variety of answers; for example, mainstream classrooms are not adapted to teaching children with special needs. But why? Teachers are not trained to educate children with special needs. But why? Aside from teacher credential programs for special needs teachers, general teacher credential programs and in-service trainings do not include content on teaching children with special needs. But why? Funding has not been allocated to develop training materials for teachers and to fund training sessions. But why? National legislation has not mandated mainstreaming children with special needs and preparing schools to do so. This line of questioning might lead to the introduction of legislation, such as the National Education Development Plan (2006–2010) in Malaysia that mandated greater integration of special needs children in regular school settings (Taib, n.d.).

Problem Tree

A *problem tree* is another tool for analyzing a problem. This approach expands upon the "but why?" approach by asking about consequences as well as causes. As with the other methods, it is most productive to do this exercise with allies and other stakeholders on the issue. This method of inquiry asks participants to consider what led to the problem (the roots) and the consequences of the problem (the branches). You can use a diagram or a drawing of a tree to frame the discussion. The problem statement will go in the center—the trunk or central box of the diagram. Then, brainstorm the causes of the problem—these will be written below the problem as roots or boxes connected to the problem statement with arrows. Next, brainstorm about the consequences of the problem—these will go above the problem statement as branches or another set of boxes connected to the problem statement with arrows. See Box 4.4 for an example of a problem tree diagram. A variation of this exercise is to develop an objective or solution tree, which places a goal in the center;

solutions to reach the goal in the lower half of the diagram; and consequences of meeting the goal in the upper half of the diagram (Hovland, 2005). This tool can be used to develop your summary sheet (Chapter 6, Step 3), identifying the causes of the issue and the consequences if solutions are not pursued.

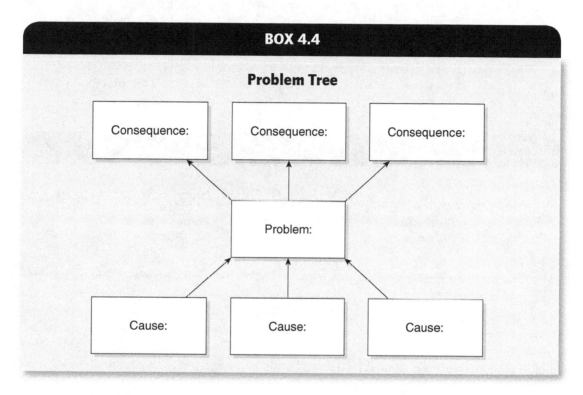

BOX 4.4

Problem Tree

Returning to the Malaysia example, a problem tree analysis would begin by placing the problem of children with special needs educated in separate schools or separate special needs classrooms rather than integrated into mainstream classrooms in the center of the analysis. Participants knowledgeable about this issue would then brainstorm causes and consequences. Causes might include the previous legislative framework that provided funding and infrastructure for separate facilities; public perception of individuals with special needs and lack of awareness of how they could be integrated into regular schools; and lack of infrastructure within mainstream classrooms to accommodate children with special needs, such as ramps for children with physical disabilities and accessible curriculum for children with sensory issues. Consequences of educating children with special needs separately from typically developing children might include the following: perpetuation of separation and lack of integration for individuals with special needs in society; reduced educational opportunities for children with special needs; and fewer friendships between children with special needs and typically developing children, which can provide role modeling for the former and promote empathy for the latter.

Force Field Analysis

Part of understanding a problem is understanding why it persists and the likelihood for change. *Force field analysis* is an approach originating from the social sciences (Lewin, 1951) to identify forces for and against a possible change. Begin by writing the goal in the center of the paper. In the left column, identify forces that may be in support of the change and driving it forward. In the right column, identify forces that may be against change and holding it back. Assign a score to each force in favor or against change, from weakest to strongest (1–5). See Box 4.5 for an example of a force field analysis diagram. This information can be used for your advocacy by building on the forces that are promoting change while being prepared to address the barriers that may hold change back.

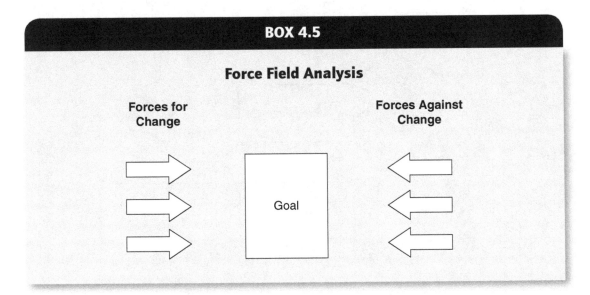

BOX 4.5

Force Field Analysis

Forces for Change

Forces Against Change

Goal

In the Malaysia example, force field analysis would begin by putting the goal in the center: inclusion of special needs children in educational settings. Next, participants would identify forces promoting change. These might include pressure from a parliament member with disabilities to promote inclusion and the rights of children with special needs, parental advocacy that demands more educational opportunities for children, and leadership by educational and nongovernmental leaders to follow best practices in special education. Then, forces acting against change would be identified. These might include lack of funding for teacher training and infrastructure improvement, concerns by parents of typically developing children that educational time will be diverted from their children, and lack of community support and understanding of the capabilities of children with special needs.

Analyzing the problem is an important process to inform your advocacy campaign and solutions. Each of these approaches offers potentially different angles and insights into the problem, and more than one may be warranted for your advocacy project. Problem analysis is most useful when conducted in partnership with stakeholders. In addition to understanding the problem, it is essential to understand who else is engaged in your issue. As the force field analysis suggests, some stakeholders may be opposed to change while others will act as forces to create change. The next section describes how to identify stakeholders related to your advocacy issue.

ANALYZING STAKEHOLDERS

Once you know what problem will be your focus, it is useful to understand the social landscape of individuals, groups, and other entities that may impact the success of your advocacy effort. A *stakeholder* is a person or organization with an interest in a particular issue who may be affected by changes related to that issue. Stakeholder analysis emerged from organizational and management research in the 1970s and 1980s and was adopted as a type of policy analysis focused on the influence of policy actors (Brugha & Varvasovszky, 2000). Chapter 2 already identified two key types of stakeholders for an advocacy effort: *allies*, other individuals, groups, and organizations already working on your issue who can become collaborators, and *decision makers and gatekeepers*, those who will become the target of your advocacy efforts to win a favorable decision. Two other important types of stakeholders are *beneficiaries*, those who will benefit from the advocacy effort, such as a particular child or group of children, and *opponents*, those who are against the change that you seek and could block your efforts.

A basic stakeholder analysis has four components: identifying, prioritizing, understanding, and managing stakeholders (NHS Institute for Innovation and Improvement, 2008). The first stage is to brainstorm which individuals, groups, and organizations would fall into the categories of allies, decision makers and gatekeepers, beneficiaries, and opponents. Consider actors in the public sector, which would include local governing bodies, government officials, civil servants and members of the bureaucracy, courts, and international bodies like the United Nations. Depending on your issue, the private sector may also be influential; this would include business leaders, corporations, small businesses, and business associations. Civil society, sometimes called the third sector to distinguish it from government and business, includes a wide category of potential actors, including media, religious institutions and figures, schools and universities, other advocacy organizations, trade unions, and national or international nongovernmental organizations (ODI, 2009).

When you have a list of stakeholders, prioritize the effort you will invest in each one and how you will involve them in your project. Consider the level of power and interest each stakeholder has on your issue. Write in the names of each of your stakeholders in the stakeholder analysis grid; color code your notes by using green for allies and beneficiaries, red for opponents, and blue for those who are neutral (decision makers or gatekeepers may fall into any of these categories). See Box 4.6 for a visual depiction of this grid. Those with high power and high interest should be actively engaged in the advocacy project, involving them in communications and consulting them on key decisions.

This group would be ideal champions for your project—these are likely to be the decision makers who have access over your issue or gatekeepers who have influence over those decision makers. If opponents have high power and high interest, then you know they will be important targets of your advocacy, to persuade them in favor of your views if possible, or at least encourage them to take a more neutral stance. Individuals and organizations with low power but high interest should be kept informed on your project and invited to be involved. These may become allies and join your coalition. Beneficiaries of your advocacy effort are also likely to fall into this category and should be consulted and involved as much as possible. Those with high power but low interest should be kept satisfied with what is happening. This group is likely to include opinion leaders, such as the media, so keep them aware of your project. The last category, those with low power and low interest, can generally be ignored given your limited time and resources. However, revisit your stakeholder analysis from time to time; keep on top of whether the status of an individual or group shifts and if they assume more power or gain more interest in your issue (ODI, 2009).

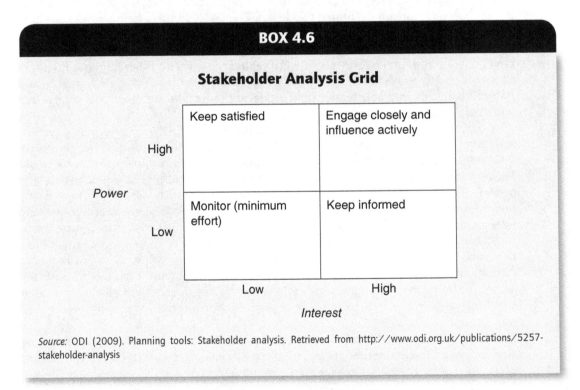

BOX 4.6

Stakeholder Analysis Grid

	Low	High
High	Keep satisfied	Engage closely and influence actively
Low	Monitor (minimum effort)	Keep informed

Power (vertical axis); *Interest* (horizontal axis)

Source: ODI (2009). Planning tools: Stakeholder analysis. Retrieved from http://www.odi.org.uk/publications/5257-stakeholder-analysis

Develop your understanding of the stakeholders so that you will know how to engage them and communicate with them in your advocacy project. Find out more about the nature of their interest in this topic, what motivates them, and how best to connect with them. Asking people directly is one way to learn about them and to start building relationships. See Chapter 5, "Step 2—Research for Background and Impact," for information on carrying out key stakeholder interviews. If there is a large group whose interests you would like to understand, then a survey may be appropriate. In addition to primary research, you might engage in secondary research to find out the views of stakeholders like decision makers or other advocacy organizations. Search their websites or look for news articles that report their views on your advocacy subject. Use what you understand about your key stakeholders to start mapping out what they know and think about your advocacy topic as well as other competing issues that that they also care about. See Box 4.7, Map Out Interests of Key Stakeholders, for a table to guide your analysis (Sharma, n.d.).

BOX 4.7

Map Out Interests of Key Stakeholders

Advocacy Goal:

Audience	Audience knowledge about issue/objective	Audience beliefs and attitudes about issue/objective	Audience cares about other issues (may be unrelated to your advocacy issue)
	KNOWS	THINKS	HAS COMPETING ISSUES
Allies			
Decision makers and gatekeepers			
Beneficiaries			
Opponents			

Source: Sharma, R. R. (n.d.). An introduction to advocacy. Retrieved from http://www.globalhealthcommunication.org/tool_docs/15/an_introduction_to_advocacy_-_training_guide_(full_document).pdf

---

The purpose of identifying, prioritizing, and understanding your stakeholders is ultimately to manage them in terms of their involvement in your advocacy project. Use the stakeholder analysis grid to identify the opponents you will need to win over to your cause and the allies, beneficiaries, and potential supporters that you will need to engage, communicate with, motivate, and inform to sustain their involvement in your project. Use the map of key stakeholders' interests to develop messages on your issue for various audiences (discussed later in this chapter, in the section called Framing the Issue). If you are working with others on your advocacy project, strategize who will communicate with different stakeholders, the messages you will use, and how you will follow up (ODI, 2009).

Going back to the Malaysia example, the Minister of Education would be an important decision maker on the topic of inclusion of children with special needs in mainstream education. In a hypothetical scenario, you might find out based on researching his published views and asking people who know him that he has attended several international conferences on education of special needs children and is aware of research and best practices in this area (knowledge). In his remarks, he has expressed his positive views about the rights of individuals with disabilities to be integrated into society but has also encouraged caution about implementation so that local schools and teachers are not overwhelmed with new responsibilities (beliefs and attitudes). The Minister of Education has prioritized science education and technology during his tenure in this position (competing interests). Having this information on your key stakeholders will help you craft messages that will appeal specifically to them and encourage their support. In addition to the primary people and institutions involved in your issue, it is also important to understand the wider policy context.

ANALYZING THE POLICY CONTEXT

Whether advocating on the micro level for a specific child, the mezzo level for a group of children or community, or the macro level for a category of children or a social issue, policy is a crucial part of advocacy. In terms of micro advocacy, advocates are often trying to ensure that children receive the rights to which they are entitled under public policy. For example, advocacy on behalf of a child in foster care by a Court Appointed Special Advocate (CASA) volunteer promotes a child's best interests and ensures that the child receives the health, educational, and other social services to which he or she has a legal right. With mezzo or macro advocacy, advocates are typically trying to affect organizational or public policy by encouraging the passage of new policy, stopping the passing of unfavorable policy, or promoting the proper implementation of existing policy. For these reasons, analyzing the policy context is an important step after you have identified and analyzed your issue.

The first step to understanding the policy context of your advocacy issue is to understand the political structure in your country. The United States, like many countries, has a three-part federal system with an executive, bicameral (meaning two chambers, in this case the Senate and House of Representatives) legislature, and judiciary. This is mirrored on the state level with a governor as executive, unicameral or bicameral legislature, and judiciary. A bill or proposed law must go through several steps before it is passed and gains the force of law. On the federal level, new legislation is introduced in one of the two chambers of the legislature and then referred to one or more committees for study and hearings. Bills are considered in detail at this stage and may be referred to subcommittees for additional study. Bills may be rejected by being ignored by the committee and are said to have died in committee. After studying the bill, the committee may amend the bill and report on it to the Senate or House of Representatives. It then goes to the floor of the originating house for debate and voting. If it is approved, the bill is sent to the other chamber of the legislature to repeat the process. If the second chamber changes the bill significantly, the two versions of the bill will be reconciled and a compromise version will be written in conference committee. If the conference committee cannot agree on a compromise, the bill may die there, or if agreement is reached, the compromise version of the bill will be sent to both chambers for another floor vote and may not be amended. If both chambers pass the bill, it goes to the president for approval or veto. Interest groups also play a powerful role in American politics through the process of lobbying for or against legislation. In some states, citizens and interest groups can initiate new legislation through a ballot initiative. If the target of your advocacy is the passage or defeat of legislation, there are databases to find pending state and federal legislation. In the United States, www.thomas.gov is a source to find bills being considered by the current session of Congress.

Policy is developed through a deliberate process known as the *policy process model* that is generally pictured as a circle because it is cyclical or continuous. As conditions change, new information is discovered, and opinions shift, policy can be reexamined and revised. It is important to understand the policy process if you hope to influence legislation that is currently pending or may go through reauthorization and be reconsidered and possibly amended. Policy development goes through several stages; however, in real life, stages may overlap or be skipped. The first stage is *problem definition and agenda setting*, which involves defining public problems and determining whether a particular problem is selected for government intervention. Defining problems and decisions about whether they will be targets for policy action are political decisions. For example, the issue of school violence has been contentious in the United States, with some defining the problem as resulting from access to firearms, while others encourage more availability of firearms for school officials to protect children. With fraught issues, it can be difficult to get agreement on a policy strategy. *Policy formulation* is the development of a proposed course of action to address a public problem. This is the stage where policy analysis comes in as alternatives are considered and weighed (see the section called Policy Research, in Chapter 5). During the stage of *policy legitimation*, potential policy approaches are weighed within government and debated within the larger society until government officials act through majority vote in the legislature, formal executive or bureaucratic decisions, or judicial decisions. These decisions give force of law to a bill, regulation, or court decision while larger societal debates assess the appropriateness of government actions in terms of popular support and compatibility with current law and public values. *Policy implementation* is the stage where the policy is put into effect with programs initiated and money spent. In the United States, the executive branch and bureaucracy is involved in developing regulations during this stage to add detail to bills developed by Congress. Ideally, *policy evaluation and policy change* follows implementation to measure whether a policy is meeting its stated goals and objectives, though this is a step that is often disregarded and skipped. Policy evaluation may result in incremental change to policies and programs (Kraft & Furlong, 2013). There are several opportunities for advocacy throughout this process, from defining a problem and getting it onto the government agenda, to promoting policy alternatives during the policy formulation stage, to careful monitoring and commenting when regulations are developed and policies are implemented.

Government has certain types of policy instruments available to address social problems. Based on the policy goal, one or more strategies may be most effective. Governments can *regulate* through sanctions, like fines or imprisonment, to require or prevent certain actions by citizens. An example related to child advocacy is regulation of child care facilities and group homes, which must generally meet health and safety standards. Another instrument is *government management*, or directly providing services or managing resources. This is a common category of policy and includes public education, public parks, and municipal services such as police and fire protection. Government management can be transferred to the private sector as when services like foster care are contracted out to nonprofit organizations. Governments can *tax and spend*, to tax an activity to encourage or discourage it, and subsidize certain actions through loans, direct payments, and price supports. Taxes have been used to discourage unhealthy behaviors like smoking and, more recently, consumption of high-calorie beverages related to obesity. Subsidies, on the other hand, have been used to encourage participation in higher education through government-provided grants and loans. Governments can use *market mechanisms* to meet social problems by allowing the market to take care of an issue and not to intervene. In the United States, paying for early childhood care has been primarily left up to the market and to parents with little intervention by government except on behalf of very low income families. Finally, governments can *educate, inform, and persuade* by providing information through formal programs and encouraging people to act in certain ways (Kraft & Furlong, 2013). Examples include government-funded research on issues related to children as well as public education campaigns on topics such as drug use.

How does your problem relate to the policy context? Are there existing policies that are adequate but need better enforcement? Or is new policy needed to better address the problem? Another possibility is that policy is being considered that would negatively impact your advocacy issue. Policy analysis is a way of assessing whether a policy has or will achieve its goals. The most common criteria (discussed in Chapter 5) are whether the policy works (effectiveness), whether it is a good use of limited resources (efficiency), and whether it is fair (equity). Analyzing policy and presenting alternatives is a significant strategy for policy advocacy at the mezzo or macro levels. See Chapter 5, "Step 2—Research for Background and Impact," for a description of policy analysis. Values are also critical for understanding policies. Policies can be understood as having three levels: 1) values, 2) social issues, and 3) policies (see later discussion in Framing the Issue section). A particular policy is ultimately informed by a moral reason about how to act about a particular social issue (Patent & Lakoff, 2006). Major American value orientations include individuality, freedom, the importance of activity and work, and achievement and success (Popple & Leighninger, 2010). These values are manifested in social policies like the Temporary Assistance to Needy Families program that replaced welfare, formerly called Aid to Families with Dependent Children, by instituting time limits and work requirements supporting the American values of independence, rather than dependence on government support, and the importance of work. Understanding the values that lie beneath policy can help you frame your issue. See Box 4.8 for a description of how one advocacy organization addresses cultural values in its work.

BOX 4.8

Advocacy Work in India for Women and Families

By Vijaya Murthy, Founder-President, Stree Chetna (India)

Stree Chetna is a nongovernmental organization that has been working for the welfare and empowerment of women since the 1980s. *Stree Chetna* means *Women's Awareness* in Hindi, the national language of India. Our organization has been proactive and we have been involved with the Ministry of Women and Child Development in its policy-making committees. We work not only for women, but also for the society as a whole, strengthening every fiber of the social fabric, including children, youth, elders, and men. The Indian values of strengthening family, marriage, and living together have been the basis of our functioning.

Issues revolving around women are the main focus of our work. In dealing with these issues, we adopted a three-pronged strategy: curative, rehabilitative, and preventive. Women in distress had to be counseled and assisted with rehabilitation. At the same time, advocacy is needed to change societal conditions. Like the way the health field succeeded only when it focused on preventing illnesses through vaccines rather than merely trying to cure them, we too have focused on efforts to prevent problems and eliminate their root causes. We have worked to create awareness about women's welfare and development in every sector of society, including about women who are battered, abandoned, or harassed. We have offered counseling to thousands of families and training programs to professionals in many fields including teachers, professors, counselors, social workers, doctors, and police.

The cultural challenges regarding awareness around women's issues are considerable. These include intense preference for sons and human rights abuses of girls, including child-marriage, female feticide and infanticide, and dowry harassment. Considering the magnitude of India's population and the enormity of problems, coupled with the age-old belief system and ancient cultural norms considering women as the weaker sex, it was prudent to focus on awareness programs. These were not just for women but for men as well, to remove the erroneous beliefs embedded in their minds. Awareness programs were conducted for the public in general: for example, trainings for the young girls in schools on hygiene and care during the menstrual cycle; for college youth on family life education; for married couples on positive interactions, expectations, and conflict resolution; and for seniors on successful aging.

Advocacy needs to be done in different ways for different people. We have found the most effective way to generate awareness and empowerment has been through direct contacts in the form of training sessions, workshops, and seminars. For the illiterate and semiliterate, we have discussion groups, which can include question and answer sessions. We even lure them under the pretext of having a demonstration on cooking or beauty tips and along with these topics mention caring for a daughter properly, including developing rapport so she can report abuse immediately, not marrying her too early but instead giving her proper education, and so on.

(Continued)

(Continued)

We envision a society where subjugation and harassment of women is eradicated; girls are valued, welcomed, and given equal opportunity from birth; and every girl lives a life of dignity to blossom into womanhood and contribute constructively toward the progress of humanity.

FRAMING THE ISSUE

According to rhetoricians, people make sense of the world using mental shortcuts called *frames*. The contents of these shortcuts often come from the way an issue is portrayed in the media and by politicians, using certain types of metaphors, tone, and values. Exposure over time to dominant ways of describing social issues makes certain mental images entrenched, as the methods used to describe social issues act as cues in terms of how to understand and mentally file information (FrameWorks Institute, 2002). When the patterns associated with familiar frames are identified, that activates the frame. Schank (1995) explains: "Understanding means finding a story you already know and saying, 'Oh yeah, that one.' Once we have found (the) story, we stop processing" (p. 71). George Lakoff (2004) famously illustrated this concept with the following directive: "Don't think of an elephant," (p. 3). The instructions are impossible to follow. The word elephant brings up the mental image of an elephant and knowledge about elephants: for example, a large animal with floppy ears and a trunk, often found in circuses. This exercise illustrates a few core concepts about frames. First, words associated with a frame evoke the frame. Mentioning peanuts, trunk, or circus would also bring up the elephant frame. Second, evoking a frame reinforces the frame. Frames become dominant ways of understanding the world when they are repeated again and again. If you use language associated with a frame, you reinforce this way of thinking for your audience. Finally, negating a frame evokes the frame. Using words and images associated with the elephant frame bring this frame to mind even if you are trying to counteract stereotypes of elephants and introduce a different way of thinking. It is not possible to change thinking when evoking an undesired frame; the only option is to reframe the issue by promoting connections to new knowledge and images (Lakoff, 2004).

Another core idea is that frames incorporate three levels of understanding. The first level is big ideas, often connected to values like freedom, justice, and prevention. The second level is the type or category of issue like child care or the environment. The third level is the specific issue like income support for single parents and protection of rainforests (FrameWorks Institute, 2002). See Box 4.9 for a visual depiction of these three levels. An example would be child maltreatment. Child abuse as a specific Level 3 issue is often framed as relating to Level 1 values of justice, protection, and authority and as part of Level 2 issue categories like law enforcement and child protective services. This frame suggests certain ways of thinking about the issue, like blaming or criminalizing parents, and certain actions, like removing children and putting them in foster care. To reframe this issue as child abuse prevention, Level 3 values can be invoked related to thinking about children as the future and involving the community as well as Level 2 issue categories like education and child development to identify broader ways to prevent child maltreatment through parental education and community awareness of children's development (FRIENDS, 2005).

BOX 4.9

Three Levels of Framing

Level 1: Values	Responsibility, community
Level 2: Issue Area	Child care, child maltreatment
Level 3: Policy	Universal preschool, home visiting program

Source: Adapted from Patent, J., & Lakoff, G. (2006). Conceptual levels: Bringing it down to values. Retrieved from http://www.cognitivepolicyworks.com/resource-center/frame-analysis-framing-tutorials/conceptual-levels-bringing-it-home-to-values/

Metaphors and analogies are the key ingredients of framing, and they are used to simplify complex ideas. For example, explaining neuroscience by describing a baby's brain as formed of complex architecture, rather than the more obtuse concepts of dendrites and neurons, gives people a mental image that they can understand. These types of metaphors are useful in part because most people simply do not understand the processes associated with children's development, particularly those associated with brain development. This often results in defaulting to dominant paradigms, such as a tendency to blame parents for children's problems (see Box 4.10), which can go against an advocate's strategy of encouraging greater community responsibility. A common frame used by advocates, school readiness, falls into this trap because of the lack of broad public understanding of child development. This concept is meant to convey the early experiences that children need to prepare them with the skills, knowledge, and qualities that will allow them to succeed in school. However, research by the FrameWorks Institute suggests that this frame does not resonant with the public, and they may misinterpret it to think that children are unable or unwilling to learn (Axelbrun & Grady, 2002). Metaphors that work fit with the way that people already think about an issue. For example, the issue of early childhood development may bear similarities to a manufacturing process, but that metaphor fails to capture the feelings of tenderness and nurturance associated with early childhood. A metaphor like caring for seedlings conveys a similar notion of careful inputs into a process but strikes the right tone (Auburn, Grady, & Bales, 2004).

BOX 4.10

Framing Children's Issues

Dominant frames for children's issues in American society[1]

- The self-made child: The goal of child rearing is to promote the development of self-reliance, emphasizing autonomy over interdependence, with this domain of development perceived as more significant than others, such as socioemotional development.
- The family frame: Raising children belongs within the private realm of the family. Parenting is an individual choice and responsibility, with negative outcomes experienced by children as the result of parental failure.
- The safety frame: Keeping children safe is the primary goal of child rearing, with physical development and safety as more observable than other domains and better understood by the general public.

Alternate frames for children's issues in American society[2]

- The parenting frame: Parenting is a skill that is learned rather than comes naturally, and society benefits when people are educated and supported to be good parents.
- The child development frame: Understanding how children develop, such as the process of bonding and attachment, helps people understand what children need to thrive.
- The community frame: The relationships and connections in a community and its resources, such as libraries, benefit children and their families.

Sources:

1. FrameWorks Institute (n.d.). Changing the public conversation about kids. Retrieved from http://www.frameworksinstitute.org/127.html
2. Bostrom, M. (2003). *Discipline and development: A meta-analysis of public perceptions of parents, parenting, child development and child abuse.* Prepared for the FrameWorks Institute. Retrieved from http://www.frameworksinstitute.org/toolkits/canp/resources/pdf/DisciplineAndDevelopment.pdf

Advocates frame ideas to persuade others to support their cause and to avoid playing into undesired ways of thinking about the issue. Framing is particularly crucial for issues advocates at the mezzo and macro levels, who are often seeking policy change. Careful framing can encourage others to think of an issue in a way that supports your proposed solution. Ryan (1991) points out that "every frame defines the issue, explains who is responsible, and suggests potential solutions. All of these are conveyed by images, stereotypes, or anecdotes" (p. 59). Consider how children are depicted in the media. A content analysis of local media coverage in cities across the United States by FrameWorks Institute uncovered a frame of the *imperiled child*. The media stories in this study showed the world as a dangerous place for children, with stories emphasizing risks to children's safety from crime, accidents, and their own risky behaviors. In this example, the frame of the imperiled child defines childhood as fraught with dangers, suggesting parents are responsible for finding ways to ensure their safety. This can create an urge to bubble wrap children and find ways to protect them, from regulating safety of playground equipment to ensuring the presence of metal detectors in schools. The downside of this frame is that it can create unwarranted anxiety despite statistically greater safety of the current generation compared with previous ones, and it can leave out other important issues around children's developmental needs, overshadowing and obscuring other important stories (Gilliam, 2003). As an advocate for children's issues, you must understand the dominant frames of your society so you can handle these carefully by either using the dominant frames when warranted or intentionally reframing an issue to avoid these frames. See Box 4.10 for other examples of dominant frames for children's issues in American society.

The media generally present children's issues using episodic thinking whereas advocates are often better served by using thematic thinking. Episodic thinking describes a moment in time: a homeless mother and her children seeking shelter for the night. The episodic approach may emphasize how cold it is outside or when the family had their last meal but does not explore the broader context of homelessness. Contrast this to a thematic approach that would describe the rate of homelessness in an area, trends in whether the problem is increasing or decreasing, and causes of homelessness. People respond differently to an episodic versus thematic frame. An episodic frame tends to suggest an individualistic solution—fix the person, rather than a societal solution—seek environmental or institutional approaches instead. Describing issues using a thematic frame can prime people to view solutions through the government as appropriate (FrameWorks Institute, 2002).

As a child advocate, consider how to use the elements of framing to present your issue in the best possible way to your target decision maker. Consider the big Level 1 values as you frame your issue, and use images, metaphors, and tone to present your case as you develop effective materials (Chapter 6, Step 3). Prior to receiving your materials at a meeting (Chapter 7, Step 4), your decision maker may have been exposed to a very different way of thinking from the media or his political party. You can address his or her potentially skewed views by reframing the issue in a way that connects with the solution you seek. Make an issue "yes-able" or "no-able" to a decision maker so that you can get support for a desired solution or defeat an unwanted solution.

Here is where research on the decision maker can be very helpful. For example, if you are seeking policy change, investigate the policy maker. What are his or her influences—for example, is there another politician with whom your decision maker often cosponsors bills or votes together in a block? Are there quotes out in the media that describe this person's views on the issue? Is it well known that the decision maker's political party tends to see your issue in a particular way? As you get to know the decision maker through all six steps of your advocacy campaign, you may return to this issue of framing and tweak your materials and revise and expand your frame to meet the needs of the decision makers and help them gain a better understanding of your advocacy goals.

Identifying, Analyzing, and Framing an Issue:
A Case Study of Paniamor in Costa Rica

Costa Rica is sometimes called the Switzerland of Central America. This nickname is often misunderstood. While the country has one of the world's oldest democracies and abolished its army permanently in 1949 to protect its democracy (Grillo, 2010), it nevertheless has significant social problems. The country has a high rate of violence against children. A telephone survey of a representative sample of Costa Ricans found that 74.2% verbally abused their children and 65.3% used physical violence. Children are often beaten with the rationale that this will straighten up their behavior (Economic Commission for Latin America and the Caribbean [ELAC] & UNICEF, 2009).

Fundación Paniamor (Bread and Love Foundation) was started in 1987. Its mission is to:

> Achieve compliance with the rights of minors in Costa Rica, through the development of social mobilization programs aimed to strengthen them in the exercise of their rights and responsibilities, and their ability to contribute to national development; prevent violence against among and from them; and encourage the development of public policies and institutional practices that contribute to advancing compliance. (Fundación Paniamor, 2013)

Paniamor uses a human rights framework to guide its work. The organization's activities include information sharing, education, training, lobbying, and public information campaigns (Belfer & Rohde, 2005).

Paniamor developed a clear message for its work by identifying, analyzing, and framing its primary and secondary issues. It conducted research on the prevalence of child rearing strategies and sexual abuse through two separate nationwide surveys (Krugman, Mata, & Krugman, 1992). The final messaging focused on protection of children against violence. The reason for arriving at this message was that, with the assistance of public relations and journalism experts, it was determined that Costa Rican society could better grasp the concepts of protection of children from violence rather than child abuse prevention. All messages were linked to this approach to ending violence against children including by abuse from their parents, bullying in schools, and sexual exploitation and trafficking.

Paniamor lobbied for national legislation to protect children's rights by assembling dossiers of research on the effects of physical violence on children and delivering these personally to legislators. The organization also reached out to the media with information on how banning physical punishment against children would promote equal protection under the law, keep children from turning to violence as a means of achieving their personal goals, and achieve progress in terms of realizing Costa Rica's commitment to the United Nations Convention on the Rights of the Child. In 2008, Costa Rica passed legislation protecting children against all forms of corporal punishment and humiliating treatment in all settings, including the family. A national survey conducted by Paniamor found the majority of the public supported the new law but were concerned about the potential for negative consequences for children if they are allowed to grow up less disciplined and more impulsive. Paniamor is now focused on advocacy that will help the country achieve the vision of this legislation through educating and supporting families with new knowledge and skills to discipline their children humanely (Grillo, 2010).

In its more than 20 years of operation, Paniamor has achieved many outcomes, including greater public awareness and prevention of child maltreatment, new legislation to protect children's rights, programs to reintegrate high-risk adolescents into school or train them for employment, and creation of the largest child welfare database in Central America (Belfer & Rohde, 2005). It has reached a venerable position in promoting policies and practices that protect children from violence.

Activity: Developing a Hub-and-Spoke Diagram

Use the diagram in Box 4.3 to identify your core issue (the hub) and all the issues that it touches (the spokes). Start with the hub: What is the irreducible issue related to your advocacy project? Then ask the question, "If this is the core issue, what issues are interlinked with it?" Continue this line of questioning by asking "Yes, and what other issues connect to that problem?" This will identify the spokes of your issue that expand on the core issue. Look beyond the obvious by considering other potential impacts of your advocacy issue. The purpose is to come up with alternative angles that may resonate with potential allies, supporters, and funders. More spokes give you a greater opportunity to appeal to a wide audience.

REFERENCES

Auburn, A., Grady, J., & Bales, S. (2004). *Opening up the black box: A case study in simplifying models.* Washington, DC: FrameWorks Institute. Retrieved from http://www.frameworksinstitute.org/assets/files/eZines/Case_Study_in_Simplifying_Models.pdf

Axelbrun, A. & Grady, J. (2002). *Promoting school readiness and early child development: Findings from cognitive elicitations.* Washington, DC: FrameWorks Institute. Retrieved from http://www.frameworksinstitute.org/assets/files/ECD/school_readiness_and_ecd.pdf

Belfer, M. L., & Rohde, L. A. (2005). Child and adolescent mental health in Latin America and the Caribbean: Problems, progress, and policy research. *Revista Panamericana de Salud Pública, 18*(4–5), 359–365.

Bostrom, M. (2003). *Discipline and development: A meta-analysis of public perceptions of parents, parenting, child development and child abuse.* Washington, DC: FrameWorks Institute. Retrieved from http://www.frameworksinstitute.org/toolkits/canp/resources/pdf/DisciplineAndDevelopment.pdf

Brugha, R., & Varvasovszky, Z. (2000). Stakeholder analysis: A review. *Health Policy and Planning, 15*(3), 239–246.

Economic Commission for Latin America and the Caribbean [ELAC] & UNICEF (2009). Child abuse: A painful reality behind closed doors. *Challenges: A newsletter on progress toward the Millenium Development Goals from a child rights perspective, 9.* Retrieved from http://www.cepal.org/dds/noticias/desafios/0/37890/Challenges9-cepal-unicef.pdf

FrameWorks Institute (2002). *Framing public issues.* Washington, DC: FrameWorks Institute. Retrieved from http://www.frameworksinstitute.org/assets/files/PDF/FramingPublicIssuesfinal.pdf

FrameWorks Institute (n.d.). *Changing the public conversation about kids.* Washington, DC: FrameWorks Institute Retrieved from http://www.frameworksinstitute.org/127.html

FRIENDS (2005). *Reframing child abuse and neglect: A practical toolkit.* Retrieved from http://www.pcain .org/files/Council_Documents/Marketing_and_Public_Relations/FramingTheoryExplained.pdf

Fundación Paniamor (2013). *About Panimor (Google Translate).* Retrieved from http://paniamor.org/ generales/nosotros.html

Gilliam, F. (2003). *A new dominant frame: "The imperiled child."* Washington, DC: FrameWorks Institute. Retrieved from http://www.frameworksinstitute.org/assets/files/eZines/The_Imperiled_Child.pdf

Grillo, M. (2010). Ending physical and humiliating punishment in a Central American Country. In J. E. Durrant & A. B. Smith (Eds.), *Global pathways to abolishing physical punishment: Realizing children's rights* (pp. 112–121). New York, NY: Taylor & Francis.

Hovland, I. (2005). *Successful communication: A toolkit for researchers and civil society organisations.* Retrieved from http://www.odi.org.uk/sites/odi.org.uk/files/odi-assets/publications-opinion-files/192.pdf

Kaufman, R. A., Rojas, A. M., & Mayer, H. (1993). *Needs assessment: A user's guide.* Englewood Cliffs, NJ: Educational Technology.

Kraft, M. E., & Furlong, S. R. (2013). *Public policy: Politics, analysis, and alternatives* (4th ed.). Washington, DC: CQ Press.

Krugman, S., Mata, L., & Krugman, R. (1992). Sexual abuse and corporal punishment during childhood: A pilot retrospective survey of university students in Costa Rica. *Pediatrics, 90*(1), 157–161.

Lakoff, G. (2004). *Don't think of an elephant: Know your values and frame the debate: The essential guide for progressives.* White River Junction, VT: Chelsea Green.

Lewin, K. (1951). *Field theory in social science: Selected theoretical papers.* New York, NY: Harper Bros.

Lopez, C. (2013). Analyzing root causes of problems: The "but why?" technique. *Community Toolbox.* Retrieved from http://ctb.ku.edu/en/tablecontents/sub_section_main_1128.aspx

Nagy, J. (2013). Defining and analyzing the problem. *Community Toolbox.* Retrieved from http://ctb .ku.edu/en/tablecontents/sub_section_main_1124.aspx

NHS Institute for Innovation and Improvement (2008). *Stakeholder analysis.* Retrieved from http:// www.institute.nhs.uk/quality_and_service_improvement_tools/quality_and_service_improvement_ tools/stakeholder_analysis.html

ODI (2009). *Planning tools: Stakeholder analysis.* Retrieved from http://www.odi.org.uk/publications/ 5257-stakeholder-analysis

Patent, J., & Lakoff, G. (2006). *Conceptual levels: Bringing it down to values.* Retrieved from http://www. cognitivepolicyworks.com/resource-center/frame-analysis-framing-tutorials/conceptual-levels-bringing-it-home-to-values/

Popple, P. R., & Leighninger, L. (2010). *The policy-based profession: An introduction to social welfare policy analysis for social workers* (5th ed.). Boston, MA: Pearson/Allyn and Bacon.

Ryan, C. (1991). *Prime time activism: Media strategies for grassroots organizing.* Boston, MA: South End Press.

Schank, R. C. (1995). *Tell me a story: Narrative and intelligence.* Evanston, IL: Northwestern University Press.

Serrat, O. (2009). *The five whys technique.* Washington, DC: Asian Development Bank. Retrieved from http://www.adb.org/sites/default/files/pub/2009/the-five-whys-technique.pdf

Sharma, R. R. (n.d.). *An introduction to advocacy.* Retrieved from http://www.globalhealthcommunication .org/tool_docs/15/an_introduction_to_advocacy_-_training_guide_(full_document).pdf

Taib, M. N. B. M. (n.d.). *School management concerning collaboration with social resources in the community—Its approaches and problem.* Retrieved from http://www.nise.go.jp/kenshuka/josa/ kankobutsu/pub_d/d-266/d-266_15.pdf

CHAPTER 5

Step 2—Research
for Background and Impact

In order to present a decisionable issue before a decision maker, it is necessary to conduct sufficient research to convey the breadth and depth of concern on the advocacy topic and the impact on children. It is critical that the need specific to the issue be clearly understood and depicted through this research. This chapter discusses the importance of using objective information, such as facts and expert opinion, to build your advocacy case. This research can be conducted in several ways. In many cases, libraries and the Internet can provide access to useful secondary data and statistics. When information available on a topic is insufficient, original data may be collected. This may include focus groups, interviews, or surveys. Capturing the experiences and voices of individuals and families in a community may also be persuasive to decision makers. Quotes from both experts and local leaders on the advocacy issue can be compiled and later used in persuasive communication tools. The information you collect can be summarized narratively in a summary sheet (described in Chapter 6) as well as using images. If your advocacy goal is to influence policy, it can be helpful to write a policy memo, which is described in this chapter. The value of research is highlighted in a case study about an advocacy effort in Sweden that identified job skills needed by local employers which could be filled through specialized training of youth with disabilities. Readers are encouraged to explore websites and print sources with information relevant to the advocacy topic of interest, with help from a list of useful Internet websites and guiding discussion questions.

CONDUCTING RESEARCH FOR ADVOCACY

Advocacy research is different from typical academic research because the intent is to persuade as well as to inform. Speaking of the principles that guided his work on *The Other America*, a powerful book on poverty in America that sparked significant social change, author Michael Harrington noted that his efforts were intended "to be as honest and objective as possible about the figures; to speak emotionally in the name of the common humanities of those who dwell in the culture of poverty" (Harrington, 1962, p. 177). This quote describes the type of principled stance that advocates must assume in terms of reporting facts honestly without manipulation or inflation. It also hints at the most effective type of case for advocacy, which is an approach that combines facts and figures with emotional appeal. When making a case for your issue, look for information that will help you describe the big picture as well as highlight the personal impact of your advocacy issue. Dry research will never win the day—the information needs to be conveyed using the elements of framing described in Chapter 4 (in the section called Framing the Issue) and appeals to logic and emotion discussed in Chapter 6 (in the section called Persuasive Communication).

Conducting research for advocacy is part of a larger tradition of action research that seeks knowledge to address social problems rather than simply knowledge for its own sake. Research for advocacy is a means to an end, allowing the advocate to present objective, hard-hitting information in a clear and passionate manner. *Action research* is an approach that cuts across academic fields and has been applied to a variety of social problems, including labor organizing, social justice, and institutional change. The principles of action research include doing research with, for, and by populations in a participatory and democratic manner; addressing issues of broad social and human significance; and being open to research as an emergent process that changes as new information is discovered and new questions come up (Reason & Bradbury, 2007). These principles also apply to advocacy research and highlight the value of directly involving the population for whom you are advocating as much as possible in informing your research effort. See Box 5.1 for an example of an action research project that highlighted local voices.

BOX 5.1

The Importance of Local Voices

By Dr. Alan Pence, UNESCO Chair for Early Childhood Education,
Care and Development and Professor in the School of Child and
Youth Care at the University of Victoria (Canada)

Early childhood education, care, and development (ECD) is at an exciting point in its development internationally. To an unprecedented degree, one encounters arguments put forward by scholars from neuroscientists to economists and from a multitude of United Nations and other international organizations in support of ECD services. The voices, however, that are often overlooked in these high-end pronouncements are those at the most local level: voices from children, families, and local communities. And if programs are to be effective and sustainable, it is these voices, and these perspectives, that matter most.

The importance of local voices came through to me clearly in a program we codeveloped in the early 1990s with an indigenous tribal council in northern Canada. The council was concerned that postsecondary education, typically understood by society as a key tool for capacity development, was having a capacity depleting impact. Part of the problem was that individuals were being pulled away from their communities and many did not return, but even when the courses were offered in the community, the content was based on cultures and contexts far removed from their own with no opportunity to include their own communities' views, values, and understandings.

Cooperatively, we developed an educational training program that was based on multiple knowledges—knowledge and understandings from the West but also knowledge from respected individuals in the communities. Students, encountering more than one source of knowledge, were in a situation where they could, and did, generate their own knowledge based on multiple sources of information. The approach taken, which we came to call the *generative curriculum,* had benefits far beyond graduation rates that were 4 to 5 times higher than the norm for indigenous education in Canada at that time (over 85% completion rates for the 1-year, and over 75% for the 2-year program), but even more importantly, the respected knowledge holders at the local level became part of a community revitalization impact. Here are the words of a tribal administrator:

> Because the community was invited into the classroom and the students' learning extended into the community, the impacts of the training were not limited to the students. There was a ripple effect that reached out to all aspects of the way we as a community think and act with respect to young children and families. Everyone was transformed. (Personal communication, M. McCallum, January 15, 1992)

The results attracted the attention of the United Nations Children's Fund (UNICEF), and I was invited in 1994 to undertake ECD capacity building work through their auspices in the majority (developing) world. Africa became the primary focus for this work, and through ECD seminars and the subsequently developed Early Childhood Development Virtual University (ECDVU), we have seen the continuation of remarkable completion rates (over 95% across four deliveries in sub-Saharan Africa), but even more notable have been transformations in policies, programs, and educational opportunities at country levels that underline the power and importance of local leadership. Such leadership may be at a community or a country level, but what is important is that it is determined, guided, and implemented by those from within.

There are a number of reasons to do research to support your advocacy—both to establish your reputation as an advocate and to make your advocacy more effective. Decision makers are not typically moved by shows of emotion. Combining your passion for the cause with solid research will build your credibility and help to establish you as an expert on an issue. This will make decision makers more likely to take your advocacy efforts seriously. Backing up your arguments with research will also give you a clearer sense of the issue as well as help you identify the courses of action you will recommend to the decision maker. Through research, you can also become informed about opposing arguments so that you can be prepared with counterarguments. Ultimately, the research that you conduct can contribute to your advocacy activities, such as educating the public, supporting a particular piece of legislation, testifying on behalf of legislation, informing lawsuits, and seeking media coverage (Padgett, 2008). See Box 5.2 for an example of how research informs the advocacy work of one organization

---

BOX 5.2

Conducting Research to Inform Advocacy in Latin America

By Alejandro Acosta Ayerbe, Regional Director CINDE Bogota (Colombia)

The International Center for Education and Human Development (CINDE) is a research and development center created in Colombia in 1977 by Glen Nimnicht and Martha Arango. Its purpose is to position the public agenda in countries like Colombia, overall in Latin America, and in the developing world to perceive issues related to children, youth, and families as the fundamental basis of human development. The organization highlights education in the broadest sense as the common thread among economic, social, and human development. Education must be at the service of children by creating a suitable environment for their healthy development in families, communities, and institutions.

To promote these objectives, CINDE works not only with and for children and their families but also with all levels in society directly and indirectly related to their quality of life. This includes caregivers, teachers, and health providers that work with children and families as well as the decision makers who influence their lives through planning, budgeting, and management processes at the local, regional, national, and international levels.

A priority of CINDE's work is to generate innovative social programs that are high quality, sustainable, and consonant with the human, technical, financial, and institutional resources of their countries. To generate this type of innovation, it is necessary to promote research, systematization, and monitoring and evaluation approaches to identify approaches that promote developmental processes and enhance the capabilities of social actors to promote the integral development of children and youth. This requires human talent at all levels, including the children themselves and their caregivers. CINDE has designed and has worked within educational programs for the children themselves, their families, and caregivers and has also designed Masters, PhD, and postdoctoral programs in partnership with universities.

The intention is that the knowledge generated and the innovations created from these programs reach the population on a large scale. CINDE has strategies to disseminate its research and advocacy to many audiences, including various government levels, civil society organizations, and international institutions so that this information may be translated into policies, programs, and projects.

Your research will have different purposes, depending on whether your focus is micro, mezzo, or macro advocacy. For micro advocacy on behalf of a particular child, your goals may include understanding the child's legal rights, finding out best practices for meeting the child's needs, and identifying local resources to meet the child's needs. For example, advocacy on behalf of a child with special needs might involve assessing the child's legal rights to accommodation within a school setting, determining the types of educational interventions appropriate for the child's disability, and finding out whether there are materials and trained individuals to carry out that intervention within the child's school district. For mezzo advocacy for a group of children or a community or macro advocacy related to a social issue affecting a large number of children, your research will entail identifying the scope of the problem, how best to address it, and support and opposition on the issue. It can also make sense to do research on the economic benefit or harm related to the issue as a way of strengthening your advocacy case. Decision makers are often more influenced by economic impact than any other type of evidence.

A 3-step process is recommended for your research. First, develop your research question and possibly subquestions. Your research questions should connect to your advocacy goal and objectives so that you will have the information you need to make a strong case. Then, review the available information on your issue, which can be found through Internet and library research (this is called secondary research). Finally, conduct original (primary) research as needed to fill in the gaps. As much as possible, involve your allies and your advocacy population in the process.

Try this approach to developing your research question. Take your problem statement from Step 1 (Chapter 4). Then consider what you need to know on this issue to make a persuasive case to others that change is needed. Phrase this as a question that is open-ended, meaning that it cannot be answered by "yes" or "no." Make sure your question is clear and focused, such that it can be understood by others and has a narrow emphasis on your topic of interest. See Box 5.3 for examples.

BOX 5.3

Examples of Moving From Advocacy Goals to Research Question(s)

Advocacy Goal	Problem Description	Research Question(s)
A child with special needs is able to participate in an afterschool program	The child would benefit from socialization and academic enrichment activities with peers but requires accommodations.	What are the child's legal rights to accommodations? What types of accommodations would best facilitate his participation given his specific needs? How can the afterschool program implement those accommodations?
Children in a community have a safe and appropriate place to play	There is a lack of safe, public, open space for children in the community. The parks that do exist are not well kept and lack adequate play structures.	What would be the best location for a public park given the geographic concentration of the child population? Should the gap be addressed through improving existing parks or developing new ones?

(Continued)

(Continued)		
Advocacy Goal	Problem Description	Research Question(s)
Youth in state juvenile detention facilities receive education and rehabilitative services	A state is under pressure to reform its juvenile justice system after negative media coverage and class action lawsuits alleging lack of appropriate services.	What evidence-based programs have been found to be effective in providing educational and other services in a juvenile detention facility?

As you review the information that already exists on your topic and plan your own original research as needed, you will encounter two broad types of research. *Quantitative research* involves the collection of numerical data that is analyzed using statistics. This type of research is helpful for identifying the big picture of how a social problem impacts society through statistics that demonstrate the scope of the problem, its consequences, and changes over time. *Qualitative research* is the collection of narrative data on how people understand social problems, which is analyzed by identifying general themes that emerge (Creswell, 2008). This type of research is helpful for identifying the personal impact of a social problem through documented stories and powerful quotes.

Before moving on to specific strategies for research, here is a word of caution: An advocate is only as good as his or her reputation. Carefully consider the credibility and integrity of the information that you use. You put your reputation on the line when you share your information and research with others through the materials you will develop (Chapter 6). Be careful when seeking information on the Internet and from other sources, and try to confirm information so that you can be sure of its accuracy. It is also crucial to be honest in reporting your research findings and avoid the temptation of inflating the problem, which can ultimately come back to haunt you.

SECONDARY RESEARCH

Today's advocate is fortunate to have an enormous amount of information available via the Internet and libraries that can be used to support one's cause. Make a thorough survey of the material that is already out there on your topic. This is *secondary research*, the type of research that you can do at a desk. This type of research will educate you on the topic and reveal the gaps that will need to be filled by primary research that you will conduct yourself. Types of secondary research and data for advocacy include demographic data, statistics, indicators, polling data, research studies, and policy analyses. Your job in this phase is to pull information together by synthesizing and summarizing. When in doubt, cast the net broadly. Some small piece of information may be the thing that makes the difference in your campaign.

Demographic data is statistical information about populations, such as population size, level of education, employment, and other characteristics. These types of data are generally available at a national level from a census that is collected at regular intervals. A *census* is an official government count of the total population often with additional demographic information collected such as age, household formation, and other details. For example, the United States Constitution mandates that a census be taken every 10 years, and this information is supplemented with a yearly survey with a small sample of the total population called the American Community Survey. Aggregated data is available for geographic locations at the census tract, zip code, Congressional district, city, county, state, and national levels on the U.S. census website, and this is also the case in many other countries. Local bodies such as municipal governments may also collect demographic data that can be used to inform mezzo advocacy efforts; search the Internet for your locality of interest. Demographic data is helpful when you need to know about the population of an area and its characteristics, such as the total number of children or the percentage living in poverty.

It can be helpful to supplement demographic data on a population with more specific statistical data related to the extent of social problems. You can search for statistics on the prevalence of a social problem at a particular point in time or find trend data that shows how a social problem has changed over a time period. For example, in 2009 and 2010, more than one in six American children ages 6 to 11 were overweight, and children in this time period were nearly 3 times as likely to be overweight as children of the same age from 1976 to 1980 (Child Trends Databank, 2012). This information shows that being overweight is common among American children and that this is a problem that has grown significantly worse over time. Statistics on social problems affecting children and youth are available through government and private research institutes. In the United States, sources include the Federal Interagency Forum on Child and Family Statistics and Child Trends Databank for national data and Kids Count for data within and across states (see the activity at the end of this chapter for websites). In other countries, useful sources of statistics include the Australian Institute of Family Studies, the Canadian Children's Rights Council, and United Kingdom National Statistics Hub. The United Nations Children's Fund (especially the Innocenti Research Centre) and the World Bank also provide statistics on children and youth by country.

Certain statistics are known as *indicators* because they indicate something about the well-being of a nation. These statistics may be expressed as a percentage of the total population, a rate of occurrence per standardized number of the population (e.g., per 1,000), or a rank comparing nations. Statistics such as gross national product and per capita income are often used as indicators about the health and size of a nation's economy. Likewise, statistics like the infant mortality rate (children born alive who die before the age of 1), percentage of infants with low birth weight, and the percentage of children of primary school age enrolled in school indicate something about the well-being of children in a nation. Indicators can be used to make various kinds of comparisons. They can be used to make comparisons with past historical values: for example, comparing the rate of infant mortality for a nation over a 100-year time frame or two points in time. Indicators can also be used to compare contemporaneous units (e.g., comparisons among subpopulations, states, regions, or countries): for example, a comparison of child poverty rates among ethnic/racial groups. Finally, they can be used to compare a unit or multiple units with goals or other externally established standards; for example, progress made on meeting children's needs as outlined in the United Nations Convention on the Rights of the Child, described in Chapter 1. When multiple indicators are put together, they form an *index*, a ratio or other number derived from a series of observations and used as an indicator or measure. This allows for aggregating a number of statistics that all relate to the same concept to give a more sophisticated picture of a subject like poverty or health. For example, Save the Children issues a yearly "State of the World's Mothers" index that ranks the best and worst countries in which to be a mother based on aggregating indicators such as lifetime risk of maternal death, availability of skilled attendants at birth, and maternity leave benefits.

After quantifying the size of a problem and how it has changed over time, it can be useful to find out about public opinion on the problem. *Public opinion polling* data provides a snapshot of what people think about an issue at a particular time. This information is typically collected through a survey of a random sample of the public. Polls may be conducted by research institutes, newspapers, and polling institutes such as Gallup and Rasmussen. Polls are often conducted to assess public support for a social policy, such as nutrition programs. If your advocacy is focused on supporting legislation or opposing cuts or changes to current legislation, polling data may bolster your case by showing the percentage of the population that supports your views.

To show the human dimension of a problem, you can search for documented stories and powerful quotes. You may need to gather this information yourself, depending on what is already available; this will be addressed in the next section on primary research. However, there may already be stories and quotes out there that illustrate the problem. Look for stories in news articles and websites on your advocacy topic. Some organizations have *story banks* that collect stories on a particular topic that powerfully illustrate how people are impacted by a problem. Examples include Half in Ten's project, the Road to Shared Prosperity, that collects stories from throughout the United States on how federal programs address the economic and other needs of vulnerable populations; FamilyUSA's collection of stories that illustrate the need for health care reform; and the Family Values at Work story bank that shows the impact of workplace policies on working families, including paid sick days and family leave. Good sources of quotes include interviews and op-eds from well-known figures, such as politicians. Select quotes that are powerfully worded and create impact rather than just convey information. A quote that is often used to support the value of early childhood education programs comes from Nobel Prize winning economist James Heckman (2000): "The real question is how to use the available funds wisely. The best evidence supports the policy prescription: Invest in the Very Young" (p. 1).

Research studies are another valuable source of support for your advocacy topic. Research findings can be used to demonstrate the importance of a topic or the effectiveness of a social intervention. Search for published literature through academic journals, research reports, and books. If you belong to a university as a student or alumnus, you may have access to journal articles through an institutional subscription. Otherwise, as a member of the general public, you may be required to pay for access to journal articles. Specialized academic search engines can be customized to bring up only peer-reviewed journal articles. Search engines available through paid subscriptions include ProQuest and JSTOR whereas Google Scholar is free to search, but articles shown may be available only for payment without an institutional subscription. Research studies can provide powerful and persuasive information on your topic. For example, studies of the Perry Preschool project and Abecedarian program are frequently cited by advocates to demonstrate the economic benefits of early childhood programs for low-income children. These programs randomized treatment by assigning some children to early childhood programs while other children were also tracked who did not receive these services. Then both populations were followed for a number of years, revealing that the groups who received early childhood services did better on a host of outcomes, including educational completion, and had lower rates of negative outcomes such as smoking as adults. The net benefits compared with the net costs greatly favored these early childhood programs (Barnett & Masse, 2007).

Research studies can also help you identify the best interventions to address the social problem based on what has been tried in other jurisdictions. As discussed in Chapter 2, evidence-based programs are supported by high-quality research that suggests that the program is responsible for achieving the desired outcomes. A list of sources for evidence-based programs is included in the activity at the end of the chapter. This will help your research by allowing you to present options to the decision maker on how to address the social problem and will give you evidence to support the effectiveness of your recommendations.

If you are attempting to influence policy making, or even if you are trying to ascertain how a policy would affect a specific child or community, then policy analysis is another type of research to seek. Conducting your own basic policy analysis is discussed later in this chapter. Policy research institutes, often called *think tanks*, are a source of policy analyses, but be careful. Such institutes may have a particular political slant; for example, the Heritage Institute in the United States is well known for its conservative views whereas the Public Citizen has a more liberal flavor. A major purpose of think tanks is to generate new ideas on policy change, so you may find that reports from think tanks are a good source of information for developing alternatives to present to a decision maker if you are engaged in mezzo or macro advocacy. A helpful source that lists influential think tanks is the yearly "Global Go To Think Tanks Rankings" produced by the University of Pennsylvania (International Relations Program University of Pennsylvania, 2013) based on feedback from think tanks themselves from around the world. The "Harvard Kennedy School Library Think Tank Search," an online list of U.S. and non-U.S. think tank websites, is another way to locate reputable partisan and nonpartisan sources.

PRIMARY RESEARCH

Once you have surveyed what is out there through secondary research, the next step is to fill in the gaps through your own original *primary research*. While it may seem overwhelming, focus on the types of research that will provide the most impact for your cause. Ultimately, advocacy research is a means to an end, and that end is social change rather than a research report. Research can strengthen your advocacy case by providing empirical support (Padgett, 2008). See Box 5.4 for suggestions on the most impactful types of research for different levels of advocacy. As mentioned previously, there are two forms of research: quantitative and qualitative. *Quantitative research* asks questions that can be answered with numbers like how many people are affected. For advocacy research, a common quantitative research approach would be a survey or poll with a sample of the total population affected; surveys can also provide qualitative data through inclusion of open-ended questions. *Qualitative research* generally answers questions of what, why, and how. The resulting data is in the form of words, opinions, anecdotes, and case studies. Types of qualitative research helpful for advocacy include interviews, focus groups, observation, and participatory research activities. This section provides a brief overview of various forms of research and data collection; if you choose to pursue one of these approaches, find a text that covers the topic in depth so that you can be systematic, thorough, and ethical in your use of the research technique.

BOX 5.4

Examples of Research for Different Levels of Advocacy

Micro Level

- Information about the child's situation or condition
- Quotable quotes from experts
- Evidence-based programs

Mezzo Level

- Demographic data on the local community
- Stories or case studies demonstrating impact of the problem
- Quotable quotes from local officials

Macro Level

- Demographic data on the scope of the problem
- Indicators or trend data to show change in the problem over time
- Research studies to back up your proposed solution

The story of shipping magnate and research pioneer Charles Booth exemplifies the use of multiple research methods to understand a social problem so that the problem can ultimately be addressed. Called the founding father of empirical research in the social sciences, Booth developed an interest in the poor and unemployed of London after moving there in 1875. He found that conversations with politicians, socialists, and social workers were fruitless in answering his concerns about how the poor lived and how they might be helped. So he sought answers to these questions himself through analyzing existing census data, gathering information from London School Board visitors on families with young children, interviewing numerous individuals in low-income areas, and conducting what would now be called focus groups with key informants. He and his associates used this information to develop an economic classification system, define a poverty level, and use the economic classification system to create color coded maps of the city; these materials were published in a four-set series of books called the *Poverty Series*. His findings on the association between poverty and old age directly influenced the passage of the 1908 Old Age Pensions

Act in Britain (Andres, 2012). Like Booth, you may find that the answers to your questions about social problems have not yet been collected but that the answers are out there.

Since advocacy research projects rarely go through the vetting process of a human subjects institutional review board common to academic or institutional research, it is up to the advocate to observe ethical standards. You must obtain *informed consent* from anyone participating in your research. This means disclosing the purpose of the research, the procedures involved, the expected duration of the subject's participation, foreseeable risks (including psychological discomfort), benefits to the participant or broader society, manner of protection for the participant's confidentiality, and notification of the option to stop participating at any time without consequence. Ask the participant to give consent for participation orally or in writing. If you plan to use the person's name when reporting your research, be certain to ask permission beforehand. If the information will be reported in the aggregate (e.g., attributing viewpoints to parents at a school) or using nonspecific titles (e.g., a preschool teacher), let the person know that his or her responses will be confidential and findings will be reported anonymously. Protect any information that you collect by ensuring that only the person collecting the data has access to it, whether it is electronic or hard copy (Israel & Hay, 2006).

Survey research involves the collection of data on a relatively large group of people, either the entire population of interest or a sample of the population, through questionnaires or structured interviews. This approach is useful when you want to understand an issue at a particular point in time, such as public opinion or the prevalence of a social problem. A survey will ask respondents to respond to a set of questions. Closed-ended questions present a set of options, such as a rating scale for their level of agreement with a statement. Open-ended questions ask the respondent to write a reply. Analysis of responses to closed-ended questions tends to involve descriptive statistics that count and rank responses whereas content analysis can be used for responses to open-ended questions to identify the major themes that emerge. Surveys can be administered face-to-face or by mail, Internet, and phone. The advantages of using a survey include being a low-cost and efficient means of collecting information that can be representative and therefore generalized to the population. The drawbacks include the challenges of getting people to complete your survey and capturing information at a general rather than detailed level. It is important to be careful about sampling from a larger population so that you can select a subsample that is representative of the overall sample. The findings of your research will also be most valid if you take time to pilot your instrument by sharing it with a small subsample of your population and to check whether questions and concepts are uniformly understood (Kelley, Clark, Brown, & Sitzia, 2003).

For advocates, interviews can be a great way of gathering stories or *case studies* that illustrate your issue. Just like the story banks mentioned earlier, you can create your own repository of powerful stories. Rather than seeking a sample that is representative of the population as a whole as with surveys, finding people with compelling stories is a type of purposive sampling. You might seek people through organizations that address specific social issues, specialized outreach via social media, or membership organizations (Community Catalyst, 2012). Seek people who have experiences that can be crafted into stories that demonstrate personal impact and are credible and sympathetic to the possible audience (Families USA, 1999). Develop an interview script with questions, but be prepared to go with the flow of the interview and ask follow-up questions as interesting angles come up. Pace the interview so that you are able to establish rapport with your interviewee; start the interview with easier questions, display genuine enthusiasm and interest in the interviewee, and use active listening techniques like paraphrasing to show that you are listening. Interviews for collecting stories can be recorded by taking notes, or making a video or audiotape. You may also wish to supplement with photographs of the interviewee. Be sure to notify the person that he or she may be contacted by media if you use the media to disseminate your information. Use the interview responses to craft a truthful and coherent narrative that relates to the main ideas of your advocacy project. A strength of this approach is depth—you can explore an issue and its impact on people's lives in a meaningful way. However, the number of stories will be limited and may be criticized as *cherry picking*, meaning that stories have been selected that reinforce a particular position while ignoring other facets of an issue.

Key stakeholder interviews are another way to use interviews to gather helpful information. Stakeholders are people who have an interest or concern in your issue (see the Analyzing Stakeholders section in Chapter 4). Seek out decision makers, journalists who have reported on the issue, and experts for in-depth interviews on your advocacy issue. It can be helpful to first do some research on your target decision maker and find out which individuals he or she holds in high esteem, and seek out those potentially influential voices. Request an appointment, typically 30 to 60 minutes, at a location of his or her convenience or by phone. Craft open-ended questions for the interviews, but as with interviewing for stories, be prepared to go with the flow of the conversation and ask spontaneous follow-up questions. This type of data collection can be a way to collect *quotable quotes,* pithy statements that support your advocacy case. If you hear a particular choice phrase that you would like to quote directly with attribution, request a signed statement acknowledging the quote and permission to use it. After your interview, be sure to follow up with an email or note thanking the interviewee. Summarize the main ideas that came out of your interviews and note any differences of opinion among stakeholders. The downside of this approach is that key stakeholder interviews require some skill at interviewing and building rapport and can be time-consuming. The payoff is that beyond the useful information that you gather, key stakeholder interviews can be a way to establish or deepen a relationship with a possible ally.

Focus groups are group interviews that are particularly useful when you would like to capture the views of a category of people, such as parents or youth in a particular community, and utilize group dynamics to generate compelling data. Focus groups feature a group of participants and a moderator who asks a set of structured questions and keeps the conversation on track. It is best to audiotape a focus group and have it transcribed or have a second person in attendance who takes notes on participants' statements. An advantage of the focus group approach is the potential synergy created by bringing respondents together; this can spark new ideas and encourage deeper conversations than you would get interviewing people on their own. A related drawback can be that some people might feel more reluctant to share in a group setting, particularly if the information is personal, and may be less likely to state views that run counter to the group (Kitzinger, 1994). Particularly vocal members may also skew the results and have a strong influence on other participants. Design considerations for using focus groups include sampling to include a representative number of the types of people whose views you wish to understand, considering potentially meaningful characteristics that relate to your advocacy topic like age or gender. Focus groups are usually kept fairly small to enable contributions by all participants. While the number of focus groups to conduct varies based on the amount of information desired, a standard rule of thumb is four to six focus groups to reach *data saturation*, or the point where ideas begin to repeat (Morgan, 1996). As with interview data, you can analyze focus group data for major ideas and themes that emerge, and you may note differences in ideas depending on the backgrounds of the groups that you talk to (for example, different community priorities for the elderly and youth).

In addition to eliciting people's perspectives, *observation* can be a way to gain an understanding of an issue. You might engage in *participant observation* by putting yourself into a social situation and experiencing it the way that others are experiencing the event. This form of data collection may be useful for informing advocacy work when you wish to understand how a social setting functions, such as a school. While some researchers have engaged in covert observation, overt observation in which people are aware of the reason for the presence of the research is more ethical. The main form of data collection with this method is collecting *field notes* that describe the social setting as well as the feelings and reactions of the observer. These may be supplemented in the moment with photographs and audio materials and later added to by the observer based on memory (Coffey, 2006). Another form of observation is a *windshield survey,* involving making systematic observations of a community by car, or *walking survey*, doing the same thing on foot. This type of data may be useful if you are planning advocacy that involves community improvement and you need to get a deeper sense of a neighborhood. Decide on the goal of your windshield or walking survey in advance so you know what to take notes on. Ideas might be the number, location, and conditions of parks or street safety conditions like crosswalks and traffic patterns (Rabinowitz, 2013). A downside of observation is that the presence of an observer might change people's behaviors in a social setting. The benefits are a recording of the actual events or conditions of a social setting or community.

Photographs or videos are another way to document a social issue. *Photovoice* is a method of engaging people in documenting their communities' strengths and challenges through photography, engaging in dialogue about those photographs, and attempting to influence decision makers, particularly policy makers. Participants should be trained in using cameras as well as the broader intent of the Photovoice approach and given specific parameters for the project. After participants have taken photos, a facilitated group discussion involves a three-step process of selecting images that reflect the community's strengths and challenges, providing stories to contextualize the images, and identifying the main themes that emerge across the images and stories captured. Photovoice offers the advantages of engaging individuals, particularly from marginalized groups, in assessing the needs of their own community through the accessible medium of photography, which does not require a high degree of literacy. This approach has been used frequently and with great success with children and youth and can be a powerful way to involve them in advocacy efforts on their own behalf. The limitations of Photovoice include the subjectivity of those taking the photographs and the potential for self-censorship around sensitive topics (Wang & Buriss, 1997). Analyzing and summarizing the data you receive through photographs can be difficult, but you may find that this technique provides powerful images that can be used in Chapter 6, "Step 3—Preparing Effective Materials."

Beyond the benefits of supporting your advocacy campaign with compelling informa-tion, research can also be a way of finding and engaging new allies for your cause. For example, people whom you interview for their personal stories can become spokespeople for the advocacy cause, giving interviews to media and speaking with decision makers (Community Catalyst, 2012). The stakeholders you interview or include in your focus groups may become collaborators as they learn about your work. *Participatory action research* is a way of directly involving beneficiaries of advocacy or stakeholders such as community members in a research effort. This method engages a group in a process of identifying a problem, collecting and analyzing information, and then finding solutions and acting on the problem. Any of the research methods previously described, such as Photovoice and wind-shield or walking surveys, might be used as part of a participatory action research effort. This manner of research is particularly appropriate for efforts to create community change because it can encourage buy-in and ownership over the process. Participatory action research is also frequently used to create organizational change from the inside out and to transform educational practices or schools by empowering educators (Selener, 1997).

Build a library of the information you have collected in either electronic or hard-copy format. After you have completed your secondary and primary research, write up your main findings in a brief and accessible format. The recommended format for your write-up is a summary sheet, described in Chapter 6, Step 3. If you are seeking policy change, you may also prepare a policy memo as described in the next section.

POLICY RESEARCH

If your goal is policy change, at the mezzo or macro levels, a very specific type of research and write-up is called for. A *policy memorandum* (or memo) has three major components: a problem description section that describes the scope of the problem and why it is of policy importance, a recommendations section that discusses how the problem can be addressed through legislation, and an executive summary that summarizes main points. A helpful guide that provides greater detail on the process of developing a policy memo is Eugene Bardach's (2011) *A Practical Guide for Policy Analysis: The Eightfold Path to More Effective Problem Solving*. This section will provide an overview of how to develop a policy memo. See Box 5.5 for a policy memo outline.

BOX 5.5

Policy Memorandum Outline

Heading

To:

From:

Subject:

Date:

Executive Summary

- What is the issue?
- Why is a decision needed?
- What key information is contained in this memorandum?
- What course of action is recommended?

Problem Description

- What is the nature of the problem/issue?
- Why is it of public policy concern?
- What is the current policy?

Options/Recommendation

- What are the plausible courses of action along with the pros and cons of each?
- What are the risks and potential opposition that might result from choosing an option?
- What is your recommended course of action and why?
- What resources would be necessary to implement your recommendation?
- Who would be helped and who would be hurt by your proposal?

Conclusion

- Summary of main points

Policy memos are often produced by advocacy organizations and think tanks in order to influence policy makers and the gatekeepers who have access to them at the local, state/regional, national and international levels. The audience for a policy memo is a decision maker who has jurisdiction over the issue. This may mean that the person is in a position to introduce new legislation on a topic, serves on a committee that will study and revise a bill on this topic, or is eligible to vote in favor of or against the legislation. When writing a policy memo, it is important to keep in mind the needs of the audience, which is either the decision maker or a gatekeeper such as a legislative aide who advises the decision maker. Decision makers and gatekeepers need to master complex, substantive issues in a short amount of time as they consider an array of legislation across a range of topics. Since they review policy on numerous issues and face time constraints, they must make decisions such as whether to introduce a bill or vote for or against it based on partial or imperfect information. They are motivated to please a constituency, in the case of a decision maker, or a boss, in the case of a gatekeeper. Given your audience, keep these guidelines in mind: Be brief, avoid technical jargon, and present your case for a clear course of action supported by research. You can provide valuable information and potentially win allies if you can produce and disseminate clear, brief, and well-researched policy memos.

The problem description should identify a significant problem facing children and families, describe why it is of public policy concern, and address the current policy. Begin by defining the problem with a problem statement (see the section in Chapter 4 titled Identifying the Issue for a discussion of how to write a problem statement). It can be helpful to define a problem in terms of deficit and excess: for example, by describing how there are too few resources to address a problem or too many people using a scarce resource (Bardach, 2011). Use the secondary and primary data research methods described earlier in this chapter to find statistics and illustrative anecdotes about the scope of the problem and who is affected. Help the reader understand how this problem has developed over time by describing its causes and trends. Not all problems are appropriate for government intervention. Make a case that this problem is appropriate and amenable to public policy solutions by considering reasons for government involvement: political reasons, moral or ethical reasons, and economic and market failures. *Political reasons* can include pressure from the public and social movements; an example in the United States is changes to civil rights legislation as a result of the Civil Rights Movement of the 1960s. *Moral and ethical reasons* are often invoked for legislation that is enacted because it protects a vulnerable group and is perceived as the right thing to do; this is often the rationale used for policy on behalf of children and families. *Economic and market failures* exist when the private market economy cannot meet certain social needs; one significant example relevant to child advocacy is the provision of public goods, which are available to all with no economic incentive, such as public parks (Kraft & Furlong, 2013). Then describe the current policy related to this social problem and its limitations that need to be addressed with new legislation. Identify current policy through secondary research, including looking for reports from advocacy organizations and think tanks and journal articles from academic sources.

Once you have established the significance of the problem, the next step is to make recommendations on how to address the problem. The basic argument of this section is as follows: *The* (who should do it—state legislator, the governor, a state department) *should* (what should they do—hold hearings, introduce legislation, appropriate funds) *in order to* (for what benefit—reduce dropout rates, increase access to child care). Provide two or more options for the decision maker and support your discussion with evidence, reasoning, and analysis. The options you provide may be mutually exclusive or complimentary. For example, you could present one option to let the status quo continue without policy intervention. Project current trends in terms of how this problem might continue to develop and contrast this to your recommended course of action. The other approach is to present two or more acceptable options. To generate ideas for recommendations, it is first necessary to understand what governments can do. Governments can regulate, manage services, tax and spend, utilize market mechanisms, and educate, inform, or persuade (see the section in Chapter 4 titled Analyzing the Policy Context for definitions of these terms). You can propose new or modified legislation that uses one or more of these strategies. Once you understand the repertoire of policy instruments, research can turn up policy approaches that have worked elsewhere. Conduct a review of the research literature to learn what others have proposed in terms of addressing your problem. Research articles often include implications for policy development. The journal *Future of Children*, available for free on their website, includes a policy brief in each issue that summarizes the research articles covering a particular theme and offers policy recommendations. Another source of ideas is to look at what has worked in similar situations. If you are interested in the issue of universal preschool, for example, you could learn about regions and countries that have adopted universal preschool and how it has worked. Similarly, you could see what has worked in other policy areas to see if ideas can be adapted. For example, if you are interested in promoting professionalization and training of afterschool care providers, you might see how this has been done in the field of early childhood care and education. If these approaches don't generate any ideas, try envisioning an ideal scenario to address the problem and use this to brainstorm solutions.

Part of making a case for your recommendations is to support your recommendations with analysis. *Policy analysis* is a way of assessing whether a policy has or will achieve its goals; the most common criteria are effectiveness, efficiency, and equity. Other criteria include ethics, political feasibility, social acceptability, administrative feasibility, and technical feasibility. The main idea of *effectiveness* is whether a policy can reach its goals and objectives. An effectiveness question would be the following: Has a city's use of school vouchers raised the quality of education? *Efficiency* is concerned with keeping costs within reason, weighing benefits against cost. An efficiency question would be the following: Does the social and economic value of a higher education loan program for underrepresented youth justify its cost to the taxpayer? *Equity* considers the distribution of costs and benefits to groups and individuals and whether it is fair. *Process equity* considers whether decision-making processes about social policy are open and accessible to all participants so various voices are represented. *Outcomes equity* relates to the end results of how societal resources are distributed and whether this is fair (Kraft & Furlong, 2013). A process equity question would be the following: Were all parents in the district consulted about the change to school policy? An outcomes equity question would be the following: Should a city have lottery based or neighborhood-based criteria for public school enrollment? Present your reasoning and evidence in terms of how the options presented to the decision maker would be assessed using the major policy criteria as well as the other criteria as needed (for example, political feasibility to convince a legislator to support a controversial bill). Be clear about the potential impact on populations, both winners and losers. Finish your recommendations section with a clear call to action to the decision maker, reiterating the main reasons in support of your recommendation.

Finally, understand that the decision maker and gatekeeper audience are busy and may not read the entire policy memo; for this reason, condense, simplify, and highlight main points in an *executive summary*. Write your executive summary last after completing your policy memo. An executive summary should be a brief (one-page) description of the contents of the policy memo, using a similar structure as the memo; that is, briefly describe the problem first; then present alternatives and recommendations. Do not include new information—simply condense the information in the memo to the main points. Prepare an outline for the summary by making a bulleted list of the main points of the memo. Edit the outline to eliminate secondary or minor points. Review the summary to make sure it is concise. Assess your final draft and the overall policy memo by considering these questions:

- What is the main message?
- What do I want the policy maker to remember?
- Have I made a case for why a policy change is necessary?
- Are the recommendations I have made feasible? Convincing? Supported with evidence?

The case study in the next section demonstrates how research can be used to inform advocacy and policy development for children and youth.

Using Research to Influence Policy: A Case Study of Specialized Job Training for Youth With Disabilities in Sweden

Sweden is a country that values data and statistics. When a need for children and families arises, either from an interest group or government study, the next stage is to call for national debate related to the subject area. Unlike the election-style debate common in other parts of the world, these debates are a method of bringing together parties representing all sides of an issue in order to study it and develop consensus regarding strategies to address the issue.

Advocates inside and outside of government in the county of Uppsala, Sweden, brought attention to the future adult life of special needs youth during the 1970s. A group of professionals who worked with special needs youth wanted to ensure that the youth could gain employment, live independently, and become an active part of society. These goals were shared by the local government. Debates were launched to determine how youth with motor challenges or developmental delays could gain and maintain paid employment.

The advocates working with youth conducted extensive research to learn about potential employment opportunities. This entailed secondary research to review existing forecasts of emerging market trends and surveys of businesses on their employment-related needs. Primary research was used to supplement this information, including interviews with employment specialists. The group of advocates used this information to develop a plan that identified economic opportunities for employment in manufacturing thermoses, assembling jewelry, and stone cutting for jewelry.

The advocates, in partnership with the government, developed trainings with local businesses to prepare youth for these occupations. The jewelry making training, for example, provided a 4-year program for youth age 14 that would enable them at age 18 to enter the market with a valued skill. The first cohort of young people graduated into jobs, for which not only were they paid, but as shown by follow-up evaluation by the Swedish government, they also became taxpayers.

The Uppsala experience illustrates how the process from research to debate to policy development to evaluation can conclude with solid new programs for children and families.

Activity: Review Websites to Look for Information on Your Advocacy Topic

Explore the websites in this section and search for additional websites for information on your advocacy topic. Use the discussion questions below to guide your research.

1. What is the prevalence of the social problem? How many people are affected? Are certain groups more affected by this problem based on race/ethnicity, gender, socioeconomic status, geography, and other background factors?

2. What is the history of the problem? What are some of the root causes of this problem? How has it changed over time?

3. What are possible solutions to address this problem?

Finding stories

- Our Head Start (Head Start/early childhood care & education): http://www.ourheadstart.org/
- National Foster Care Month (foster care): https://www.childwelfare.gov/fostercaremonth/reallifestories/
- The Beat Within (juvenile justice): http://www.thebeatwithin.org/

Statistics and trend data

- The Federal Interagency Forum on Child and Family Statistics (U.S. national level): http://www.childstats.gov/index.asp
- Kids Count (data by and across states in the U.S.): http://datacenter.kidscount.org/gf
- Child Trends (U.S. national level, trend data): http://www.childtrendsdatabank.org/
- Children's Defense Fund (by state and national in U.S.): http://www.childrens defense.org/
- Children Now (U.S. national level): http://www.childrennow.org/index.php/
- Zero to Three (U.S. national level): http://www.zerotothree.org/public-policy/
- World Health Organization (international): http://www.who.int/topics/child_health/en/
- United Nations Children's Fund (international): http://www.unicef.org/statistics/index.html

Geographic and demographic data

- United States Census (census data by zip code, census tract): http://factfinder2.census.gov

Polling data

- Polling Report: http://www.pollingreport.com/
- Rasmussen Reports: http://www.rasmussenreports.com/
- Gallup: http://www.gallup.com/

Research studies

- The Future of Children (general): http://futureofchildren.org/
- The Children's Bureau (child welfare): http://www.acf.hhs.gov/programs/cb/stats_research/index.htm
- Child Welfare League of America (child welfare): http://www.cwla.org/programs/researchdata/default.htm
- Chapin Hall (child welfare, home visitation, juvenile justice): http://www.chapinhall.org/research
- National Dissemination Center for Children with Disabilities (disability): http://nichcy.org/research/summaries
- National Association for the Education of Young Children (early childhood care & education): http://www.naeyc.org/files/naeyc/ResearchStudies.pdf
- Pre-K Now (early childhood education): http://www.preknow.org/
- Kaiser Family Foundation (health): http://www.kff.org/
- National Criminal Justice Reference Service (juvenile justice): http://www.ncjrs.gov/
- National Center for Children in Poverty (poverty): http://www.nccp.org/
- International Society for the Prevention of Child Abuse and Neglect (child welfare): http://www.ispcan.org/
- UNICEF Innocenti Research Centre (general): http://www.unicef-irc.org/

Evidence-based prevention and intervention

- What Works Clearinghouse (education): http://ies.ed.gov/ncee/wwc/
- Promising Practices Network on Children, Families, and Communities (general): http://www.promisingpractices.net/
- National Governors Association Center for Best Practices (general): http://www.nga.org/cms/center
- California Evidence-based Clearinghouse for Child Welfare (child welfare): http://www.cebc4cw.org/

REFERENCES

Andres, L. (2012). *Designing and doing survey research*. Thousand Oaks, CA: SAGE.

Bardach, E. (2011). *A practical guide for policy analysis: The eightfold path to more effective problem solving*. Thousand Oaks, CA: CQ Press.

Barnett, W. S., & Masse, L. N. (2007). Comparative benefit–cost analysis of the Abecedarian program and its policy implications. *Economics of Education Review, 26*(1), 113–125.

Child Trends Databank (2012). *Overweight children and youth*. Retrieved from www.childtrendsdatabank.org/alphalist?q = node/70

Coffey, A. (2006). Participant observation. In V. Jupp (Ed.), *The Sage dictionary of social research methods* (pp. 214–216). Thousand Oaks, CA: SAGE.

Community Catalyst (2012). *Storybanking: A critical activity for advocates.* Retrieved from http://www .communitycatalyst.org/resources/storybank?id = 0003

Creswell, J. W. (2008). *Research design: Qualitative, quantitative, and mixed methods approaches.* Thousand Oaks, CA: SAGE.

Families USA (1999). *The art of storybanking.* Retrieved from http://familiesusa2.org/assets/pdfs/ ImPRESS_story_banking6de2.pdf

Harrington, M. (1962). *The other America.* New York, NY: Simon and Schuster.

Heckman, J. (2000). *The real question is how to use the available funds wisely. The best evidence supports the policy prescription: Invest in the very young.* Ounce of Prevention Fund and the University of Chicago Harris School of Public Policy Studies. Retrieved from http://www.ounceofprevention .org/news/pdfs/HeckmanInvestInVeryYoung.pdf

International Relations Program University of Pennsylvania (2013). *2012 Global go to think tanks report and policy advice.* Retrieved from http://www.gotothinktank.com/wp-content/uploads/ 2013/01/2012-Global-Go-To-Think-Tank-Report.pdf

Israel, M., & Hay, I. (2006). *Research ethics for social scientists.* Thousand Oaks, CA: SAGE.

Kelley, K., Clark, B., Brown, V., & Sitzia, J. (2003). Good practice in the conduct and reporting of survey research. *International Journal for Quality in Health Care, 15*(3), 261–266.

Kitzinger, J. (1994). The methodology of focus groups: The importance of interaction between research participants. *Sociology of Health & Illness, 16*(1), 103–121.

Kraft, M. E., & Furlong, S. R. (2013). *Public policy: Politics, analysis, and alternatives* (4th ed.). Washington, DC: CQ Press.

Morgan, D. L. (1996). Focus groups. *Annual Review of Sociology, 22,* 129–152.

Padgett, D. K. (2008). *Qualitative methods in social work research* (Vol. 36). Thousand Oaks, CA: SAGE.

Rabinowitz, P. (2013). Windshield and walking surveys. *Community Toolbox.* Retrieved from http://ctb .ku.edu/en/tablecontents/chapter3-section21-main.aspx

Reason, P., & Bradbury, H. (Eds.). (2007). *The Sage Handbook of action research: Participative inquiry and practice* (2nd ed.). Thousand Oaks, CA: SAGE.

Selener, D. (1997). *Participatory action research and social change* (2nd ed.). Ithaca, NY: The Cornell Participatory Action Research Network, Cornell University.

Wang, C., & Burris, M. A. (1997). Photovoice: Concept, methodology, and use for participatory needs assessment. *Health Education & Behavior, 24*(3), 369–387.

CHAPTER 6

Step 3—Preparing
Effective Materials

After developing an understanding of the issue and conducting the necessary research to support your advocacy on that issue, the next step is to prepare tools that will effectively communicate the issue to decision makers. It is first essential to understand the components of persuasive communication, then to see how these elements can be used in different forms to present the issue to potential allies and supporters. Research and persuasion are means to getting to the "yes"—the decision that you are seeking. Child advocates have many mediums by which to spread their message; a few examples are presentations, videos, and legislative testimony. Summary sheets can be an effective way of communicating with a decision maker. This chapter will lay out the elements of persuasive communication, how to craft your message, types of advocacy tools, and how to develop a summary sheet to coalesce your advocacy argument.

PERSUASIVE COMMUNICATION

How can advocates make their issues prominent among all the potential causes vying for scarce attention from decision makers and the public? Tools for communication with decision makers and potential allies must be both informative and persuasive. Persuasive communication is "any message that is intended to shape, reinforce, or change the responses of another, or others . . . [through] changes to cognition, attitudes, and behaviors" (Miller, 1980, p. 11). In this context, cognition means someone's beliefs about the meaning of an issue, such as how it is defined, interpreted, or attributed; attitude relates to how someone evaluates an issue, whether positively or negatively; and behavior is how someone overtly acts with regard to an issue. In other words, we are trying to change how people think, feel, and act. Persuasion methods involve appeals to logic and emotion as well as factors related to the messenger (Stiff & Mongeau, 2003).

The classic text on persuasion, Aristotle's *On Rhetoric*, identifies three modes of persuasion. *Logos* (Greek: word) refers to reasoning and supporting evidence, such as facts and statistics, which constitute the logical aspect of an argument. *Pathos* (Greek: suffering or experience) is an emotional appeal that provokes the sympathy and imagination of listeners, allows them to identify with the speaker's point of view, and ultimately moves them to respond. *Ethos* (Greek: character) is the messenger and what gives this person the authority and credibility to speak on the issue (Ramage & Bean, 1998). Marshaling each element of persuasion makes for a compelling case. In terms of child advocacy, this can involve encouraging others to join your efforts through sharing stories that stir compassion (pathos), explaining how their assistance will make a difference (logos), and demonstrating your personal characteristics and qualifications suitable for the task (ethos) (Booher, 2003).

Think about it as a head, heart, and gut check. Head: Does the evidence make sense and does it support the case being made? Heart: Does the evidence connect with your audience emotionally and invoke a reaction like warmth, fear, or guilt? Gut: Does the way that you are presenting yourself help people to trust you and have faith in the information you are providing? There are many ways to utilize these three elements of persuasion, and most messages rely on more than one type of appeal.

Appeal to Logic

From the previous chapter, you have learned various ways to conduct primary and secondary research. Facts and statistics can be used to make a compelling appeal to logic. Compare these statements:

Statement without data: "In recent years, South Dakota has seen both a need and a demand for low-cost, high quality child care. South Dakota has a high number of females with children who are in the workforce. The need for child care touches the lives of every South Dakotan. The child care industry is an essential part of the state's economic development strategy." (Cochran, 2006, p. 1)

Statement with data: "Without child care, most South Dakota businesses would be hard-pressed to find enough employees. That's because in South Dakota 73 percent of children under age 6 have one or both parents who are in the workforce. South Dakota leads the nation in the percentage of women in the workforce who have children younger than 6. In our state, the percentage is 77.5%, compared to 63.5% for the United States as a whole. At 47 percent, South Dakota also leads the nation with the highest percentage of children under age 6 in paid child care. That's almost twice the national average of 26 percent. Licensed or registered child care itself is a significant industry in South Dakota that:

- Generates $100.6 million in gross annual receipts.
- Creates 4,410 jobs in South Dakota.
- Yields $124.5 million in direct economic activity" (Cochran, 2006, p. 1).

If you were a decision maker, would you respond to vague concern or a clearly worded argument supported by evidence? Yet rattling off numbers can be dry, and constant exposure to statistics in the news has left much of the public desensitized to numbers. Social math is a way to make numbers meaningful by creating a frame of reference with other numbers that are smaller and part of everyday experience or placing the number in the context of other events or costs (Center for Health Improvement, 2004). Rather than only giving the numbers and percentages of children killed through gun violence, the Children's Defense Fund uses an image familiar to the public and puts this statistic in terms of classrooms: "The number of children and teens killed by guns in 2007 would fill more than 122 public school classrooms of 25 students each" (Children's Defense Fund, 2010, p. 2). The report's authors also use time, noting that this is the equivalent of one child killed every 3 hours. Social math can also be useful in terms of making the case for financial costs of interventions. In *The Life You Can Save,* Singer (2009) suggests that $125 billion would cut global poverty in half, and Americans spend $116 billion annually on alcohol. Bringing it to more familiar terms, child sponsorship programs often frame the cost of paying for a child's education or material needs in a developing country as less than the cost of a daily cup of coffee.

Other forms of evidence include research studies, theories, analogies, and statements from experts and authorities. Studies on interventions in areas such as education, mental health, child welfare, and juvenile justice can demonstrate what works, and interventions with a body of supporting research are often called evidence-based programs or promising practices (as discussed in Chapter 2). Describing longitudinal research on children's experiences and their adult outcomes can be a compelling way to support high-quality social interventions; examples of longitudinal studies include the National Institute of Child Health and Development Study of Early Child Care and Youth Development in the United States and the Growing Up in Australia Longitudinal Study of Australian Children. Theories from the fields of developmental psychology, education, sociology, and even economics can also support contentions about the importance of investing in services for children. Attachment theory, for example, highlights the importance of consistent relationships and can be used to support policies such as maternity leave, foster parent retention, and measures to counter turnover in the early childhood workforce. Sometimes an analogy that demonstrates parallels to familiar or historical events can be effective. Another way the Children's Defense Fund described the effects of gun violence in the United States was to point out that in 2007 more preschool children than police officers in the line of duty were killed by firearms. Advocates might look to how other eras responded to social problems and suggest similar responses, such as responding to economic downturn by rebuilding infrastructure such as schools as a form of stimulus. Informed opinions from public figures or subject experts can also be used to make a case. The previous chapter suggests developing a file of quotable quotes on an advocacy subject. A public figure's experience and reputation can bolster support for an issue, such as this statement by New Orleans Sheriff Marlin Gusman in support of child maltreatment prevention home visitation programs: "Violence breeds violence. We need to do more to save innocent kids from harm, because if we don't, more of them will end up in the criminal justice system as juvenile delinquents and criminal offenders" (Fight Crime, Invest in Kids, 2010).

Appeal to Emotion

Another approach is an appeal to emotion. Research can support your narrative in terms of telling a compelling story. The powerful emotions societies hold toward children, such as protectiveness and anxiety, can be tapped into by child advocates. However, there is also the danger of hand-wringing that can be easily dismissed by those in power. On *The Simpsons* television show, the minister's wife, Helen Lovejoy, utters, "Won't someone please think of the children?" as a meaningless catchphrase in the context of public events. This running joke suggests that emotional arguments on behalf of children often have a knee-jerk quality that is predictable and meaningless. Successful advocates develop messages that evoke an emotional response but are not themselves emotional in delivering their arguments.

Another cautionary note is to avoid developing arguments that appear to blame the target decision maker, as such arguments are likely to trigger a defensive reaction. A group of parent advocates learned this lesson the hard way. Concerned about accidents and near accidents on a busy street that children needed to cross to get to schools, they developed a plan to get a traffic light installed and needed to plead their case to the Concord Traffic Safety Commission made up of retired sheriffs and a retired local police chief. The parent leader made one of the most egregious mistakes an advocate can make. She blurted, "My taxes pay your salaries, and if my children die, it's your fault." This comment sparked a half hour of statements from the commission about why it would not be their fault if something happened to the parents' children. After an initial refusal to vote on the initiative, followed by many apologies from the parent, the desired action was taken. While the parents learned from this mistake, their advocacy was unnecessarily delayed and they barely won in the end. As is discussed further in Chapter 7, "Step 4—Making Meetings That Work," it is important to be perceived as someone who builds up the decision maker's reputation and never as someone who makes him or her lose face by making that person appear foolish.

Emotional appeals are more likely than logical appeals to grab attention and leave the audience with a vivid and memorable image (Bettinghaus & Cody, 1994). They may play on negative emotions, such as fear and guilt, or positive ones, such as humor and warmth. *Fear appeals* describe a threat and recommend a change in attitude or behavior as a coping response. Public service announcements about substance abuse often take this tactic by demonstrating the harmful impacts of drug, alcohol, or tobacco use with a frightening image such as the physical impacts on a long-term addict, and then recommend a response of abstaining from substance use or "just say[ing] no" to pressure from peers to engage in substance use. *Guilt appeals* identify how audience members' actions may have violated their values and how to make up for this violation through changed behaviors or attitudes (Stiff & Mongeau, 2003). International organizations with child sponsorship programs that allow individuals to send money in support of a particular child frequently use guilt appeals in their advertisements with an often unspoken comparison of poverty in developing countries and affluence in Western countries and how little it would cost the viewer to provide life-saving aid. Research supports the persuasive efficacy of fear appeals but suggests that guilt appeals have more mixed results and may backfire by eliciting anger and irritation, which work against the message's persuasive intent (Stiff & Mongeau, 2003). Positive emotional appeals, such as to warmth and humor, have been less studied in commercial and social marketing (Haynes, Thornton, & Jones, 2004).

Warmth appeals include messages that suggest kindness, nostalgia, pride, and togetherness (Bettinghaus & Cody, 1994). An evocative image of a young child or family can trigger feelings of warmth. One iconic example was a series of ads produced in 1978 by Försäkringskassan, the Swedish Social Insurance Agency, to promote paid paternity leave and encourage participation by fathers. The ads featured Swedish weightlifter Lennart

"Hoa-Hoa" Dahlgren holding an infant child below the words "Maternity Dad" (Klinth, 2008). The poster and related media coverage led to huge national attention on the issue and an increase in father participation in the parental leave program. Humor may be effective to get attention and raise awareness rather than as a means of persuading audiences to pursue a course of action (Bettinghaus & Cody, 1994). The American National Responsible Fatherhood Clearinghouse used this approach in a series of public service announcements encouraging men to "take time to be a dad today." One public service announcement begins by showing an elderly woman who sees and hears an adult man doing a cheerleading routine outside her window. The camera slowly reveals that he is rehearsing the cheer with his young daughter (National Responsible Fatherhood Clearinghouse, 2011).

Appeal to Character

Audiences are influenced not only by the content of a message but also by its source and delivery. An argument may have airtight evidence and tug on the emotions, but if conveyed by a messenger deemed noncredible, it is likely to be rejected by the intended audience. Audiences judge the credibility of sources on factors such as the following:

- expertise to speak on a topic comprised of experience, formal training, subject knowledge, and intelligence;
- trustworthiness that the messenger will communicate the truth as they understand it;
- similarity to the audience, particularly when the issue is of a personal nature; and
- personal attributes such as physical attractiveness or dynamism that may enhance likability or confidence (Bettinghaus & Cody, 1994).

Celebrity spokespeople often embody these attributes, and initiatives like United Nations Children's Fund (UNICEF) Goodwill Ambassadors and Advocates program make use of the qualities of celebrities to further social causes. For example, as Audrey Hepburn stated on her appointment as Goodwill Ambassador in 1989, "I can testify to what UNICEF means to children because I was among those who received food and medical relief right after World War II" (UNICEF, 2003). This message about the efficacy of UNICEF may be persuasive to its audience because Hepburn identified her expertise from personal experience to speak on the subject. Trustworthiness is established by her reputation, and personal attributes such as her physical attractiveness increase the appeal to the audience. Her modern equivalent is Angelina Jolie, a Goodwill Ambassador for the U.N. High Commissioner on Refugees, who has visited refugee camps, spoken widely on the issue, and adopted children from orphanages in Cambodia, Ethiopia, and Vietnam (UNHCR, 2011).

Establish your own credibility with the audience that you are attempting to persuade. Identify your relevant credentials, such as education and job positions. Depending on the cultural context, these types of credentials may have more resonance. But don't limit yourself to professional work alone. A string of letters behind your name, suggesting multiple degrees, or a fancy title can be helpful but not necessary. Draw on your personal experience as a parent, a volunteer, or someone who has dealt with a problem like community violence. Provide some evidence of your expertise that gives you the grounds to speak on the topic.

Know Your Audience

Communication research supports the receiver of persuasive messages as a fourth element of persuasion. This can be expressed in the aphorism "know your audience." Personality, social, and demographic characteristics may influence how audience members react to persuasive messages. For example, individuals with high self-esteem may be persuaded by requests that help them maintain esteem whereas individuals with low self-esteem may be persuaded by requests that help them gain others' approval. Social and demographic characteristics can lead to similarities among members of a group, creating shared values and a social referent to compare one's attitudes and behaviors with others who are similar. Gender, race/ethnicity, age, social class, education, occupation, and income are all variables that may be relevant to making a persuasive case (Bettinghaus & Cody, 1994). These ideas can be applied when preparing materials or presentations for a specific audience. As a hypothetical scenario, consider preparing an oral presentation for the local Rotary Club comprised of local business people who perceive themselves to be community leaders. It could be helpful to develop an argument that takes into account their political views, social class, and personality traits to make a request that affirms their leadership stance and fits with their values. Analyze your particular audiences and assess what types of messages and advocacy approaches will most appeal to them.

You may find yourself facing audiences with different attitudes on your issue, whether hostile, apathetic, or highly knowledgeable as experts. Different tactics of persuasion may be effective with these various types of crowds. With a hostile audience, establishing credibility through one's background and citing respected authorities may help. Likewise, identifying shared values with the group may build rapport. For example, while specific policy preferences may differ, a speaker and her audience may be able to agree about a higher value such as caring for others. For an apathetic audience, a surfeit of data may be overwhelming and increase disengagement. Emotional stories may be a better hook or another novel piece of evidence that can capture the audience's attention. It may be better to stick to a simple format and argument. Expert audiences are likely to have heard the standard arguments and evidence before. A more nuanced discussion, acknowledging alternatives and soliciting thoughts from the audience, can encourage buy-in and interest (Jansson, 2008).

Moreover, each advocacy effort is likely to encounter multiple types of audiences, such as bureaucrats, legislators, and media. Each audience requires the advocacy message to be packaged in different ways. Bureaucrats, for example, may be looking for analysis on how best to implement legislation. Legislators, whom you are approaching to champion your proposed bill, need summaries of the problem and proposed solutions. Members of the media, who can give you a megaphone for your message, are often looking for facts and anecdotes to bring an issue alive. Keep these various needs in mind as you prepare your arsenal of advocacy tools.

Something also to consider is whether to develop a one-sided or two-sided argument—that is, whether to note the opposition's argument as well as your own. For example, an advocate arguing on behalf of national parental leave policy following childbirth or adoption can note the benefits for parent-child bonding while also acknowledging the costs to industry and other objections. Communications research suggests that one-sided arguments may be more persuasive to those already convinced on the issue whereas two-sided arguments are more effective with audiences who initially disagree with the pro argument or are likely to be exposed to the opposing view anyway. Educational level may also play a factor: Some research suggests that more highly educated audiences find two-sided arguments preferable (Bettinghaus & Cody, 1994). It is important to know both sides of an issue whether or not you include counterarguments in your communication.

CRAFTING YOUR MESSAGE

After thinking about the content you want to include and the types of persuasive methods you may employ, it is necessary to make decisions about argument, format, and style. It is important to be clear about your argument and its underlying elements: the claim, the evidence, and the warrant. The format is how you structure your message and the elements you include. The style includes tone, register, and use of literary devices. Being thoughtful about these elements can help you craft a more powerful message.

Argument

The bare bones of a persuasive argument consist of a claim, evidence, and warrant (Toulmin, 2003). The claim is the point you are trying to make. A fact claim is a statement of what is or was. Child advocates are making a fact claim when they are trying to explain conditions for a child or group of children. A micro level advocate for a specific child makes a fact claim by arguing that the child is being discriminated against or is not having her educational needs met. A values claim judges or evaluates existing conditions against a value or ideal condition. The idea that we should not allow a group of children to suffer relies on a humanitarian value claim. A policy claim suggests what should be. An assertion that families should have access to a new local child care subsidy is a policy claim (Toulmin, Rieke, & Janik, 1984). Particularly in the case of fact claims, the point you are trying to make may not be absolute. A *qualifier* limits the scope of a claim, using words like "mostly," "unless," and "usually" as in this example: This child has not had her educational needs met most of the time in her current school. You may also anticipate a counterclaim or rebuttal and include that in your argument, as in this example: While there are significant costs associated with providing the necessary accommodations, that is no excuse for not meeting this child's educational needs. The rebuttal itself is a claim that will need to be supported (Toulmin, 2003).

Support your claim with *evidence*. Here is where you use the research and stories you gathered in Chapter 5, Step 2. Share an anecdote to illustrate your claim and put a human face on the issue. For example, to support a claim that a new local child care subsidy is needed, tell the story of a family who struggles to pay for high-quality care. Provide a fact or statistic that supports your argument to show the scale of the problem. Another piece of evidence in support of a child care subsidy may be the number of parents who are on a wait list for a subsidy or the average percentage of income that parents spend on child care. Testimony or quotations from experts are another form of evidence. The claim for a child care subsidy could be bolstered by a quote from a local official about the number of phone calls she has received inquiring about support for child care. Anecdotes, facts, statistics, testimony, and quotes are all common forms of evidence for persuasive arguments (Flacks & Rasberry, 1982).

A *warrant* is a principle that bridges the claim and evidence (Toulmin, 2003); it is the underlying assumption about why the evidence proves the claim. Often, warrants assume that particular values are held by the audience; this is called a *motivational warrant*. For example, an argument that uses an anecdote about a family struggling to pay for child care will only move an audience if its members believe in a communal responsibility for children that supports the idea that parents should be able to work and therefore need affordable child care or some other shared understanding that would make the audience sympathetic. Sometimes a warrant needs *backing* to ensure a compelling case; this involves making the warrant explicit and providing support for it. For a motivational warrant, you can make it clear that you are drawing on a particular value, such as equality or humanitarianism, and remind your audience of the importance of these ideals within the society. As was discussed in Chapter 4, "Step 1—Knowing Your Issue," it is essential to be aware of major value orientations in the society in which you are conducting your advocacy and use these values to shape your advocacy messages (Lakoff, 2004).

Format

Drape your argument over a logical framework. Consider your audience's need for structure—to be able to follow your argument and remember it. A random jumble of anecdotes and facts is confusing and irritating. Develop an outline for your argument and use signals to give your audience clues about the direction you are taking them.

Often, your intention as an advocate is to identify and explain a problem and how to address it. This is the case with the summary sheet (see activity at the end of the chapter). The summary sheet includes the following components: informative title, statement of the problem, discussion of the need for change, description of two or more proposed solutions, list of organizations and key individuals in support of these solutions, and likely outcomes if the proposed solutions are not or are implemented. Begin by identifying the problem. A way to do this is to use the *problem-solution* format, or a slight variation called *problem-cause-solution* format (Verderber, Verderber, & Sellnow, 2007). You might use *chronology* to sequence your description of the problem and how it has changed over time. Then, elaborate by providing evidence. Describe the breadth, or the scope and scale of the problem, by noting who is affected and how the problem has changed over time. Or you might use *criticism* to describe criteria that show you have a problem; commonly used criteria in policy analysis include equity, efficiency, and effectiveness (described in Chapter 5, in the section called Policy Research). Address the scope of the problem by detailing its consequences. If relevant or useful, mention the cause of the problem. Discussing the cause of a problem may reinforce the solution you suggest or allow you to correct misconceptions about a problem. Identify one or more solutions. If someone else has suggested another solution, you might use *refutation* to describe a problem, the competing solution, and problems with the solution, and then your own solution. End with a call to action for your audience. Think about trying different outline structures until you find one that seems to fit (Jansson, 2008).

As you structure your argument, keep in mind the rule of three. A classic rhetorical device, effective arguments often use groupings of three. The frequent use of three in mythology and religion suggest the compelling and memorable quality of this number. Develop three supporting points for your argument, and consider using three pieces of evidence for each supporting point. For example, a child advocate concerned about after-school care for elementary school children might use a basic problem-solution argument format with the rule of three as shown in Box 6.1.

BOX 6.1

Problem-Cause-Solution Format

A. *Problem*: We must increase the number of afterschool programs in our state

   a. Supporting point 1: The time period between 3 p.m. (end of school) and 6 p.m. (parents' work day) is a time that children frequently engage in risky behaviors

      i. Statistics on correlation between lack of supervision and injury

      ii. Statistics on correlation between lack of supervision and sexual activity

      iii. Statistics on correlation between lack of supervision and drug usage

   b. Supporting point 2: Afterschool time can be used productively to engage in recreational and academic pursuits

      i. Anecdotes about how children spend their time in existing afterschool programs

      ii. Research on connection between school achievement and involvement in afterschool programs

      iii. Research on cost-benefit analyses of afterschool programs, comparing cost of services with benefits of decreased antisocial behaviors and increased prosocial behaviors

   c. Supporting point 3: Demand for afterschool program slots exceeds existing supply

      i. Percentage of children in the state currently served by afterschool programs

      ii. Number of children on wait lists for afterschool programs and average duration that they have been on the wait list

      iii. Quote from a mother about her family's need for afterschool care

B. *Cause* (optional): Legislators have not responded to the need for safe, stimulating afterschool care while parents work due to fiscal concerns

C. *Solution*: Pass pending state legislation to create a new funding stream for afterschool care

D. *Call to action* (depends on audience):

   a. For voters: Contact your legislator by phone, email, or letter and ask them to vote in favor of the legislation; inform others on the issue

   b. For advocates: Bolster support for the legislation through the media, reach out to stakeholders like parents, and contact legislators to ask for their commitment to vote for the legislation

   c. For legislators: Vote for the legislation and become a cosponsor

Another format often used in persuasive communication is Monroe's Motivated Sequence. The idea is to lead your audience through a series of steps that will motivate them to act. First is the *attention* step to engage the interest of the audience using an anecdote, humor, surprising fact or statistic, or some other hook. This is also the moment to establish your credibility as a speaker and why the audience should listen to you in particular. Provide an overview of your argument as part of your introduction. Second, establish the *need* for change by describing the potential ramifications if the problem is ignored and allowed to continue. Hint at how the audience will have a role in addressing this need. Third, propose *satisfaction* of the need by describing your solution and how it will address the facets of the problem that you have identified. Use examples in which the solution has been used successfully in other contexts, if you know of any. Fourth, promote *visualization* of your proposed solution by describing what will happen if it is adopted, or alternatively, the consequences if it is not. You could describe both and use the power of contrast to support your case: buttercups and daisies if your recommendation is adopted, doom and gloom if it is not. Try to create an image in the minds of your audience by using graphic detail. Fifth and finally, make an *action appeal* to encourage your audience to do specific and concrete things to help realize your goal. This may also be a moment to acknowledge and dismiss criticisms of your solution. End on a high note with a quote or story that lends emotional impact (Verderber, Verderber, & Sellnow, 2007). See Box 6.2 for the previous argument about afterschool care, this time using Monroe's Motivated Sequence.

BOX 6.2

Monroe's Motivated Sequence

1. *Attention*:
   a. Anecdote about children engaging in risky behaviors between 3 p.m. and 6 p.m.
   b. Speaker introduction and description of relevant credentials
   c. Overview of presentation

2. *Need*:
   We must increase the number of afterschool programs in our state
   a. Ramifications of lack of supervision leading to risky behaviors
   b. Ramifications of lost opportunity for recreational and academic activities
   c. Ramifications of unmet need for safe and stimulating care while parents work

(Continued)

(Continued)

3. *Satisfaction*:

   a. Increased availability of afterschool programs will provide supervision and curtail risky behavior

   b. Increased availability of afterschool programs will create opportunities for recreational and academic activities

   c. Increased availability of afterschool programs will enable parents to work while their children receive care

4. *Visualization*:

   a. Imagine a child happily engaged in arts and crafts projects, sports activities, and academic tutoring, being safely cared for and making productive use of her time between the end of the school day and when her parents arrive after work to pick her up

   b. Imagine a child leaving school on her own with 3 hours until her parents return home and peers who may pressure her into dangerous and illicit activities

   c. Imagine this was your child which would you choose?

5. *Action Appeal*:

   a. Acknowledge detractors' argument about limited resources and dismiss by pointing to the societal costs of risky and illicit behavior and the cost of lost opportunities to promote positive social and academic skills

   b. What you can do right now:

      i. For voters: Contact your legislators by phone, email, or letter and ask them to vote in favor of the legislation; inform others on the issue

      ii. For advocates: Bolster support for the legislation through the media, direct outreach to stakeholders like parents, and contacting legislators to ask for their commitment to vote for the legislation

      iii. For legislators: Vote for the legislation and become a cosponsor

   c. End with a quote from a mother about the importance of afterschool care

Whichever format you select for your argument, help your audience by *signposting*, or using language that signals where you are in your argument. This helps your audience have a mental map to orient themselves in your argument and understand where to put the new information you present. Begin by previewing where you are going by introducing the subject with words like "start" and "begin." During the body of your argument, indicate where you are with sequencing language like "first," "second," "third," and "finally." Indicate shifts in focus with statements preceded by "turning to," "moving to," and "next." Before introducing new points and in your wrap-up, remind your audience where you've been by summarizing your arguments, using phrases like "in conclusion," "to sum up," and "let's recap" (Turk, 1985).

Style

Use of literary devices and careful selection of language can give your message a vividness that leaves an impression with your audience. Capture your audience's attention by posing a *rhetorical question* for effect rather than an answer: "Don't we all bear responsibility for children?" You can use words to create an image by using *metaphors* and *similes* to compare an issue to something else, perhaps more familiar to the reader. For example, when talking about parenting, you might say that it is "like tending a garden" (simile) and that children "are seeds whose personalities and potential unfold" (metaphor). Attributing human characteristics to nonhumans, called *personification*, can also create a mental image: "The compassionate tree provides shade for the park." Another way to create a mental image is through *allusion*, or making a reference, often to a historical, literary, or popular source. Say the word "Dickensian," for example, and people think of bleak institutions from the work of Charles Dickens. Make your argument more memorable by using *alliteration*, repeating similar sounds, for a catchy statement like "working women." Contrasting two ideas using *antithesis* can also make an argument interesting: "Investing in poor children can enrich our society." *Repetition* is another way of making an argument memorable, using the same word or phrase while building up to a climax of an argument; we remember Martin Luther King Jr.'s statement "I have a dream" in part because his speech repeats this phrase over and over (Lens, 2005).

Avoid language that undermines your argument by provoking boredom or offense. Clichéd phrases that have been overused to the point of losing meaning are an easy way to lose your audience's attention. Common clichés about children include "growing like a weed" and "following in [a parent's] footsteps." Another way to alienate your audience is to use emotional opinion-based statements: for example, labeling an opposing view "stupid" or an opposing side "wrong." Show that your opponents are wrong through your arguments and evidence rather than using labels and insults. Be aware of how you refer to groups and avoid invoking stereotypes through sexist or racist language (Daniels & Daniels, 1993). If you use a hypothetical scenario, like a typical family affected by your issue, consider if you are playing into assumptions about particular groups—for example, that only certain ethnic groups use government programs or that care for children is the sole responsibility of women.

Tone and Voice

Tone conveys the writer's attitude toward the subject and audience, like tone of voice in a conversation. In daily life, we vary how we speak to a child, a friend, a colleague, or a supervisor. Our tone also varies to reflect our emotions and perspective on an issue. Part of what is conveyed through tone is formality and informality. Most advocacy communications strive for a conversational tone that is engaging and direct, in the manner you would speak. Your tone needs to match the circumstance and cultural context in which you are communicating; some cultures tend to be more formal than others in their preferred communication styles. Keep in mind that unless you are addressing an audience that is highly expert on your issue, specialized professional language should be defined or replaced by simplified terms, and abbreviations should at minimum be spelled out at least once and preferably avoided (Daniels & Daniels, 1993).

Selection of narrative voice, expressed through selection of pronouns, can also contribute to a sense of formality or informality. First person can create a sense of personal relationship between the narrator and audience; the pronoun "I" is used for a single narrator and "we" for multiple narrators or narrator(s) plus audience. For example, "we must ensure the children who attend this school get the resources they need" includes the writer and reader in a shared mission. Second person uses "you" when addressing the audience, providing the opportunity to make an argument immediate and relevant to their lives: "Your child needs educational resources to succeed." Third person removes emphasis from the narrator and places it on the people being spoken of, avoiding "I" and "we" and using the pronouns "he/she," "one," and "they": "They [the parents] must ensure the children who attend this school get the resources they need". (Daniels & Daniels, 1993).

Length

Concise and clear writing is generally preferable in advocacy materials. As Thomas Jefferson famously said, "If I had more time, I would have written a shorter letter." In an information age, attention is in short supply and a host of other interests compete with your efforts. The executive summary (described in Chapter 5, in the section called Policy Research) is a short version of a report intended for an executive with little time. Consider all your materials "executive" for audiences with busy lives. While it may be necessary to repeat your central idea to describe, illustrate, and support your argument, avoid redundancy or needless repetition. Try to vary your choice of words and omit ones that are unnecessary. Scrutinize your sentences. Could you reword them to make them clearer, shorter, and less redundant?

Practice your argument verbally as an elevator pitch. The premise of an elevator pitch is the imagined scenario that you find yourself in an elevator with your key decision maker, and you have only the time until she reaches her floor to deliver your advocacy message, about 60 seconds. Policy makers in the California legislature have been known to take the stairs to avoid the elevator pitch, but an apt advocate may observe this and accompany the policy maker for more time, less competition, and more exercise. Even if you don't find yourself in an elevator or a stairwell with a decision maker, there may be other opportunities to share your pitch, such as running into a decision maker or other key stakeholder at an event or introducing yourself at the beginning of a meeting. Practice your elevator speech so that it comes naturally if an opportunity arises. Be aware of your body language so that you can send signals that you are engaged with your audience, such as eye contact, and avoid signals that you may be nervous, such as foot tapping. See Box 6.3 for an activity to guide you through the development of an elevator pitch.

These stylistic elements come together in your advocacy tools. The medium is how you transmit your message and can include various forms of written communication, oral communication, and visual communication.

BOX 6.3

Activity: Practicing Your Message by Developing an Elevator Pitch

Write a brief (around 150 words) statement that encapsulates your advocacy message. Read the message aloud, and time yourself. Limit yourself to about 60 seconds, and cut it down if it exceeds that time frame. Include the following information:

- Who are you?
- What is the social issue that you are addressing?
- What is the goal of your advocacy?
- Why are this issue and your goal important?
- How does this issue connect to broader issues that might concern a decision maker?
- What support are you seeking?

Here's an example:

I am a second grade teacher at McKinley Elementary. My goal is to create a community garden in an unused municipal lot that can be a living laboratory to teach children and families about environmental stewardship, cultivation of crops, and eating seasonally. This is important because a community survey revealed that 65% of children in this community are overweight and are mostly sedentary after school and on weekends. Fewer than 30% of households maintain gardens. This issue connects with childhood health, nutrition, and community development. I am seeking support from city council members, like yourself, to allow the municipal lot to be used for this purpose and to allocate funds for clearing the lot and planting crops. With volunteer time and labor, the estimated initial cost would be $10,000 and $5,000 for yearly maintenance, partially recouped by donations of crops to city-run soup kitchens as well as saved health care costs.

Your work in previous chapters will inform your pitch, drawing on your problem statement, goal, and hub-and-spoke diagram from Chapter 4 ("Step 1—Knowing Your Issue"). Role play with a partner, taking turns presenting and giving each other specific feedback on content, length, and body language.

DEVELOPING COMMUNICATION TOOLS

Communication can be oral, written, or visual, and these forms may be combined to develop an array of advocacy tools. Each comes with advantages and disadvantages. Verbal communication can be more spontaneous and informal, such as an elevator speech given at an opportune moment to a potential supporter. However, if not recorded, it may be forgotten or remembered incorrectly later. Written communication allows for precise content and wording and leaves a record. It is also easier to communicate with distant parties or large audiences. A drawback is that it may not allow the sender to know her audience's immediate reaction when they are not present in the same location. Visual aids are often used to supplement oral and written communication. An image, symbol, or map may be used to enhance understanding. See Box 6.4 for one advocate's perspective on developing effective advocacy materials.

BOX 6.4

Effective Materials for Promoting Early Childhood Care and Education for Children in Conflict Areas

By Maysoun Chehab, Early Childhood Specialist (Lebanon)

Many countries in the Arab Region are facing short or long term conflicts and emergencies, leaving millions of young children at risk of not reaching their full potential and threatening their lives and well-being. Despite the overwhelming impact of emergencies on young children, only very few government and civil society actors give attention to this specific age group. Raising public awareness about the needs of young children living in emergencies among national and international organizations, funders, families, and community actors has become a vital mission. Successful advocacy requires knowledge about the situation, a plan of action, trained human resources, and effective advocacy materials to deliver the desired messages.

Advocacy materials should be developed to enable stakeholders to position early childhood care and education as a core intervention and make it integral to all national emergency responses. Since 2005, I have been working with many partners in Lebanon, Palestine, Iraq, and recently, Syria on supporting young children and their families living in conflict affected areas. Developing and sharing advocacy materials has been a key way to sway public opinions, mobilize community resources, and establish networks of allies. Depending on the situation and context of each emergency as well as the audience, I learned to use different tools and materials such as press releases, policy papers, summary sheets, posters, newsletters, editorials for media, and watch reports. Recently, the use of digital materials and social media outlets such as Facebook, Twitter, and blogs have proven to be effective and efficient in terms of cost and time. Regardless of the tool, there are a number of key elements and guidelines that should be followed:

1. It is important to have accurate, trusted, and up-to-date local data.

2. Messages should be spelled out in a brief, direct, and clear manner. Most decision makers do not have much time to read materials if messages are not easily discernible.

3. Materials should voice children and community issues and concerns. Whenever possible, include quotes from children, parents, or decision makers as well as children's drawings or writings.

4. Ensure confidentiality is protected when sharing photos or case studies.

5. If the materials are intended for the general public, use familiar vocabulary and avoid the use of technical terminology.

6. If the materials are intended for the parents of young children, include as many tips, instructions, and frequently asked questions as possible.

7. Remember to be holistic in your approach! The message should encourage that rights to health, nutrition, protection, and cognitive and psychosocial development are met for all children, including girls and children with special needs.

When advocacy materials are finalized, it is as important to identify a local and knowledgeable messenger. It is preferable to train messengers who have mobility within the community and to select champions to speak to the media. Since emergencies are unstable and unpredictable, updating the materials and relevant data about young children should be an ongoing process.

Advocates have numerous mediums to express their message. The next section describes different methods of communication with examples from child advocacy; these are summarized in Box 6.5.

BOX 6.5

Communication Tools: Pros and Cons

Type of Communication Tool	Pros	Cons
Direct correspondence	Bring an issue to a decision maker's attention, particularly if many communiqués are received	Potentially low impact, particularly for one or few communiqués
Presentations	Connect with a specific audience relevant to your cause	May reach fewer people than other forms of communication
Legislative testimony	Influence legislators directly on proposed legislation	May not be invited or selected to give testimony
Graphics	Convey an idea memorably with an image	Generally a complement to other advocacy materials, not a stand-alone form of communication
Media	Reach a broad audience with your advocacy message	Can be difficult to access the mainstream media

(Continued)

| (Continued) | | |
Type of Communication Tool	Pros	Cons
Video	Tell a story using emotional appeals about your advocacy issue	Requires money, effort, and technical know-how
Social media	Communicate with a potentially large audience on a real-time basis	Need to update your materials frequently to keep audience engaged
Arts	Share your advocacy message in a novel way	Necessitates creativity and runs the risk of cliché

Direct Correspondence

Citizens in a representative system of governance often use direct correspondence like letters, phone calls, emails, faxes, and petitions to communicate with their representatives. This form of communication makes sense when your aim is to bring an issue to the attention of legislators. A single email or letter is low effort but potentially low yield in terms of advocacy results. Better results may be garnered through encouraging others to join your effort. Beyond expressing a constituent's preferred course of action, the volume of letters or emails received on a given subject signals public concern on an issue and may influence the representative's actions. Advocacy organizations recognize the value of flooding a legislator's office with emails and often provide an email script or automated forms to which the sender adds her contact information. Examples abound of organizations with websites that include a "take action" or advocacy section, including Save the Children, Zero to Three, and Children's Rights Information Network, as well as many more organizations with a national or international advocacy focus. Amnesty International, which advocates on children's rights such as putting a stop to child execution and use of children as soldiers, organizes *letter writing marathons* worldwide to encourage the public to write personal letters about human rights violations. A similar approach is a *phone bank*, gathering many people together to use landlines or cell phones to make calls using a script. While not a common scenario, you might know you've won if you get a phone call from the staff of a decision maker asking you to call off the phone bank because they get the message and will support the change you are seeking.

Your written correspondence is more likely to be taken seriously if you follow certain conventions. Find the contact information for your representatives and direct your correspondence to them; legislators are most interested in the views of potential voters. For this reason, include your return address. Be courteous and use your representative's proper title in the address as well as salutation line (for example, in the United States, it is customary to address members of Congress as "The Honorable . . . "). Address a single topic, such as pending legislation or your suggestions for potential legislation, and ask for a specific action. If you have personal or professional experience on the topic, mention it. Keep the letter brief and to the point. Follow up on your initial correspondence with another, expressing appreciation if the legislator adopted your stance or concern if the outcome was unsatisfactory. If you are making a phone call, many of the same conventions still apply about courtesy, relevance, and brevity.

Presentations

Child advocates often make oral presentations in the form of speeches before groups like local business leaders, testimony before representative bodies like legislatures, and informative presentations to their own allies and supporters. For oral presentations, it is particularly important to know your audience as discussed previously. Are you addressing a room of experts or neophytes? Will you be met with potential allies or foes? Do your homework and learn about the groups that you will be addressing.

Give careful consideration to the elements of your presentation, including your verbal remarks, visuals, and body language. Your own personal preference will dictate how you prepare your remarks: Some speakers like to write out their presentations word for word and then rehearse to memorize or get the general feel for the speech whereas others use an outline and develop the wording as they go, and still others are extemporaneous speakers who do not prepare written remarks. Until you are very comfortable as a public speaker, it is a safer option to write out or prepare an outline of your speech rather than winging it. Consider using one of the formats previously described as you structure your remarks (see Boxes 6.1 and 6.2). Visual aids, such as slides or handouts, are frequently used to back up the main points of an argument and help the audience to follow the discussion. If you choose to use slides, like the ubiquitous PowerPoint, keep them simple. If you jam your slides with information, you are likely to distract your audience from your verbal remarks as they struggle to read the slides. If you want to explain concepts in some detail, it is best to have a separate handout. Use of a handout also allows your audience to focus on listening to your speech without the need to take notes to retain the information. Keep in mind how you hold yourself during your presentation. Body language can lend impact to your argument—for example, by using your hands to emphasize important points (palms toward audience) or signal where you are in your argument (hold up fingers for point 1, point 2). Nonverbal communication can also be distracting when it communicates lack of confidence: for example, rocking the body, avoiding eye contact, or fidgeting. As an alternative to in-person presentations, the Internet provides an opportunity to share presentations via narrated PowerPoints.

Legislative Testimony

Giving legislative testimony is a specific type of oral presentation and can be highly impactful in terms of advocacy for or against a proposed new policy. Advocates may have an opportunity to testify before a city council, a state or regional legislature, or a national legislature (these will be generically referred to as a legislature). Depending on the jurisdiction, people may be invited to testify, or there may be a sign-up sheet or lottery process at the hearing. Check the legislature's website for rules regarding providing testimony and a schedule of hearings. It is a good idea to attend a hearing before the same legislature to familiarize yourself with standard procedures before the hearing on the legislation that concerns you. Prepare written remarks that you can submit to the legislature to enter the record for the hearing and for distribution as a handout to the legislators (call ahead to find out the number of copies to bring). However, do not read your comments during your testimony. Instead, prepare a bullet list of your main points, and practice your speech so that you convey these points. Keep your remarks short, usually 3 to 5 minutes total (check with the legislature on the allotted time for each speaker). Be aware of your body language, and try to make eye contact with the members of the legislature. Dress appropriately, in business attire, to demonstrate respect for the committee members and to make a positive impression.

Cover these main points in your testimony. Begin by introducing yourself and identifying the constituency and/or organization that you represent. Then, clearly state your position on the legislation, whether in support or opposition, and identify the bill by its name and number. Make a case for your position by explaining the potential impacts of the legislation, providing evidence in the form of facts, statistics, and research, as well as personal experience and anecdotes. Describe other solutions and alternatives to address the social problem, if any. Close by reiterating your position: "Therefore, I urge the legislature to support/oppose [name of legislation]." Utilize the elements of persuasion described earlier in this chapter by establishing ethos as you introduce yourself and establish your character through your appearance, demeanor, and preparation. Incorporate elements of logos by using relevant factual information that relates to the provisions of the proposed legislation and pathos by connecting to personal stories that evoke values in support of your position.

Use the research you have conducted on decision makers (Chapter 5, Step 2) to tailor your presentation to appeal to particular legislators. Keep in mind that you may be asked questions following your testimony. Try to anticipate possible questions and be prepared to answer them. If you do not know the answer to a question, offer to follow up with the legislator and provide the information as soon as possible. Be sure to address members of the committee with their proper titles. If possible, get other allies to join you at the hearing and also testify to provide additional information on the issue and demonstrate greater support for your position (but avoid repetition).

Graphics

An image or symbol can often convey a point more simply and directly than words. There is a rich history of photographs as tools of advocacy. For example, the photographs of Lewis Hine in the early 20th century revealed conditions for working children in the United States and helped secure the passage of child labor laws. A historian noted that Hine's photography "[brought] into view what normal social vision has been conditioned to ignore" (Gutman, 1967, p. 5). Symbols, images or concepts that stand for something else, can also be impactful for advocacy purposes. In the Western context, for example, apples are used to symbolize education; thus, advocacy groups protesting educational cuts may use an apple core to suggest that education funding is being decimated. Maps are another way to present information visually. Geographic information, like crime rates or child abuse reporting by zip code, can depict a problem in the context of a region. Consider using graphics to complement your written or verbal communications or as a logo for your advocacy efforts.

Information design can be another way to convey information using pictures. Examples of information design include timelines, maps, charts, graphs, and word clouds. This approach to sharing information has the advantages of clarifying complex information, attracting people's attention, and being more persuasive to certain people than numbers or words alone. Information design can also be used as part of analysis to make patterns more evident. For example, you might collect geographic data and then map this data using a commonly available program like Google Maps. Mapping the data might show associations like clustering of a social problem or correlations between one issue and another (like child maltreatment reporting and liquor outlets). Information design can also be used for planning how to address a social problem; for example, charts can be used to project future trends and decide the target of advocacy. Information design is particularly effective for educating others by using pictures to compare and contrast and simplify issues like the consequences of specific choices. For example, information design was used historically for public education and advocacy on issues such as the conditions on slave ships, as in Thomas Clarkson's 1786 "Essay on the Slavery and Commerce of Human Species," by showing schematics of the interior of a slave ship and how people were crammed together in inhumane conditions (Emerson, 2008).

Media

Advocates can use the media through newspapers, magazines, radio, and television to convey their message. Ways to reach out to the media include press releases and op-eds. A *press release* is a statement that can be used as the basis of a news story; you might write a press release about a newsworthy aspect of your advocacy issue or campaign. Begin with an attention-getting title. Open your press release with a lead (or lede) paragraph that lays out the 5 W's and 1 H of journalism: Who, What, When, Where, Why, and How. Be sure to address why your topic qualifies as news—in other words, why is this an interesting story that a reporter will want to tell and the audience will want to read? Keep your press release brief, one or two pages, and include facts or quotes that could be included in the news story. End by mentioning your name, organizational affiliation (if you have one), and contact information so the news outlet can follow up.

In contrast to a press release, an op-ed allows you to cut the reporter out of the equation and write directly for the media audience. An *op-ed* (short for "opposite the editorial page") is a brief article that communicates the writer's opinion on an issue and often proposes a solution or action. The typical structure of an op-ed is to open with a lead that connects your issue to a current news topic; make an argument with three main points supported by evidence such as anecdotes, facts, and quotes; include a "to be sure" statement that anticipates likely opposing arguments; and draw a conclusion that may hearken back to the lead.

Make sure your article is interesting and engaging; the use of different types of appeals (logic, emotion, and character) is valuable, as are literary devices that can convey a complex idea in a metaphor or catchy alliterative statement. Include a brief biographical statement at the conclusion of your op-ed. Pitch your op-ed to an editorial editor via email by describing why the issue is important and timely, and why you are qualified to speak on it (OpEd Project, n.d.). Tips on writing op-eds, examples, and submission information for top (American) media outlets can be found at the OpEd project, http://www.theopedproject.org. Some radio or television stations may also accept opinion pieces that can be read on air. See Box 6.6 for an example of an op-ed about federal budget cuts to a maternal and child nutrition program.

BOX 6.6

Example of an Op-Ed

If human capital is the wealth of nations, the House GOP's proposed federal budget will leave us poorer.

Economists know that what separates wealthy and poor countries is not simply their natural resources like oil and minerals, but their human capacities, like initiative and ingenuity. Many Americans fear that our status in the world is slipping.

In that context, the last thing we should do is accept the GOP's proposed federal budget cuts leveled at the poor, particularly those aimed at children, such as cutting about 10 percent, or $758 million, from the Women, Infants and Children program.

WIC is a federal nutrition program, established in the mid-1970s, aimed at improving the health of young children and pregnant or postpartum women through education, nutrition and referrals. To qualify, participants must be at or below 185 percent of the federal poverty line ($34,280 for a family of three) and assessed by a health professional to be at "nutrition risk" for medical or dietary reasons. Children and mothers receive an average of $41 a month in food assistance that meets common nutritional deficits in WIC participants, including protein-rich foods such as peanut butter and eggs.

Cuts to WIC might work with voters in the short term by delivering immediate and visible spending reductions, but they will cost us in the long run.

Here's why.

Thanks to recent advances in our understanding of nutrition, we now know that when it comes to nutrition, a child's first five years last a lifetime. These are the years of the most intense growth and development, particularly for the brain.

The types of nutritional assistance provided and promoted by WIC are key to brain development. Nutrients consumed before birth and during early childhood become part of the architecture of the brain, such as the essential fats used to grow myelin, the insulation between brain cells. These essential fats can be found in the breast milk of mothers with adequate diets, as well as whole milk and other items in the WIC food package.

Like fixing a house without a solid foundation, undoing damage caused by poor early childhood nutrition is more difficult than providing a nutritious diet in the first place. While some effects of malnutrition can be repaired by a proper diet, poor nutrition during sensitive periods of development can alter children's developmental trajectories.

Children may make height or weight gains, but their basic physiology and brain structure remain affected by early nutritional deficits. This can result in cognitive impairment, as well as behavioral emotional problems.

What's more, investments in federal food-assistance programs such as WIC are more important in our current economy than ever before. Soaring enrollment in the federal food stamps program, which now serves one in seven Americans, attests to the vital role that food assistance plays in the American safety net. And states are slashing their social programs to close budget gaps, leaving federal food-assistance programs as one of the few resources that Americans can count on to keep them going in a time of need.

If anything, the federal government should be investing more funds, not less, in programs such as WIC.

Children are not passive little recipients of charity. They are actors in a social contract that says invest in children now and they in turn will grow into productive citizens.

If we renege on our part of the contract, we deprive these children of what they need to develop their full human potential. For the cost of a dozen eggs and a gallon of milk, we're investing in their, and our, futures.

Amy Conley Wright is an assistant professor of Child and Adolescent Development at San Francisco State University, where she teaches courses and conducts research on child and family policy, the social ecology of childhood, and child advocacy.

Source: Wright, A. C. (2011,February 23). Opinion: GOP budget cuts will cost us in the long run. *AOL News.* Retrieved from http://www.aolnews.com/2011/02/23/opinion-gop-budget-cuts-will-cost-us-in-the-long-run/

Video

Video has several advantages as well as some drawbacks as an advocacy medium and can be used in many ways. This medium lends itself to storytelling and making an emotional connection with an issue. It can be packaged in a variety of forms, allowing multiple uses from a full broadcast documentary to a brief segment for a news station to a public service announcement just a few seconds long. Video can also provide access to new audiences through its ability to reach a wide variety of people regardless of literacy. The YouTube website, for example, is a way to share videos with people around the world.

However, advocates considering this approach should consider whether they have access to the people and situations that will help to craft a compelling story (Caldwell, 2005). Cost and effort may also be a factor, though with the decreasing costs for digital cameras and editing software and the growth of outlets such as YouTube, videos are becoming a more accessible advocacy tool. With a few dollars and an idea, a video can become an Internet sensation. Websites like xtranormal.com allow budding auteurs to select animated characters, facial expressions, and voices to act out a typed script (Kurwa, 2011). Some uses for advocacy video include participatory efforts that allow communities to define their own challenges; outreach efforts that connect video footage with an advocacy campaign online; information efforts that utilize video to educate particular audiences, particularly decision makers; and influencing efforts that submit video as evidence for a court or tribunal (Caldwell, 2005).

Social Media

Social media is growing in importance as a way to spread a message and keep allies informed (see the section in Chapter 8, Effective Use of Social Media, for an in-depth discussion). Social networking sites like Facebook and Twitter allow people and organizations to share information with those in their networks. Consider creating an account for your group, using an application like Facebook Causes, to allow interested parties to follow your updates. You can share relevant information in the news or your current activities. One big advantage is the ability to reach an audience quickly and encourage them to do something to aid your advocacy efforts. Consider, for example, this Twitter update: "Take Action: The House is voting on the Debt Relief for Earthquake Recovery Act for #Haiti tomorrow!" Blogs are another way to share your advocacy efforts in a narrative description. Audio material, like interviews, can be shared via podcast and distributed through a website or through iTunes. Video materials can be shared on sites like YouTube; by creating a channel you can allow supporters to subscribe to your updates. With a creative product, you may succeed in becoming a viral Internet sensation, gaining popularity as viewers spread your message to each other. If you choose to utilize social media, update your materials frequently to keep your audience engaged.

Arts

People are used to advocacy messages being transmitted through presentations or op-eds. Artistic expressions of advocacy messages can feel more fresh and interesting. The novelty of this approach may connect with audiences on an emotional or aesthetic level. Artistic advocacy may take many forms, including music, performance, and visual art. You can write a report arguing that materialism is prioritized over the needs of children and provide evidence in the form of research and statistics. Or you could write a song like Cat Stevens's "Where do the children play?" that makes this case in a more poignant way. Visual art is sometimes used in marches and strikes, including large puppets that have a symbolic purpose like the grim reaper in a "death of public education" march. Performances may have an advocacy intent, as with a play that encourages compassion toward those with HIV/AIDS. Flash mobs, with choreographed performances, may make a point through their music and movements; protests against 2011 proposed cuts to public higher education in California included flash mob dance performances to the song "Stayin' Alive."

Activity: Putting It All Together in a Summary Sheet

A summary sheet is a simple and succinct way to inform others about your advocacy issue and is a helpful tool for Chapter 7, "Step 4—Making Meetings That Work." Prepare a summary sheet with the following components, drawing on the research you did in Chapter 5, "Step 2—Research for Background and Impact." Your final summary sheet should be brief, one page if possible, and written in a simple and clear manner without jargon. See Box 6.7 for an example that includes these components.

- *Informative title:* Here is your first chance to grab your reader's attention. Choose a title that makes the topic of your summary sheet completely clear: for example, "The Need for Child Care Licensing Enforcement in [region or state]" or "Additional Signal Lights at Three Critical Intersections in [city]."
- *Statement of the problem:* Document the problem, including who is affected and the prevalence of the problem.
- *Discussion of the need for change:* Discuss the need for change, using appeals to logic in the form of statistics or facts and appeals to emotion in the form of anecdote or metaphor.
- *Description of two or more proposed solutions:* Describe two or more options for the problem so that the decision maker is given a choice and support your recommended option(s).
- *List of organizations and key individuals in support of these solutions:* Identify your allies, particularly those who are likely to be respected by your audience.
- *Likely outcomes if the proposed solutions are or are not implemented:* Paint a dark outcome if one of your solutions is not accepted, and end on a rosy outcome that will occur if one of your solutions is accepted. This is your call to action.

BOX 6.7

Summary Sheet Example: The Risks and Opportunities of Juvenile Justice Realignment in California

Issues Related to Realignment

As part of his 2012–2013 budget plan, California's Governor Jerry Brown proposed shifting responsibility for juvenile justice to counties, stopping new admissions to the Division of Juvenile Justice (DJJ) after January 1, 2013, and phasing out the DJJ by 2014. This strategy, called "realignment,"

(Continued)

(Continued)

would send youth formerly held in state institutions for serious, violent, or sexual offenses to county institutions (Legislative Analyst's Office, 2012b). Currently, between 1,000 and 1,130 youth are in the custody of DJJ. According to Burns Institute Founder and Executive Director James Bell, these are youth with serious emotional problems or who have committed serious offenses, and are not considered appropriate for county facilities (Kernan, 2012). Certain counties, particularly less populated ones, are more dependent on the DJJ for housing juvenile offenders (California Sentencing Institute, 2012).

The Impact of Realignment on Youth

The decision to realign the Division of Juvenile Justice could increase the likelihood of youth being sent into adult prisons. According to current laws, prosecutors can charge youth as adults for crimes. Advocates worry that with realignment, this could occur more frequently, exposing youth to harsher circumstances with older, more experienced inmates.

Alternatively, realignment could keep youth at a local level, which would help families remain in contact and increase the chances of rehabilitation. As it stands now, there are youth from counties like Stockton living in facilities as far as Los Angeles. This means they are separated from their families by distance, and if there are family financial difficulties, it is unlikely that they receive family visits. Keeping youth at the local level could enable them and their families to access more services intended to prevent recidivism (meaning the rate at which offenders commit subsequent crimes).

A Call to Action

For years, advocates, community leaders, and former inmates have called for the closure of the DJJ. The system has been massively expensive, costing about $179,400 per youth each year (Legislative Analyst's Office, 2012a), while delivering recidivism rates above 80%, demonstrating that the DJJ has not met the mission of the juvenile justice system to rehabilitate young offenders (Barrows, n.d.). Yet until the current budget situation, political will to change the system was lacking.

Two options are recommended. One option is the the legislature could pass legislation mandating that youth offenders are segregated from adult prisoners and are housed within their counties until they reach the age of 18 or for the duration of their sentences if expected to end before the age of 21. Studies have shown that youth are more likely to be assaulted, raped, and commit suicide if incarcerated with adults (Schiraldi & Zeidenberg, 1997). As part of this legislation, sufficient funding must be allocated to counties to meet the increased costs of housing youth offenders. This course of action is recommended by the Legislative Analyst's Office (2012b), which notes that a decision to house juveniles in state prisons would potentially be very expensive and expose the state to lawsuits.

Another option is that the legislature could require that counties develop community-based reentry strategies using evidence-based or promising programs that reduce recidivism and improve long-term outcomes for youth offenders, including educational attainment and preparation for the job market. San Francisco, Santa Cruz, Marin, Placer, and Santa Clara counties have implemented innovative programs that have resulted in a reduction in recidivism (Barrows, n.d.). Research shows that gainful employment is associated with a lower likelihood of reoffending. Prominent research and advocacy organizations have joined together on the Assembly Select Committee on the Status of Boys and Men of Color in California (n.d.), including the Center on Juvenile and Criminal Justice and the W. Haywood Burns Institute, and support this recommendation.

The question for California's decision makers is not "if" DJJ closure will happen but rather "how." There are risks and opportunities with the Governor's realignment of the juvenile justice system. The state must avoid imperiling youth by housing them with adult offenders. Instead, legislators can use this opportunity to rehabilitate and reintegrate them back into their communities through access to effective services. If this change is made, youth will have improved chances to grow up and contribute to California as responsible citizens.

Source: This summary sheet is adapted from one developed by students in the course, CAD 650: Child Advocacy, at San Francisco State University as part of a community service learning project.

REFERENCES

The Assembly Select Committee on the Status of Boys and Men of Color in California (n.d.). *Equity and criminal justice realignment in California: A position paper of the Assembly Select Committee on the Status of Boys and Men of Color in California.* Retrieved from http://www.policylink .org/atf/cf/%7B97c6d565-bb43-406d-a6d5-eca3bbf35af0%7D/BMOC%20SELECT%20COMMITTEE %20REALIGNMENT%20POSITION%20PAPER.PDF

Barrows, T. (n.d.). *Addicted to incarceration but can't afford the habit.* Retrieved from http://www .burnsinstitute.org/article.php?id = 332

Bettinghaus, E. P., & Cody, M. J. (1994). *Persuasive communication* (5th ed.). Fort Worth, TX: Harcourt Brace College.

Booher, D. (2003). The power of persuasion: Emotion, logic, and character. *Expert Magazine.* Retrieved from http://www.expertmagazine.com/artman/publish/article_326.shtml

Caldwell, G. (2005). Using video for advocacy. In S. Gregory, G. Caldwell, R. Avni, & T. Harding (Eds.), *Video for change: A guide for advocacy and activism* (pp. 1–19). Ann Arbor, MI: Pluto Press.

California Sentencing Institute (2012). *State confinement rate 2010.* Retrieved from http://casi.cjcj.org/ Juvenile/2010

Center for Health Improvement. (2004). *Using data strategically: Social math.* Retrieved from http:// www.chipolicy.org/pdf/TA5.pdf

Children's Defense Fund (2010, August). *Protect children not guns 2010.* Retrieved from http://www .childrensdefense.org/child-research-data-publications/data/protect-children-not-guns.html

Cochran, C. (2006). *How to be a voice for babies: Using data effectively.* Zero to Three Policy Center. Retrieved from http://zttcfn.convio.net/site/DocServer/Using_data_effectively.pdf?docID = 1686 &AddInterest = 1159

Daniels, D. I., & Daniels, B. J. (1993). *Persuasive writing.* New York, NY: HarperCollins.

Emerson, J. (2008). *Visualizing information for advocacy: An introduction to advocacy design.* Retrieved from http://www.opensocietyfoundations.org/sites/default/files/visualizing_20080311.pdf

Fight Crime, Invest in Kids (2010, November). *New Orleans law enforcement leaders say child abuse linked to future crime.* Retrieved from http://www.fightcrime.org/state/louisiana/news/new -orleans-law-enforcement-leaders-say-child-abuse-linked-future-crime

Flacks, N., & Rasberry, R. W. (1982). *Power talk: How to use theater techniques to win your audience.* New York, NY: The Free Press.

Gutman, J. M. (1967). *Lewis W. Hine and the American social conscience.* New York, NY: Walker and Company.

Haynes, M., Thornton, J., & Jones, S. C. (2004). An exploratory study on the effect of positive (warmth appeal) and negative (guilt appeal) print imagery on donation behaviour in animal welfare. *Faculty of Health & Behavioural Sciences—Papers,* 80.

Jansson, B. S. (2008). *Becoming an effective policy advocate* (5th ed.). Pacific Grove, CA: Thompson Brooks/Cole.

Kernan, H. (2012, February 9). *Q&A: James Bell on what to do with California's youth prisons.* Retrieved from http://www.kalw.org/post/what-should-be-done-youth-prisons-interview-james-bell

Klinth, R. (2008) The best of both worlds? Fatherhood and gender equality in Swedish paternity leave campaigns, 1976–2006. *Fathering, 6*(1), 20–38.

Kurwa, N. (2011, January 5). *Behind rise of xtranormal, a hilarious DIY deadpan.* NPR All Things Considered. Retrieved from http://www.npr.org/2011/01/05/132653525/behind-rise-of-xtranor- mal-a-hilarious-diy-deadpan

Lakoff, G. (2004). *Don't think of an elephant! Know your values and frame the debate.* White River Junction, VT: Chelsea Green.

Legislative Analyst's Office (2012a, March 22). *Governor's proposal to complete juvenile justice realign- ment.* Retrieved from http://www.lao.ca.gov/handouts/crimjust/2012/Completing_Juvenile_ Realignment_03_22_12.pdf

Legislative Analyst's Office (2012b, February 15). *2012–13 budget: Completing juvenile justice realign- ment.* Retrieved from http://www.lao.ca.gov/analysis/2012/crim_justice/juvenile-justice-021512. pdf

Lens, V. (2005). Advocacy and argumentation in the public arena: A guide for social workers. *Social Work, 50*(3), 231–238.

Miller, G. R. (1980). On being persuaded: Some basic distinctions. In M. Roloff & G. R. Miller (Eds.), *Persuasion: New directions in theory and research* (pp. 11–28). Beverly Hills, CA: SAGE.

National Responsible Fatherhood Clearinghouse (2011). *Fatherhood involvement PSA.* Retrieved from http://www.fatherhood.gov/media/303/3

OpEd Project (n.d.). *Basic op-ed structure.* Retrieved from http://theopedproject.org/index.php? option = com_content&view = article&id = 68&Itemid = 80

Ramage, J. D., & Bean, J. C. (1998). *Writing arguments* (4th ed.). Needham Heights, MA: Allyn & Bacon.

Schiraldi, V. & Zeidenberg, J. (1997). *The risks juveniles face when they are incarcerated with adults.* Retrieved from http://www.justicepolicy.org/images/upload/97-02_REP_RiskJuvenilesFace_ JJ.pdf

Singer, P. (2009). *The life you can save: Acting now to end world poverty*. New York, NY: Random House.

Stiff, J. B., & Mongeau, P. A. (2003). *Persuasive communication* (2nd ed.). New York, NY: Guilford.

Toulmin, S. (2003). *The uses of argument* (Updated ed.). London, UK: Cambridge University Press.

Toulmin, S., Rieke, R., & Janik, A. (1984). *An introduction to reasoning* (2nd ed.). New York, NY: MacMillan.

Turk, C. (1985). *Effective speaking, communicating in speech*. London, UK: Chapman & Hall.

UNHCR (2011). *Goodwill ambassadors*. Retrieved from http://www.unhcr.org/pages/49c3646c3e.html

UNICEF (2003, June). *UNICEF people Audrey Hepburn*. Retrieved from http://www.unicef.org/people/people_audrey_hepburn.html

Verderber, R. F., Verderber, K. S., & Sellnow, D. D. (2007). *The challenge of effective speaking*. Stamford, CT: Cengage Learning.

Wright, A. C. (2011, February 23). Opinion: GOP budget cuts will cost us in the long run. *AOL News*. Retrieved from http://www.aolnews.com/2011/02/23/opinion-gop-budget-cuts-will-cost-us-in-the-long-run/

CHAPTER 7

Step 4—Making Meetings That Work

The planning you completed in Step 1, the research in Step 2, and advocacy tools in Step 3 have all prepared you for Step 4, meeting with those in a position of power on your advocacy issue. The objective for these types of meetings is to have a dialogue with decision makers about the advocacy issue in order to help them become experts on your advocacy topic and to get a clear understanding of what steps will be necessary to secure their support. This chapter will cover how to set up a meeting, including whom to bring as your advocacy team and what to do if you encounter barriers to establishing a meeting. Strategies for the actual meeting are described, focusing on how to conduct the meeting and pitfalls to avoid. Closing and memorializing the meeting by developing concrete next steps are also discussed. An opportunity to practice these tasks is provided in an activity.

SETTING UP THE MEETING

Abraham Lincoln (1907) once said the following:

> If you would win a man to your cause, first convince him that you are his sincere friend. Therein is a drop of honey that catches his heart, which, say what you will, is the great high-road to his reason, and which, when once gained, you will find but little trouble in convincing his judgment of the justice of your cause. (p. 15)

In previous chapters, you have equipped yourself with allies and an understanding of your issue. Now, it is time to identify those who have power regarding your advocacy cause, build relationships with such people, and win them over to support your cause. See Boxes 7.1 and 7.2 for perspectives on a child advocacy effort from two advocates and a decision maker.

BOX 7.1

Malaysia as a Model for the Growth and Development of Programs for Young Children

By Liew Sau Pheng, Director Emeritus of Malaysian
Child Resource Institute, and Radziah Daud, cofounder of
National Association for Early Childhood Care and Education (Malaysia)

During the early 1980s, Malaysia was a country that received funding from international agencies, such as UNICEF and Bernard Van Leer Foundation, for national surveys and research to meet better standards in maternal and child health, early childhood development, and other fields. From then until the present time, Malaysia, compared to many neighboring countries, has made the fastest growth in developing quality care and education for children under age 5. As a result of the work of numerous nongovernmental organizations for children and with the help and support of key government officials, there has been a significant transformation in the delivery of high quality services to disadvantaged groups of children and their families.

Advocates from nongovernmental organizations such as National Association for Early Childhood Care and Education, Malaysian Child Resource Institute, the Association of Registered Child Care Providers, and the Malaysian Association of Kindergartens were instrumental in sharing knowledge and best practices on early childhood care and education (ECCE) to impact decision makers and the ECCE community in Malaysia. These advocates first sought training and certifications from around the world to upgrade themselves and their programs in planning, curriculum development, design of high quality buildings, and outdoor play areas for children. The benefits of their overseas experience and training, as well as the sharing of best practices, motivated them to promote awareness of the needs of all children for developmentally appropriate early childhood programs among relevant sectors of the population. They worked with government agencies to assist them in gaining a deeper understanding of children and highlighted the need for critical services and policies to be put in place for children. Advocates rallied ECCE professionals and government officials as well as academics and took them overseas on a regular basis to world conferences, seminars, and forums in the field to gain insights and learn about new research on early childhood. These experiences and inputs informed the development of quality ECCE services adapted to Malaysia's needs. The Ministry of Women, Community, and Development was subsequently created after the general election of 2004 to encompass ECCE, child protection, and support for women and families.

The greatest boost to their advocacy effort for children came with the concern expressed by the then-Deputy Prime Minister's wife, The Honorable Datin Paduka Seri Rosmah Mansor, and her

(Continued)

(Continued)

championing of ECCE. In 2005, she was particularly concerned about the many social ills among children and young people. She believed if children were nurtured from the start with the right values, they would become responsible adolescents. In her words, "If we fail to give all our children a good start in life, we risk failure on many fronts. If we do not pay attention to our children today, they may force us to pay attention as the troubled adults of tomorrow" (Ali, 2013, p. 55). So with that in mind, she mobilized members of the ECCE community, academics, doctors, police personnel, the armed forces, and women and child activists to meet and discuss the causes of problems facing children. The conclusion was that a long-term solution should begin with addressing the needs of children at a young age.

In 2007, the PERMATA Programme was launched under the leadership of the First Lady as Policy Executive Committee Chair, with the tag line "Every Child is Precious." The programme gained Malaysian Cabinet approval in 2006 as a pilot project and has since expanded throughout the country, including Sabah and Sarawak in East Malaysia focusing on underprivileged rural and urban poor children. Being friendly to input from the nongovernmental sector, the Malaysian Government consulted with child advocates with ECCE expertise. They were invited to participate on commissions, councils, and consultative forums. With the formulation of the National Policy of Early Childhood, the roles and functions of government agencies were streamlined in order to avoid duplication of resources. The establishment of a university-based National Child Development Research Center to develop the PERMATA curriculum and to provide training for teachers and child care providers further boosted the ECCE industry and also led to ECCE departments being created in prominent universities and colleges. ECCE became a buzzword, with increasing numbers of young graduates making ECCE a first option for a university degree, when previously the field was not seen as a good choice. In 2009, the Secretariat of PERMATA was set up in the Prime Minister's Department and organized the first International Conference of ECCE, with Datin Paduka Seri Rosmah Mansor being the patron of the event.

The latest fruit of these child advocacy efforts is the government's Transformation Programme. This led to the launch of the ECCE Council to represent the industry. Another key event that boosted the ECCE industry was the First Lady's call to private employers and government agencies to invest in setting up child care centers at workplaces. This call is aligned with the Malaysian principle of social justice and the government's national agenda of promoting corporate responsibility through the 10th Malaysia Plan. Child advocates worldwide, including International Child Resource Institute, now hold up Malaysia as an outstanding model for positive growth and transformation for a country's most vulnerable citizens—its children. In the words of Datin Paduka Seri Rosmah Mansor, "Early childhood education is the foundation for quality human development. Indeed, educating our children correctly is something we must do, not just for the benefit of the children but also the future of the country" (Ali, 2013, p. 49).

BOX 7.2

Preparing Our Children for a Transformed Malaysia

By Datin Paduka Seri Rosmah Mansor, Wife of the Prime Minister (Malaysia)

As the Patron and Chair of the Coordination Working Committee for the PERMATA Programme, it is most heartening for me and for those who work with me to see this programme currently being rolled out nationally to 665 centres involving more than 27,000 children within a span of 6 years. PERMATA alludes to children as "jewels of the nation," hence they need to be exquisitely shaped and polished to bring out their brilliance and true beauty. The PERMATA Programme offers an alternative approach to early childhood care and education for children below 5 years of age from rural and under privileged urban families. It lays the foundation for the later performance and success of the child throughout his or her life. This approach has been proven successful in several developed countries in enhancing children's cognitive, intellectual, and communication abilities and also in heightening their emotional stability. Importance is given to enhancing their mental stimulation by encouraging them to learn through exploration, experimentation, and experiences by means of play. The play approach is fun and appropriate for young children and the success of the programme is evident among children who have completed their time at the PERMATA Centres.

With the theme "Every Child is Precious," we envisioned that Malaysian children should have the best possible start in life. If we fail to do this, we may lose many opportunities and risk failure on many other fronts. They may also cause us to pay attention as troubled adults of tomorrow. We believe every great future starts with how happy a child is now. And every great country is built on how it looks after its children. This was the basis and the main drive that inspired the idea for the implementation of the PERMATA Programme. The collaboration with relevant government agencies, universities, nongovernmental organizations, professionals, and child advocates has accelerated the implementation of this programme as there were already existing resources available within those institutions. We were also very fortunate to have the support of the Government of Malaysia right from the outset and the leadership provided by the Honorable Prime Minister himself. Projects such as this require political will to succeed. Without this support, especially the financial allocation, it would have been a real challenge for us to achieve so much in such a short period of time.

It has been a great pleasure to collaborate with a wonderful and dynamic team who have been working tirelessly with me to introduce the PERMATA Programme as an innovative and crucial component of the Malaysian education system. They conducted research and reviewed ECCE programmes around the world in order to develop curriculum as well as approaches that are culturally acceptable

(Continued)

(Continued)

in the Malaysian environment. The team too should be credited for conducting continuous training programmes to prepare child care providers to undertake their jobs at the PERMATA Centres. I would like to thank each and every one who has played some part in enabling me to implement this programme. As an African saying goes, "If you want to go fast, go alone, but if you want to go far, we must go together."

One of the essential tasks of an advocate is to make the right meetings in order to gain the support and commitment of decision makers. For micro advocacy, decision makers may be officials involved with educational, health, and social services systems. For mezzo and macro advocacy, decision makers are very often elected officials and other members of government. While there are cases in which economic actors, such as businesses, have power over a child advocacy issue, most typically government (at various levels) is the main recourse. Government intervention generally results for reasons related to 1) efficiency, 2) equity, and 3) ethics (Kraft & Furlong, 2013). First, *efficiency*, or market failure, explanations suggest that government action is warranted when the market is unable or unwilling to produce desired goods and services, such as public goods like clean air that are consumed by all. Second, the *equity* argument points out that even if the market produces a good or service, it may not be distributed in a fair manner, requiring government action. Third, *ethics* dictate that there is a boundary between the market and public spheres and that there are some things that should not be subject to being bought and sold in the market. Matters related to children often involve these three arguments for government intervention. Often, children need public services that the market may not provide, such as public safety and free education. Children who are poor and/or face discrimination and social exclusion may not receive an adequate share of resources. Also, children have needs, such as services to protect them from abuse and exploitation, that are not amenable to market solutions.

When contemplating whom to approach, consider which level of government may have jurisdiction over your issue. There are three primary governmental structures: unitary, confederate, and federal. In *unitary governments*, power is held by the central government; China is one such example. In *confederate governments*, central authority is weak and power is held by component members, such as states. Few such configurations exist today, except in the form of international organizations that connect nations for purposes such as trade. *Federal governments* apportion power between central and regional governments, such that two or more levels of government exercise authority over the same territory (Føllesdal, 2010). Modern examples of federal governments include the United States, India, and Australia.

With these government structures in mind, consider whether your child advocacy issue is a problem at the *international, national, regional, or local* level, and where power is held over your issue. For example, perhaps you are interested in promoting child safety. If your concern is an intersection dangerous for pedestrians, consult your local authorities. If you are interested in passing a law criminalizing drivers who do not stop for pedestrians, a regional government like a prefecture, province, or state may be responsible, or possibly the national government. If you are interested in widening your scope so that all the nations in regional governance structure reexamine their laws for pedestrians, it may be appropriate to work at the international level. Conduct research to find out who currently holds the government position of relevance to your issue by checking governmental websites or making phone calls to local governmental agencies. In this book, we refer to the person vested with authority over your issue as a decision maker (see the section in Chapter 2, Influencing Outcomes: Gatekeepers and Decision Makers, for additional discussion of decision makers).

Rarely will your first interaction be with decision makers themselves; typically, you will first seek an audience through a staff member, a person who plays the role of a gatekeeper (as discussed in Chapter 2). Like the person monitoring the gates to a city, from which this word was derived, a gatekeeper controls access to people in positions of power and thereby regulates the flow of information and political influence in political systems (Roberts & Edwards, 1991). Your initial meeting with a gatekeeper may be a sort of dress rehearsal for an audience with the decision maker. The gatekeeper may first wish to vet your presentation before allowing you to schedule a meeting with the decision maker. Your ticket to getting your foot in the door, so to speak, is to impress upon gatekeepers the value of your meeting with the decision maker. Throughout this chapter, we will refer to both gatekeepers and decision makers as potential people with whom you may be meeting.

In order to set up a meeting, it is important to understand the nature of decision makers' work. For decision makers who are elected officials, it is likely that they will have office hours within their district when they are available to meet with their constituents, who are the voters and/or potential campaign backers in their district. Why would a person in a position of power be willing to meet with you? Rational choice theory posits that those in power are pursuing their own interests when deciding on alliances (Riker, 1962). If you cannot win an ally out of pure altruism, appeal to the decision maker's enlightened self-interest, or as de Tocqueville (2000) describes it, "[the belief] that a man will be led to do what is just and good by following his own interest rightly understood" (p. 441). An instructive example is the character of Colonel Cathcart in *Catch-22* (Heller, 1961). He makes up lists of "feathers in his cap" (successes or accomplishments) and "black eyes" (embarrassments or bad news). To secure actions that will benefit your advocacy campaign, look for ways to offer "feathers in the cap" and to avoid "black eyes" for the decision maker on your issue. This raises the question of how to exercise influence over others. But first, here is a word about money: While money in the form of campaign contributions seems to be the most expeditious way to gain access to politicians in many, if not most, nations around the world, there are things you can do without it.

Sociologist Talcott Parsons (1963) suggests that there are four primary modes of influence to gain desired results in an interaction. The first, *inducement*, is offering the other person something he or she wants to encourage compliance. Offering something desirable to the decision maker, such as votes or positive attention, indicates that cooperation with your efforts may be advantageous. The second, *deterrence*, is suggesting that not providing assistance to your efforts may result in a negative outcome. This is the opposite of the previous approach; failing to cooperate with your efforts may be disadvantageous, resulting in lost votes or negative attention. The third, *persuasion*, is offering reasons why cooperation is a good in itself, separate from personal advantage. With this approach, you are encouraging the decision maker to see cooperation as the right thing to do, for the children and families in his or her district. Fourth and finally, *activation of commitments* is helping the decision maker understand why it would be harmful, separate from personal interest, to fail to provide assistance. This is the reverse of persuasion, as the decision maker comes to view not helping your cause as the wrong thing to do, resulting in harm to children and families in his or her district. All four modes of influence may come into play during your meeting with the decision maker.

In your efforts to gain influence with a decision maker, your goal is to engender a sense of reciprocity, the notion that one kind deed is returned with another. Reciprocity seems to be a universal societal norm; anthropologists have observed cultural practices of reciprocity in diverse human societies from tribal to industrial cultures (Gouldner, 1960), and expectations of reciprocity are central to social and political arrangements (Becker, 1986). Examples of how to gain influence with politicians, costing little or no money, will be discussed in the next three sections: controlling votes in the politician's district, hosting events for the politician, and making the politician look good.

Controlling Votes in the Politician's District

One of the best methods of gaining a meeting with an elected official who has a constituency is to be a voter in the district of the elected official. Being a voter in the district has a tremendous impact on whether decision makers, or their gatekeepers, believe it is necessary and even advantageous for them to meet with you. Decision makers who are required to be reelected to their positions on a regular basis, whether it be every 2 years, 4 years, 6 years, or another period of time, place great value in pleasing their constituents, especially if they also represent a voting block within their constituency. One of the main traits of elected officials is a desire to continue to be elected to either the same posts or higher posts on the local, regional, or national level. Thus, if advocates can impress upon gatekeepers the value of the information to be provided or the power of the advocate's group in assisting the decision maker in becoming reelected, there will be a far greater likelihood of securing a meeting with that decision maker and acquiring her assistance in meeting your goals.

Initiate your contact with the office of the decision maker by modifying and using the following script via phone or email:

> "Hello, my name is ____. I represent the ____ organization made up of 5,000 voters in the district of Mr. or Ms. ____. We would like to share some valuable information with [the senator, the assembly member, the city council member, etc.] that will help [him or her] to understand issues that will be coming before [him or her] shortly. We would like to have no more than 45 minutes of the decision maker's time, at a time within the next week or two that is convenient to [him or her]."

This approach will generally give decision makers or their staff great interest in having a meeting with you because you have both notified them that you are a constituent and that you have clout within their district in the form of potential control of hundreds, if not thousands, of other votes. The authors have witnessed, on many occasions, the impact of having a constituency within a district and of being voters in that district, over all other suitors for meetings with the decision maker. For example, in the California State Legislature, when one of the authors was about to start a meeting with the financial committee chair on legislation for children for that particular year, an aide to the official handed him messages from two important federal judges from outside his district; The decision maker simply looked at notes and said, "These people are not from my district, I can't be bothered with them now!" Afterward, he promptly threw the messages into the wastepaper basket. After that rude dismissal, the elected official gave the advocate his full attention and made a clear commitment to advocate for legislation on behalf of poor migrant children from agricultural workers' families (later passed into law). As this example suggests, setting up meetings is greatly helped when one can claim status as a voter in the decision maker's district and representation over one or more constituencies that shows that the advocate has a level of power and control within that decision maker's election district. Since elected officials wish to be reelected, gaining a meeting will be easiest before the crucial months leading up to an election. During that time, decision makers are most likely to agree to meetings with those with whom they are not already closely aligned in order to ensure positive relationships with all parts of their constituency and afford themselves the greatest opportunity for increasing their voting bloc within their electorate.

Please note that these efforts to develop a *constituency* within the district or area of the decision maker's control need not be highly formalized. If you have developed an advocacy effort and gone through the necessary steps to coalesce a group behind you of interested or like-minded individuals, you can have either a loosely formed or completely developed constituency group whom you can claim as part of your advocacy campaign. You can also jump-start your constituency by gaining the support of already existing associations representing neighborhoods (such as a neighborhood watch), civic interests (such as a partisan or nonpartisan political association), or child-related subject areas (such as parent-teacher associations); this may enable you to boost your list of supporters by hundreds or thousands. Be aware that the staff of decision makers will look to verify your claims by doing some research. You can honestly claim voters within a district if you have worked with them and if you have gotten their consent, preferably in writing, that they will become part of the advocacy effort. Create a form with a description of your advocacy issue, and start developing a list of supporters willing to sign on. The first few supporters may be the most challenging to secure, but once you are able to identify a few supporters (particularly if those first few supporters have high status within the community), it can be easier to get subsequent supporters. Alternatively, the growth of social media offers an additional platform for gathering support. Consider setting up a Facebook page and getting people to "like" your cause or follow your Twitter account. Keep in mind, however, that you will need to document that your supporters are from the relevant political district. Present a list of organizations and key individuals who support your cause (part of your summary sheet) to the decision maker either prior to the meeting by mail or email or during the meeting. This boosts your credibility and allows you to borrow character from your allies to make a persuasive case through an appeal to character, as discussed in Chapter 6, "Step 3—Preparing Effective Materials."

Holding Events for Decision Makers

The best time to build relationships with decision makers is when they need you and you don't need them. By holding an event, particularly prior to an election, you can provide a valuable service to a politician. Such events can include a candidates' night or a meet and greet for the politician to meet potential voters and share his or her political platform. Likewise, voters can share their own concerns with the politician. Decision makers, particularly legislators, have a desire to understand social problems and the costs of addressing those problems (Kingdon, 1984).

A *candidates' night* brings together all or most candidates for a public office before an election to allow them to share their professional backgrounds as well as intentions for their time in office with potential voters. They can convey their stances on issues in a way that is more compelling than campaign literature. It can also be a time when voters ask questions. Think of the event as a "Hyde Park Speaker's Corner" as you give people a chance to speak and listen in turn. You can't lose with a candidates' night, as such an event allows you to meet all of the possible future decision makers who could assume an elected position, each of whom would be beholden to you. With regard to your advocacy issue, such events can be a good time to gently probe how politicians feel about your issue and their intended actions. Have prepared questions and ask about the candidates' positions on issues affecting children and families. These events also allow politicians to understand their constituents and what resonates with them. What are the voters looking for in a politician? What stances will they support? Are there single-issue voters whose votes are won or lost depending on the politician's stance on a particular issue?

A *meet and greet* is an event focused on a specific politician and can be a way to build a closer relationship with a particular decision maker. These types of events are appreciated by decision makers as potential opportunities to raise funds for their reelection campaigns, so events of this nature will be of most interest prior to or during an election. Politicians are also looking for chances to be seen. For advocates, such events can be used to educate decision makers on your issue and learn about their stances on issues affecting children and youth. Hosting an event on behalf of a decision maker can also raise your profile with that person and increase the likelihood that meeting requests will be honored.

Elected officials and their potential voters often come from different worlds, and connecting in person may allow politicians to expand their understanding of who is in their district. One of the authors observed an example of this occurring. A successful insurance broker was planning to run for a state assembly position in a wealthy district in Northern California. During a meet and greet event in an upscale home, a woman approached him. She explained that she lived in the neighborhood with her three children. Her husband had left her after a long marriage that had begun when the couple met in college. She had dropped out of college after their marriage and had never held a job outside the home. She now struggled to figure out how to support her children while she received the training she needed to secure a job. From this exchange, the politician learned that his pool of voters included this single mother, who had the accoutrements of wealth, such as a fancy home and car, but no longer had the income to support her lifestyle. Once aware, he could learn more about his voters to see how many others were in this position and how he might respond.

Here is a checklist for organizing a candidates' night or meet and greet event:

☐ Contact the politician(s) and find dates when the politician(s) will be in the district and available, on an evening or weekend, which will promote high attendance.

☐ Plan a casual event in a large home (yours or another advocate's) or a public space (like an auditorium). Costs for the event should be minimal: simply some tea or coffee and perhaps some cookies or other regional treats.

☐ Advertise the event to your constituency that supports the child advocacy cause as well as more broadly to other potential voters. During the event, circulate an email list for those who may be interested in participating in your child advocacy campaign.

☐ Make sure that people knowledgeable about your advocacy topic are prepared to ask questions that steer the politician(s) to contemplate and better understand your issue.

☐ Follow up with the staff of the politician(s) by sending a thank-you note for participating. Use this opportunity to request a meeting or make an invitation to visit programs in the area that need help.

Making the Decision Maker Look Good

A positive reputation is an essential attribute for a public official. The public seems to be insatiably curious about the lives and personalities of politicians, and the media feeds this interest by creating images that are often all we know about our leaders (Bellah, 1986). Consequently, if you can play a role in enhancing the public image of a politician, you are likely to win an ally. This can be achieved in two primary ways: 1) helping the politician become an expert on children's issues and 2) facilitating positive media coverage of the politician.

Building your own reputation as an expert and change maker will indirectly help to enhance the reputations of politicians with whom you partner. If you are seen by the community as a respectable authority, politicians will want your help as much as you want theirs. All leaders are in a position where they must be generalists because the scope of their work requires that they make decisions about a broad swath of issues. By necessity, they rely on subject experts to help them make decisions about particular issues. You can become their educator about children's issues and make them look good to their constituencies on such matters.

First, you can help them develop their platforms on children's issues and make informed decisions about what types of initiatives or legislation to introduce or support. Second, when relevant initiatives or legislation are under consideration (by a city council, regional assembly, or national legislature), you can be an expert witness who presents a persuasive case in favor of the politician's position. Third, you can assist with community relations. If the politician hosts visitors who have an interest in a children's issue, such as an international delegation or a local group of professionals, you could make yourself available to speak about the politician's platform. This type of relationship, where an elected official comes to rely on you as a subject expert on children's issues, is one that can only be built over time. The relationship can be initiated and sustained by sharing accurate and timely information about children's issues and above all by maintaining your honesty and neutrality.

Relationships of this nature are easily undone if the politician hears that you have spoken against him or her about a particular vote. As an example, a prominent national child advocate in the United States came out in opposition to politicians who supported welfare reform during the Clinton administration, decrying the shift from an open-ended entitlement program that guaranteed a minimum income to poor families to a short-term employment preparation program that provided nothing for those who could not comply with the requirements. This child advocate was quoted by several publications as blaming the Chair of the Education and Workforce Committee, who had been a longtime ally on children's legislation. When the politician heard about the attacks, he ranted about what he described as smear tactics used by the advocate, claiming, "I have carried her water [i.e., favored legislation] for the last 15 years and have not spilled a drop." Take the long view and maintain your neutrality as much as possible for the good of your overall advocacy efforts. Even if others question the politician and you for supporting him or her, consider what is won and lost by coming out against your ally. It is more important to keep your eyes on the prize.

If you are able to convince the politician to be a supporter of children's issues, engage the media in his or her district to herald this person's contributions to the well-being of children. Give quotes to local reporters, making complimentary statements about the politician. Typically, elected officials assign staff to monitor their local newspapers and scan for coverage about them. Kind words can pay off in terms of appreciation from politicians. But you can't say something nice just once; politicians, like the media news cycle, seem to have short memories and need frequent feathers in their caps, or complimentary statements in the media. One way to encourage the media to pick up your positive news story is to hold a press conference or send out a press release and attribute a legislative victory to the politician. Another is to dedicate an award to a politician, on behalf of his or her work for children, and notify the media of the award. One strategy that often works well for gaining media interest is playing the *strange bedfellows* angle. A politician known for cutting taxes and funding for social programs may nevertheless want to counter that image with a few compassionate actions on behalf of children and want those contributions known to the press and his or her constituency. Engaging the media to cover advocacy successes, in the process both enhancing the decision maker's reputation and securing his or her continued support as an ally, is discussed further detail in Chapter 9, "Step 6—Reinforcing Successful Advocacy Outcomes."

Making Meetings Where Other Approaches Are Necessary

If the person who holds authority over your advocacy issue is not an elected official, approaches other than those described above will be necessary. Perhaps your advocacy issue is under the jurisdiction of the *bureaucracy*: that is, nonelected members of government who are tasked with running the government. Perhaps you are trying to create change for children in a more traditional society in which authority is not allocated by democratically run election but by some other means. Perhaps you are working to change things within a corporation or other private organization. Perhaps you need support from an informal community leader or group. Meetings with these types of decision makers can often be gained with some persistence.

Begin with research on which systems and individuals hold authority over your advocacy issue. This may require learning about how a particular governance structure or community functions. Suppose that you are interested in building a new playground and learn that the national ministry of education and welfare holds authority over your advocacy issue. Find out about the organization of that ministry and the responsibilities of various positions within it. Consider further that, in order to build that playground, you need a private sponsor. Find out about the organizations related to commerce in the area so that you can solicit funding; these organizations may include social groups like the Rotary Club as well as business groups like the Chamber of Commerce. If your plans are part of a larger effort to inform the public of the importance of free play, connect with a group that has a large and diverse membership to spread the word. To find the right players, you may need to ask a lot of questions, search the Internet, and make phone calls. You may find that a direct phone call to that person, or his or her staff, will secure a meeting.

If the target decision maker does not agree to a meeting right away, find someone within his or her network who can champion your cause. Since bureaucrats, nonelected officials, and community leaders typically have no requirement to make meetings to maintain their positions, using community connections will often be the best approach. Comb through your list of supporters or your professional and personal contacts to find a person or group who may hold sway with the decision maker. Find out whether your advocacy allies are involved in any shared community organizations with the decision maker. Your ally may be able to build on this connection and make a phone call to initiate a meeting. The following types of groups can be important in their communities: 1) civic clubs, such as Rotary or Kiwanis; 2) social clubs, such as a country club or subject area club; 3) business groups, such as the Chamber of Commerce or industrial councils; 4) religious institutions, such as your local churches, temples, and mosques; and 5) professional membership organizations, such as the National Association for the Education of Young Children or the National Association of Social Workers. It's the "who you know" club. Sometimes appealing to enlightened self-interest can win you a champion. For example, a vice president of human resources for a large multinational corporation needed child care for her own children. An advocate who was trying to convince the multinational corporation to provide subsidized care for the children of all employees was able to enlist her support and utilize her access to the president of the corporation. The key to many organizations is to find the right people and how to access them.

WHOM TO BRING TO THE MEETING

As was discussed in Chapter 2 (in the section called Reaching Out to Allies: Building a Coalition), it is essential to have allies in your advocacy effort, and they will play a starring role in the current step. While you may build a larger network of advocates who will support the advocacy campaign by educating others and contacting decision makers (particularly elected officials), it is also necessary to have a committed and active core group of advocates. Theories of collective action suggest the challenges of encouraging people to work together, even when it is in their best interests. Small, face-to-face groups can overcome some of these challenges by ensuring that each member has a significant stake in outcomes (Olson, 1965) and that their actions on behalf of the group are rewarded with high status (Berger, Cohen, & Zelditch, 1972). Think carefully about whom you recruit to your core advocacy team as you will bring members of this team to your meeting with the gatekeeper and/or decision maker.

The choice of whom to bring to the meeting will be critical to the success of the advocacy effort. Each individual who comes with you should play a unique and distinct role in the proceedings of the meeting. One person can play more than one role so that the group size is kept to no more than four or five. The following types of individuals will be particularly effective to have at a meeting: subject experts, financial experts, and allies with a personal connection to the decision maker. Individuals who are experts on the issues at hand, whether legislative, programmatic, or other related issues, are necessary when discussing the advocacy goals of your group. The subject expert member of your team can assist in helping the decision maker to become an expert by the end of the meeting, which will play a critical role in the future of the advocacy effort. Individuals who understand the costs related to the child advocacy goals will also be critical in dealing with certain decision makers, as legislators in particular will wish to know the price tag of the advocacy goals. The financial expert member of your team can educate the decision maker on costs while also emphasizing potential cost savings that may result from preventing negative outcomes. If you have an ally who has a personal relationship with the decision maker, be sure to include that person in your team. Having an understanding of the decision maker's personal life, social and economic background, and interests can help create rapport as well as help the team to tailor their messages to be particularly appealing to the decision maker. Do your homework prior to the meeting, and learn as much as you can about the decision maker or gatekeeper to make as persuasive a case as possible on your issue. Talk to people who know them, read things they have been quoted as saying, and/or attend a meeting where they are presenting. This type of preparation will improve your odds of success.

MAKING THE MEETING WORK

How to "Run" the Meeting

The most important reason for setting up advocacy meetings with gatekeepers or decision makers is to find out where they currently stand on your issue and enhance their levels of understanding so that the decision makers can gain sufficient expertise to help your cause. Therefore, the content of the meeting will be critical to achieving success on your advocacy issue. Because of the nature of their positions, decision makers will wish to run the meeting. However, as an advocate, you have a chance to have enough control over how you present information to make sure that you meet your objective. The objective is to create a dialogue. In terms of what to say, look back to Chapter 6, "Step 3—Preparing Effective Materials." From your completion of the chapter activity, you have prepared a summary sheet that will be the focal point of the meeting. The use of the summary sheet within the meeting will help to coalesce all members of the advocacy team around the issue, provide an outline of the topics to be discussed in the meeting, and allow the decision maker to understand relevant information about the advocacy issue. See Box 7.3 for a procedure to run a meeting. Use the activity at the end of this chapter to rehearse how to conduct a meeting with a decision maker, using your summary sheet from the previous chapter.

BOX 7.3

Procedure to "Run" an Advocacy Meeting

1. Greet the decision maker and other attendees

2. Introduce those at the meeting (emphasizing their affiliations and the constituencies they represent)

3. Paraphrase the summary sheet in a conversational manner

4. Make transitions from one speaker to another ("That's right, Joe, your comment ties into my remarks . . . ")

5. Show how the proposed solutions will enhance the interests of the decision maker

6. Talk about what the opposition may say, coupling this discussion with ways to counter their points

7. Close strongly with a call to action invoking appeals to logic and emotion

8. Memorialize the meeting by discussing next steps and plans for follow-up

---

In terms of how to organize the meeting, the summary sheet can be paraphrased and elucidated for the decision maker. It is very important, though, that the team doesn't merely read the information to the decision maker. Those who are nervous with this type of meeting often spend too much time reading the material to the decision maker rather than developing a dialogue and connection. Instead, present the contents of the summary sheet to the decision maker in a highly conversational style, using the elements of style discussed in Chapter 6 (in the section called Crafting Your Message). Ask different members of the team to take responsibility for sharing particular sections. This divides up the responsibilities of the advocacy team so that all who are brought to the meeting have something to contribute based on their knowledge and expertise.

A significant part of the meeting is attempting to build a relationship with the decision maker. Show respect for the decision maker by using his or her proper title (e.g., Senator, Representative) or honorific (e.g., Honorable Member); specific titles and honorifics associated with political office vary by country. Establish your own character by always following up and doing what you say that you will do in the meeting (this is discussed further in Chapter 8, "Step 5—Conducting Strategic Follow-Up"). Distinguishing yourself and your advocacy team as people who can be trusted for accurate information and assistance on political efforts will help your current and future advocacy efforts.

Potential Meeting Pitfalls

Since one of your goals of the meeting is to build a respectful relationship with the decision maker, be careful with your language. Since at least the time of the Sophists, teachers and practitioners of rhetoric in Ancient Greece (Herrick, 2001), the power of words has been well understood. In the context of meetings with decision makers and gatekeepers, words can be used to charm and make a positive impression, or they can be used to make a bad impression. In particular, avoid statements that suggest you have power over the decision maker (e.g., "My taxes pay your salary!") and statements that impugn others (e.g., "Why are you listening to those jerks?"). Do not make statements that assign blame and leave "blood on the hands" of decision makers if they do not follow your prescribed actions; for example, "If my child or another child dies because you have not voted for this traffic light, it will be your fault!" See Box 7.4 for more suggestions of things to do and things to avoid at the meeting.

BOX 7.4

A Few Always and Nevers to Make Any Meeting Work

Always . . .

. . . show respect for the gatekeeper or decision maker

. . . present in a conversational tone that establishes a dialogue between you and the decision maker

. . . assign a role to each member of the advocacy team who attends and presents at the meeting

. . . follow up when you say you will

Never . . .

. . . attack the decision maker with statements such as "my taxes pay your salary" or threats that inaction will leave "blood on his or her hands"

. . . share any information that condemns or shows disrespect for another group or organization

. . . hide opposition to your advocacy goal; instead, acknowledge the main points and dispute them with evidence

. . . leave a meeting without knowing what you should do next and how the next steps fit into your advocacy plan

---

Being outright dishonest or hiding the truth about the opposition's arguments can damage your reputation as an advocate and turn the decision maker from a friend to a foe. If there is opposition to your advocacy cause, share the main points of the case against you, and try to refute each point with evidence. Rest assured, the decision maker will find out about the opposition's arguments in any event, so concealment can only work against you. Sharing both sides of an issue makes you appear knowledgeable and trustworthy, an asset to the decision maker.

As you close the meeting, be sure you understand what the decision maker thinks about your issue and how he or she might best be able to help you. It is absolutely critical that the team allow time for the decision maker to share his or her opinions, ideas, and potential contributions to the child advocacy effort. The meeting is only successful if the team leaves the room with a good understanding of not only the ideas and opinions of the decision maker about this particular advocacy issue but also how the decision maker is willing to assist the team in moving to the next level. In many cases, the decision maker will make an effort to evade any pigeonholing or attempts to be pinned down to a series of next steps. It becomes just as critical for the advocacy team to ensure they have met the goal of enhancing the decision maker's expertise on the issue and have come to an agreement about future meetings or specific ways that the decision maker will assist with the advocacy efforts. Decision makers often have a clever ability to end a meeting in a manner such that others present have little or no idea what the decision maker is, in fact, thinking about the issues. Strategies to assess the decision maker's understanding and willingness to commit to action will be discussed in the next section.

MEMORIALIZING THE MEETING

As previously mentioned, the advocacy team must be ready to discuss follow-up steps with the decision maker at the close of the meeting, which will be acted upon in Chapter 8, "Step 5—Conducting Strategic Follow-Up." Closing or memorializing of the meeting is done by confirming the decision maker's understanding of the issue and identifying future actions.

After presenting the information from the summary sheet, check with the decision maker about his or her understanding of the issue and intended actions. This can be done by directly questioning the decision maker and pressing the issue if he or she is silent or unwilling to engage in dialogue. Simple techniques include asking, "What do you think about what we've told you, Senator?" or "Are you clear on the issues that we presented today, Senator?" or "Where do you think we should go from here, Senator?" These questions can help to avoid a scenario in which, when the decision maker thanks the group for the meeting and ushers them out the door, the advocacy team realizes with surprise and consternation that they have no idea what the decision maker is really thinking. If this conclusion is reached after the meeting, the meeting has not been a success. A successful meeting is signified by a mutual agreement regarding clear understanding of the issue and structure for next steps. Thus, it becomes critical to ask decision makers to express whether they will support the advocacy effort, whether they can offer viable next steps in order to move toward a positive conclusion to the advocacy efforts, and whether they can, in fact, become part of the continuing advocacy effort.

Another approach that has proven successful is to repeat back what has been stated in the meeting so that the decision maker and your team are clear on the current state of understanding and commitment. That way, the decision maker will understand how the advocacy team perceives the decision maker's stance on the issue and possible actions. For example, an advocate may say, "Great, Senator, we'll follow up with the head of the Ways and Means Committee, explaining that you are willing to support this new legislation for children as long as he does and will then get back to you. Is Tuesday a good day for us to have another meeting?" As you can see from this approach, you and your team will leave the meeting with marching orders for the next steps of successful advocacy, having made a meeting that worked and understanding the next steps that you will take to move forward. You should always send a note expressing thanks for the meeting and reiterating what has been said; this is described in Chapter 8, "Step 5—Conducting Strategic Follow-Up."

Activity: Meeting Role-Play

The following activity provides an opportunity to summarize and share your advocacy materials in a mock meeting. Form a group of up to five people. Refer to the summary sheet you completed in the last chapter. With your group, divide up presentation roles and responsibilities for the sections of your summary sheet. Team members should read through their relevant section(s) of the summary sheet several times so that they know the information and can describe their section(s) in a conversational manner without reading the information directly. Assign the following roles:

1. The main advocate, who will make introductions at the beginning of the meeting and steer the meeting back on track if it begins to get off topic.

2. A financial expert, who understands the fiscal implications of proposed actions and will be prepared to discuss them.

3. A personal contact of the decision maker, who is someone the decision maker knows and with whom the decision maker feels comfortable.

4. Other advocates, as needed and relevant for your topic and particular decision maker.

Select one group member to role-play a decision maker or gatekeeper. Choose one of the fact patterns below and consider how you might tailor a meeting with this specific person. Rehearse your meeting as a group; then act out before an audience for their critiques. Suggested discussion questions for processing the meeting as a small group, or together with your audience, are included below.

Decision Maker 1:

Samuel Schmirdlap has been in the legislature for many years. He is currently the chair of the finance committee of the legislature. Widely considered ambitious, he has expressed a desire to trade up to a higher political office. His attention span is short; typically, he is not able to concentrate for more than 15 minutes on a particular issue. He is divorced and the father of three children who are being raised by his ex-wife. His interests include soccer and golf. He is active on Facebook.

Decision Maker 2:

Mrs. Sarah Obi is the head of the Education Ministry. While she has been in the national government bureaucracy for a long time, she has just transferred over from another ministry and is still learning about her new role in this new ministry. She has met with staff under her direction to learn about their jobs in order to better understand her own. The reason for her appointment was that the previous head of the ministry had been perceived as incompetent, and Mrs. Obi is finding that ineptitude in the ministry is widespread. She is middle-aged and married with pictures of her children prominently displayed in her office. Religion is also important to her, and devotional images are displayed in her office.

Gatekeeper 1:

Martha Gonzalez is the administrative assistant to a very powerful elected official (state governor or equivalent). She has been in the position for 25 years. Her words and actions suggest that she feels that she has complete control over the decision maker. If people indicate that they have tried to access the decision maker directly, without going through her, she gets upset. When people contact her to arrange a meeting with the decision maker, she is often impatient and curt. She has struggled with her weight and is often trying a new diet or exercise program. Listening to opera music and reading, particularly mystery novels, are her passions.

Gatekeeper 2:

Mark Lin is a staff member for a powerful legislator and his right-hand man. He tells people that he knows the secrets of how to get to his boss and that people need to work with him. If you can play along with him, he'll go through the process with you to get you to the decision maker. As part of the process, he wants to know enough about your issue to look good to his boss. He is ambitious and enjoys working with others. During his free time, he surfs and bicycles. He is in his early 30s and is single.

Processing Questions:

- What type of research would you have done about the decision maker or gatekeeper prior to your meeting? Are there other things not included in the descriptions that you would like to have known?
- How did you use the background information to interact with the decision makers or gatekeepers in your meeting?
- What types of people did you bring to your meeting, and how did they fit with your issue and building connections with the decision maker or gatekeeper?

REFERENCES

Ali, A. (2013). *Every child is precious*. Sengalor, Malaysia: MPH Group.

Becker, L. C. (1986). *Reciprocity*. New York, NY: Routledge.

Bellah, R. N. (1986, May). The meaning of reputation in American society. Symposium: New perspectives in the law of defamation. *California Law Review*, 74(3), 743–751.

Berger, J., Cohen, B. P., & Zelditch, M. (1972). Status characteristics and social interaction. *American Sociological Review, 37*, 241–255.

de Tocqueville, A. (2000). *Democracy in America*. Chicago, IL: The University of Chicago Press.

Føllesdal, A. (2010, Spring). Federalism. In E. N. Zalta (Ed.), *The Stanford Encyclopedia of Philosophy*. Retrieved from http://plato.stanford.edu/archives/spr2010/entries/federalism/

Gouldner, A. (1960). The norm of reciprocity. *American Sociological Review, 25*, 161–178.

Heller, J. (1961). *Catch-22*. New York, NY: Simon & Schuster.

Herrick, J. A. (2001). *The history and theory of rhetoric* (2nd ed.). Boston, MA: Allyn and Bacon.

Kingdon, J. W. (1984). *Agendas, alternatives, and public policies*. Boston, MA: Little, Brown.

Kraft, M. E., & Furlong, S. R. (2013). *Public policy: Politics, analysis, and alternatives* (4th ed.). Washington, DC: CQ Press.

Lincoln, A. (1907). *Speeches and letters of Abraham Lincoln, 1832–1865*. M. Rowe (Ed.). New York, NY: E.P. Dutton & Co. Retrieved from: http://books.google.com/books?id=5zIAAAAAYAAJ&pg=PR5&source=gbs_selected_pages&cad=3#v=onepage&q&f=false

Olson, M. (1965). *The logic of collective action: Public goods and the theory of groups*. Cambridge, MA: Harvard University Press.

Parsons, T. (1963). On the concept of political power. *Proceedings of the American Philosophical Society, 107*, 232–262.

Riker, W. H. (1962). *The theory of political coalitions*. New Haven, CT: Yale University Press.

Roberts, G., & Edwards, A. (1991). *A new dictionary of political analysis*. London, UK: Edward Arnold.

CHAPTER 8

Step 5—Conducting Strategic Follow-Up

Follow-up is crucial for maintaining momentum on an issue. One type of follow-up is addressing the requests of decision makers for more information or networking with other decision makers. Another is to ensure that the advocacy coalition is involved and well prepared for subsequent steps in the decision-making process. This chapter describes a two-pronged approach to follow-up: one, to provide any further information needed by the decision maker, and two, to educate the group of advocates to keep them involved and engaged in every decision-making step. The use of social media (e.g., Twitter, e-newsletters, and blogs) is explored for its usefulness in connecting with both decision makers and advocates. A case study describes how a nonprofit organization focused on Africa uses social media for advocacy and fundraising. The chapter concludes with a self-assessment activity to consider how social media might be used in your advocacy project.

KEEPING THE DECISION MAKERS INFORMED

Follow-up is when things get done. This is the time to continue to advocate for your cause by building your relationships with decision makers and educating them on your cause to make them stronger supporters over time. See Box 8.1 for an advocate's perspective on effective follow-up. If you made a specific offer of follow-up in your initial meeting, be sure to keep your word in a timely manner. In your meeting, you might offer to provide additional information to the decision maker. This is an example of how the 6 Steps can reiterate, as you may need to go back to Chapter 5, Step 2 to conduct additional research or Chapter 6, Step 3 to prepare additional materials. Another example of follow-up would be to invite a decision maker on a site visit to a program serving children, youth, and families. You may be seeking support for legislation, and a site visit may provide a decision maker with an on-the-ground view of an issue. For example, a child care provider might invite a legislator for a site visit to an in-home child care program to demonstrate the importance of state-funded subsidies to provide nutritious meals to low-income children and to persuade the legislator to support a bill for expanded funding for the program.

BOX 8.1

The Importance of Follow-Up for Advocacy Projects

By Deepak Raj Sapkota, Child Rights Researcher (Nepal)

Advocacy is one of the most popular words that is being used in development to establish the entitlement of the beneficiary. Advocacy outcomes are the results of constant and vigorous work on specific agendas that are crucial for societal change but that are not yet mainstreamed or properly addressed by the system. The most important challenge in the development arena is to convert these outcomes into impacts on people's lives. And the only way to transform the outcomes into impacts is follow-up and reinforcement (in some cases constantly or through regular interventions) so that the commitments once made are not forgotten.

Why?

Follow-up is the key to making sure that successful advocacy outcomes are not either left out or less prioritized. Without constant follow-up, the decision makers and implementers could easily sideline or forget their promises simply because children are not a powerful political constituency. So it is essential that advocates follow up to convince the decision maker of the importance of the issue.

What Could Be the Best Way to Follow Up?

Regular and constant follow-up is crucial. In many cases, mobilizing the public through protests and other forms can be an effective form of follow-up. Another way to reinforce your outcomes is to demonstrate results through monitoring and evaluation. In any society, success matters, and once you achieve results, others will be interested in your efforts.

How Often Does One Need to Go for It?

If we are talking about follow-up for advocacy outcomes, we have to realize three main points. First, we may not have been successful in achieving the desired outcomes as planned. Second, the outcomes have lapsed, and we need to reinitiate the effort. Third, everything is going well, but in the due course of time, the effort must be reawakened, recharged, and revitalized. In case of number one, we need to go for constant follow-up with some modification if required. In the second and third scenarios, relaunching periodically and demonstrating outcomes associated with the advocacy project could be influential.

In the end, for whatever strategy we need to formulate and the situation that we need to cope with, we should return to the 6 Steps of Successful Child Advocacy and reiterate as needed: knowing the advocacy issue, researching for background and impact, preparing effective materials, making meetings that work, conducting strategic follow-up, and reinforcing successful outcomes. As part of the last step, one needs to realize that thanking and recognizing the people involved in the process is important as it is basic human nature to desire being thanked and recognized for any efforts that one is part of. More importantly, giving the feeling of belongingness to those involved in the advocacy project and sharing the credit for success encourages people to be more proactive and help the cause.

After your meeting with the decision maker, promptly send a thank-you letter to the decision maker and key gatekeepers. In this letter, thank them for their time, and summarize the discussion from your meeting. Confirm the commitments and next steps discussed during the meeting. Let them know what they can expect from you in terms of follow-up, and offer to be an ongoing resource. Conclude the letter by asking what you can do to move the decision maker toward your goal, and let them know that you will inquire after a set time about the decision maker's intended actions regarding your specific ask. Ensure that the tone of your letter is polite, friendly, and respectful, not confrontational. See Box 8.2 for an outline of a follow-up letter.

BOX 8.2

Format for a Follow-Up Letter With a Decision Maker (Macro or Mezzo Advocacy)

[Date]

[Name of staffer, if applicable]

[The Honorable or other title]

[First name, last name]

[Address]

Dear [Title] [last name]:

Thank you for meeting with [me or my colleagues and me] on [date and place]. I am pleased that we had the opportunity to discuss [advocacy topic] and your position on [issue(s)].

(Continued)

(Continued)

[Briefly restate the issue(s) and what action(s) you want the decision maker to take. Also provide any follow-up information you may have promised.]

Again, thank you for meeting with [me/us]. Please contact me at [your phone number] or [your email address] if I can be of any assistance or if I can provide any additional information. I will continue to monitor [issue(s)] and will keep in touch with your office as developments occur.

Sincerely,

[your name and any credentials]

Source: Adapted from American Speech-Language-Hearing Association (n.d.). Meeting with your members of Congress locally: Follow-up thank you letter. Retrieved from http://www.asha.org/Advocacy/grassroots/thankyouLetter/

Follow-up is important for clarifying next steps. Your thank-you note will provide a record of the meeting and keep attendees accountable for their promised actions. Keep records of meetings with decision makers. Your records can include copies of your thank-you notes. It may also be helpful to create a meeting log, noting whom you met with, when, and for what purpose, as well as follow-up for the meeting.

Your communications with the decision maker after the meeting are a way to build relationships. Being professional in your communications and maintaining credibility by completing next steps as promised will establish your reputation. The goal is to position yourself as the go-to person on your issue and build a solid relationship with your target decision maker. Keep the door open for future conversations, even if you don't achieve your desired goal right away. Make the key decision maker a star of your advocacy efforts. Invite this person to events to see and be seen, and in the case of attendance, be sure to recognize him or her by mentioning "We have Senator X in the audience" and speaking well of him or her. If you receive support from a decision maker, document this on your website, blog, or other campaign communications.

For macro or mezzo advocacy, your meetings are likely to be with elected or appointed officials, and your goal may be to support or block proposed policy. The follow-up thank-you letter can begin to cement your relationship with the important gatekeepers who work with your target decision maker. Keep in mind that staff in legislators' offices must familiarize themselves with a broad range of issues and are not typically experts in a given subject. They must turn to outside experts to learn about the issues that their bosses will address. It is to their advantage and yours that you become a trusted expert that they can turn to with questions. The Children's Defense Fund is an advocacy organization well known for its strategic follow-up with decision makers. Its members work with legislators interested in children and families to educate them by providing regular updates on important issues and offering research that can help them author legislation or present before committees.

For micro advocacy on behalf of a specific child, you may be meeting with officials in the systems that hold power in the child's life—that is, schools, social services, and the court system. The same principle of a follow-up thank-you letter applies. You may be writing the letter to express appreciation, provide information, request information, or ask for or deny an action (Wright, 2007). When the stakes are personal, and a particular child's life is deeply affected by the consequences of a meeting, it can be difficult to maintain an objective stance. This can happen, for example, with meetings to arrange special education services for a particular child. Whether meetings go as desired or not, a storytelling approach is preferable to a blame approach. A *blame approach* expresses anger and frustration, which may be understandable but is unlikely to find a sympathetic ear. You may write a blame letter to release emotions, but never send it. Not only is such a letter unlikely to achieve the desired outcome; it can also be counterproductive and put decision makers on the defensive. Instead, use a *storytelling approach* that provides the details of the case, in chronological order and without assuming prior knowledge. Stick to the facts and maintain a neutral tone. Such a letter is likely to receive a better reception from decision makers and also becomes part of a record that may be seen by others along the decision chain. Coming across as reasonable improves your chances of realizing your goal. See Box 8.3 for examples of letters from a blame and a storytelling approach, both describing the same meeting and set of events.

BOX 8.3

Follow-Up Letter, the Blame Approach Versus the Storytelling Approach

Blame Approach

Dear Dr. Smith:

You asked that I advise you about my objections to the IEP that your "professional" staff of educators wrote for my daughter. Despite my own lack of training, I found that the IEP developed by your staff was absolutely preposterous. Let me share a few observations with you.

   Your staff FAILED to include anyone on the IEP team who thoroughly understands my daughter's background, including her current teachers.

   Your staff FAILED to perform any observation on my daughter before developing the IEP.

   Your staff FAILED to develop an appropriate IEP because they failed to include information from the new testing, and relied on outdated testing completed nearly a year ago.

   Your staff FAILED to develop an IEP that targeted her specific needs and unique abilities.

   Your staff FAILED to develop an IEP that includes objective criteria to measure progress or lack of progress.

   Your staff FAILED to develop an IEP that included any evaluation procedures to measure progress, as related to the annual goals and objectives that your staff wrote.

   (This list continues for several pages.)

   Given their years of training and experience, I would expect your staff to be capable of writing a simple IEP. Although I have no training whatsoever in how to write IEPs, even I can see how inadequate this document is.

(Continued)

(Continued)

As I examine the IEP developed by your staff, I can only conclude that they are incompetent and inept. This IEP proves that your staff are incapable of teaching my daughter who is smarter than your entire team.

Sincerely,
Bob Bombastic

Storytelling Approach

Dear Dr. Smith:

First, let me thank you for allowing me to participate in the development of my daughter's IEP. I appreciate your willingness to meet with me so that I could share my concerns about her and what she needs in her education.

At the IEP meeting last week, your staff was very kind in answering my questions. Their kindness was especially appreciated since I had not met most of the people at the IEP meeting before. I was very sorry that neither of my daughter's teachers could make the meeting. I understood that one teacher was on a field trip and the other teacher had a doctor's appointment.

I had concerns that we did not have enough time to develop an IEP for Carrie. Although 25 minutes was allotted for the IEP meeting, we started more than 10 minutes late. I understand that several earlier IEP meetings ran late. I know that things get very rushed at the end of the year, which makes scheduling these meetings especially difficult.

I was also concerned that we did not have time to discuss the recent testing done on Carrie. You may recall that I had additional testing completed on her two months ago. After I received the test results, I provided you with a copy of the new testing. At that time, I shared concerns with you that Carrie had not made any progress during the two years she's been receiving special education services.

Unfortunately, the results of this testing were not included in the new IEP. The psychologist thought the new test results may have been mislaid. Perhaps this is why the school team gave me an IEP to sign that placed Carrie back into the same program. You will recall that I expressed serious concerns about her IEP and its lack of objective measures and evaluation procedures.

I'm sure you can understand why I did not sign the IEP presented to me at this meeting. Given the rushed atmosphere and general confusion at that time, I thought it would be better to schedule another IEP meeting later, so that we can discuss these issues in depth. I thought the IEP team needed to have a chance to review the new testing before trying to write an IEP. I'm including another copy of the evaluation with this letter.

Please check with your staff and send me some times so that we can get together for a productive meeting. If you have any questions, please call or write.

Sincerely,
Jim Manners

Source: Wright, P. (1998). The art of writing letters. *Wrightslaw.* Retrieved from http://www.wrightslaw.com/advoc/articles/DRAFT_Letters.html

KEEPING THE ADVOCATES ENGAGED

Follow-up with your team of allies is important to sustain the momentum of your advocacy project. Keep advocates interested, excited, and prepared to do what needs to be done to achieve the advocacy goal. This can also be a time to widen your circle of support to attract more supporters to your cause. Continue to educate your team on the issue as it develops by providing updates on your progress and additional research on the issue. This will allow them to engage in effective advocacy.

The arc of change for achieving advocacy victories can be long. Most decision making comes in layers, and it is necessary to remain involved for every phase. For example, the various stages to get a piece of legislation passed in the U.S. Congress are described in the section Analyzing the Policy Context in Chapter 4 and include introduction of new legislation into the House of Representatives or Senate, study by committees and subcommittees, debate and vote in the original chamber, referral to committees and subcommittees in the other chamber, debate and vote in the secondary chamber, conference action to reconcile different versions, another floor vote in both chambers, and approval or veto by the president. Each of these stages can be an opportunity for influence.

For mezzo and macro advocacy, your team is those who share your advocacy goal of change on behalf of a group, community, or social issue. These allies can be crucial for bringing pressure to bear on an issue with decision makers like legislators. Aim for regular contact with your advocacy allies. This can take the form of newsletters or social media, as will be discussed in the next section. Motivate them by letting them know how their actions affect victories, big and small, and express appreciation. Thank people in the way they wish to be thanked, which may include writing a letter of recommendation or acting as a reference for a job. Develop personalized messages that express the importance of the issue and why they should be involved. Educate your team by providing them with tools and resources for advocacy, including your summary sheet and research materials from other organizations. Involve them by inviting them to strategy sessions or briefings and give them the opportunity to participate and make presentations. Send out action alerts when something is needed, such as phone calls to a legislator. Describe the urgency of the issue, why they should act, and what they should do. A show of strength on an issue at a crucial moment can tilt the balance to your favor.

The ICRI Brazil Project (described in Chapter 2, Box 2.3) was effective at keeping advocates engaged. Project coordinator Caius Brandão made his advocacy allies feel like a family. Many were Brazilian expatriates living in the San Francisco Bay Area, and he created a home for them within the ICRI office by speaking Portugese (with English translation for non-Brazilian advocates), decorating with Brazilian products, and creating a welcoming environment. He made advocates feel appreciated by recognizing a volunteer of the month, who was profiled in the campaign's monthly newsletter. He would invite advocates to events like a Capoeira (Brazilian martial art) benefit and a year-end holiday party. These efforts kept the group of advocates connected to each other and to the advocacy project.

For micro advocacy on behalf of a particular child, your allies may be others who are advocates like yourself but who are advocating on behalf of other children (such as parents, teachers, and guardians ad litem). In this case, you can support each other emotionally and help each other practically by exchanging information and tips on advocacy. For example, parents who advocate on behalf of their children with special needs can join parent support groups that meet in person or via the Internet and offer each other information on disabilities and methods for approaching special education that can result in more strategic advocacy (Trainor, 2010) and support that can reduce feelings of social isolation (Black & Baker, 2011). Parent groups can also provide specialized trainings and offer a chance to join with others for collective action (Madden, 1995).

Using social media is a dynamic way to remain in contact with decision makers, engage allies, and also spread the word to other important stakeholders, such as the media. The next section will describe different types of social media and how they can be used to support your advocacy plan.

EFFECTIVE USE OF SOCIAL MEDIA

The Internet and social media have transformed advocacy, enabling a new form of electronic advocacy, or *e-advocacy*. Social media encompasses the digital tools, such as cell phones, and applications, such as networking sites, that enable interaction and connectivity among users (Fine, 2006). E-advocacy holds particular promise in rallying supporters to a cause, distributing information, and promoting regular contact. Yet it also has limitations. E-advocacy has been criticized as armchair advocacy, or *slacktivsm*, combining a slacker mentality with activism that is nothing more than a click of a computer mouse. While some people may do nothing more than like your cause on Facebook, a study that surveyed a representative group of 2,000 Americans suggests that people who use social media to engage with social causes also participate in other activities at rates similar to or greater than those who do not use social media. This study also found that participants still preferred traditional forms of engagement, such as volunteering, donating money, and talking to others about a cause, and that these forms of engagement gave them a greater feeling of being a champion for a cause (Ogilvy Public Relations Worldwide & Georgetown University's Center for Social Impact Communication, 2011). These findings suggest the importance of combining e-advocacy with traditional forms of advocacy.

The challenge with e-advocacy is to translate the awareness raised through social media into action (Morozov, 2009). Its best use is to enhance, not replace, offline, in-person activities by sharing information about events and asking people to engage in timely actions such as sending letters and attending rallies and meetings. To keep engagement and momentum at a high level for your advocacy project, offer meaningful opportunities for participation through social media and ask for input and guidance on the forms that participation may take. For example, if your project needs to raise funds or recruit volunteers, engage your supporters in a conversation through social media about how to achieve these aims (Fine, 2006). In their book *The Dragonfly Effect*, Aaker and Smith (2010) recommend a four-prong strategy to use social media to advance a change effort. First, determine a single, concrete, and measurable goal for your social media efforts. Second, grab attention through material that connects with people through novelty, imagery, and personal appeal. Third, engage and create a connection that will make the audience want to do something through establishing authenticity, telling a story, and encouraging feelings of empathy.

Fourth, empower people to take action, preferably in ways that are easy and fun, and that build on their unique strengths.

Social media options change as new platforms emerge and others fall out of favor. There are many possible tools, and it is easy to feel overwhelmed. In terms of crafting your social media strategy, focus on the principles that underlie social media: communication, collaboration, content, and collective action (Fine, 2006). These categories are not mutually exclusive, and one form of social media can enable more than one of these strategies (see Box 8.4, Uses and Examples of Social Media for Advocacy). When considering which platform to use, a good rule of thumb is to start where your supporters are. You can informally survey your allies to learn which forms of social media they already favor. When you are ready to reach out to a new audience, you might consider expanding your use of social media. Choose a core location for your activity where you can have a lot of information and centralize your activity and use social media to drive traffic toward your core. For example, your core could be a website, Facebook page, or blog, and you can use other forms of social media like Twitter and LinkedIn to encourage people to visit your core for new information and opportunities to interact.

BOX 8.4		
Uses and Examples of Social Media for Advocacy		
Principles Underlying Social Media[1]	**Definition**	**Examples of Social Media Tools**
Communicate	Enable many people to share information and participate in a conversation	• Listservs • Text messages • LinkedIn • Facebook
Collaborate	Work together online to produce joint content or aggregate and curate individual contributions	• Wikis • Storybanks • Video collages • Photo pools
Content	Create new materials in the forms of text, photographs, audio, and video	• Blogs • Twitter • YouTube • Instagram
Collective action	Enable online or offline actions such as circulating petitions, fundraising, and setting up meetings	• Change.org • Network for Good • Meetup • Twitter

[1]*Source:* Fine, A. (2006). *Momentum: Igniting social change in the connected age.* San Francisco, CA: Jossey-Bass.

Communication is enabled by many forms of social media, allowing for group conversations. Social media that enables communication can be used to stay in contact with decision makers as well as your team of advocates. A simple place to start with social media can be electronic mailing lists or e-newsletters. Electronic mailing lists, also called listservs, allow users to share information via email, whereas e-newsletters typically are sent from a centralized source out to an audience. Text messages can also be used to communicate with a group, using cell phone messaging. Start to build your list of supporters through events, or allow people to add themselves to your distribution list online. Social media networking sites, such as Facebook and LinkedIn, are also ways to promote communication. Special features on Facebook include Causes, which allows followers to make donations and add your cause to their own page, and Events, which allows you to publicize and track planned attendance at offline events. LinkedIn has a group option that allows people to connect over a shared interest. A study of social media use by advocacy organizations found Facebook to be the most popular, valued in particular for its ability to facilitate civic engagement through education and collective action (Obar, Zube, & Lampe, 2012). In addition to creating your own advocacy project site on a social network, you can also post on other people's sites in order to represent your cause. For example, decision makers who are elected officials often have official sites on platforms like Facebook that will allow you to engage with the decision maker's staff by asking questions and posting information.

Social media communication can be taken to the next level through collaboration on projects. This is a way for participants in an advocacy project to be engaged in developing the tools used to educate, inform, and persuade others. A wiki is a prime example of collaboration using social media. Users are allowed to change the content of a wiki, allowing people to create resources like Wikipedia, a user-created online encyclopedia. You can also invite and curate individual contributions, creating a final product that is greater than the sum of its parts. Video collages and photo pools are two ways that users can contribute multimedia dedicated to a specific cause, using websites like Tumblr, providing you with material that can be used to advance an advocacy campaign. Another method is storybanking (described in Chapter 5, in the section called Secondary Research). For example, Half in Ten has an online storybank that invites written or video stories that highlight how U.S. federal programs have impacted people's lives through promoting economic security and meeting basic needs. This project allows people to be part of a tapestry of stories that can be used to advocate against budget cuts.

Social media allows users to create and share content in a variety of forms and ways. One format is through web diaries known as blogs that typically share written content in the form of news and opinion and often allow viewers to leave comments. Content and collaboration can be combined through group blogs that allow a set of users to collaborate together, or individual bloggers can jointly participate in a blog week with set topics about a social issue. Twitter is an application that enables microblogs, or messages with no more than 140 characters, called a tweet. Twitter can be used to share messages, tag messages with a hashtag (using the symbol #) to signify the topic and share the conversation more widely, follow other users like influential decision makers, and repost other users' content by retweeting. Social media also allows users to share audio in the form of podcasts, photographs on websites like Instagram, and video through platforms like YouTube. Sites like Twitter and Instagram can be used to share a photo a day, keeping your supporters engaged through vivid images that show the importance of your work. An example of an advocacy campaign using YouTube is "It Gets Better," a campaign that invited lesbian, gay, bisexual, and transgender (LGBT) adults to upload videos about their lives to reassure LGBT teenagers that life can indeed get better if they can make it through the difficult experiences during adolescence of bullying and exclusion due to their sexual orientations.

Beyond creating and sharing information, social media can be used for collective action, online and offline. Collective action online can take the form of online petitions to demonstrate the level of concern about a social issue, using websites such as Change.org. Nicholas Kristof (2012) highlighted an example of schoolchildren who used a petition on Change.org to successfully pressure a major movie studio to amend the promotional website for the movie *The Lorax* to include content on the film's environmental message. Another example of online collective action is fundraising. Advocacy campaigns can integrate a "donate now" button into their websites and collect money through companies like Network for Good and use other forms of social media like Facebook to keep supporters apprised of the amount of money raised and progress toward meeting the goal. Combine these different principles of social media by creating a social media calendar with messages that you can send out to encourage timely advocacy activities. See Box 8.5 for a social media calendar designed to create awareness and activism around proposed cuts to early childhood services in California. Social media can also be a way to organize people to meet offline for events, protests, and volunteer work. Twitter has famously been used to spread the word about the time and location of protests and to communicate among activists on the ground. Meetup is another way to attract people to your cause and encourage offline meetings; users can create Meetup groups by posting a description of the group and its location, and users find groups by searching for topics within a certain location.

BOX 8.5

Example of Social Media Calendar for Campaign Against Budget Cuts for Early Childhood Care and Education in California

Day	Principles Underlying Social Media[1]	Social Media Platform	Statement
		Week 1	
Monday	Communicate, collective action	Website, Facebook, LinkedIn	Take a stand against budget cuts! Governor Brown's proposed child care realignment would dismantle California's child care system, cut 62,000 children from their child care programs, and put over 100,000 child care workers' jobs at risk! Take Action! Sign the petition: https://www.change.org/petitions/the-governor-of-ca-take-

(Continued)

(Continued)

Day	Principles Underlying Social Media[1]	Social Media Platform	Statement
			child-care-and-calworks-proposed-cuts-off-the-table?
Tuesday	Communicate, collective action	Twitter	Come out to the state capitol for #Stand for Children Day! Represent children! For more information: http://www.parentvoices.org
Wednesday	Collaborate, content	Twitter, Tumblr, Facebook	Post your photos from #Stand for Children Day on Tumblr. Tell your story about the personal impacts of cuts on Facebook. Show our strength!
Thursday	Communicate	Website, Facebook, LinkedIn	California's current child care delivery system is intended to meet the needs of diverse families, but with the proposed realignment, many of these families will lose their child care. For more information, visit the link below: http://www.lao.ca.gov/analysis/2012/ss/calworks-child-care-022212.aspx
Friday	Collective action	Facebook, LinkedIn	Take action by making a phone call to your legislator! Use the script found at: http://www.parentvoices.org/campaigns/state-budget-organizing.html as your guide.
Week 2			
Monday	Communicate	Twitter, YouTube	What do we want? CHILD CARE! When do we want it? NOW! #Child Care #Reject Governor's Proposal http://www.youtube.com/watch?v=zb5qg4KrTW0
Tuesday	Collective action	Website, Facebook, LinkedIn	Let your voice be heard! Write your representatives urging them to reject the proposal: https://secure3.convio.net/cccrrn/site/Advocacy?cmd=display&page=UserAction&id=123

Day	Principles Underlying Social Media[1]	Social Media Platform	Statement
Wednesday	Communicate, content	Facebook, LinkedIn	Learn about how the quality of subsidized preschools is being reduced. "The goal of state preschool programs is to prepare the children to thrive—socially, emotionally, and academically—in kindergarten and beyond." Check out this article and repost it on Facebook and LinkedIn as your update: http://www.mercurynews.com/ci_20360515/report-funding-cuts-are-eroding-quality-nations-subsidized?IADID
Thursday	Communicate, collective action	Website, Facebook, LinkedIn	Help people learn about the issues! Hand out the summary sheet found at: http://www.pre school california.org/resources/resource-files/californias-child.pdf in your community.
Friday	Collaborate, content	Website, Facebook	Make a submission to our story bank about how budget cuts are affecting you, your family, and your community. Share the link to the story bank with your friends and family on Facebook.

[1]*Source:* Fine, A. (2006). *Momentum: Igniting social change in the connected age.* San Francisco, CA: Jossey-Bass.

Source: This social media calendar is adapted from one developed by students in the course CAD 650: Child Advocacy, at San Francisco State University, as part of a community service learning project.

Social media is a powerful tool for connecting with potential champions and allies. When planning your social media strategy, consider your goals. Are you seeking to educate, build community around a cause, or motivate a particular kind of action? You can also monitor your effectiveness by using social media metrics. For example, you can track engagement of your supporters by observing how often people comment on your posts and which types of messages seem to attract the most attention. Explore the reach of your message by tracking your numbers of followers on Twitter and Facebook and noting the frequency of reposts (Vocell, 2012). There are also analytic sites that can help you track the exposure that your campaign is receiving; for example, you can set up a Google Alert that tracks different types of content like news and blogs and lets you know when keywords are mentioned. The activity at the end of the chapter provides some questions to consider for planning your use of social media. The next section describes a case study of how an advocacy organization uses social media to achieve its goals.

Case Study: Mama Hope in Africa

Mama Hope is a nonprofit organization serving communities throughout sub-Saharan Africa. It operates on the vision that there are enough resources in the world to enable every human being to live a healthy and happy life, and this can be achieved by sharing resources across the globe and providing tools to communities that they need to thrive. Mama Hope's model is to raise funding for local African organizations to carry out the projects that their communities need, such as construction of schools, health clinics, children's centers, clean water systems, and food security projects. The organization started in 2006 after founder Nyla Rodgers lost her mother to cancer and traveled to Kenya to see a women's project that she had sponsored. It was her mother's wish that she carry on fundraising for the project, and that was the beginning of Mama Hope and the first of many projects it has sponsored.

In addition to directly funding social programs, Mama Hope initiated an advocacy campaign called the Stop the Pity movement. The motivation behind this project is a desire to change the way that Africa is represented by the social marketing of nonprofit organizations that play on pity to encourage people to donate out of guilt. Instead, Mama Hope wants to tell a story of inspiration and the potential of communities to help themselves when they have the resources they need. Rather than giving out of guilt, Mama Hope wants people to give to projects in Africa out of a feeling that the people there are an extension of themselves and are more similar than different. Rather than showing them as deserving of pity, Mama Hope wants communities to be depicted as full of strength and possibility so that they will feel good about the way they are portrayed in social marketing materials. The goal of this project is ultimately to transform the narrative used to describe sub-Saharan Africa in the Western world from one of pity to one of partnership and to encourage people to be critical about the stereotypes used to depict Africa.

Social media is key to the Stop the Pity movement. The campaign uses a variety of social media platforms, including Facebook, Twitter, and YouTube, to spread its message. It seeks to connect with a specific audience of primarily young people who are innovative, disillusioned with traditional development practices, and interested in speaking out and getting involved. Mama Hope *communicates* with this audience with Twitter, Facebook, Instagram, and blogs that share stories and photos from the Mama Hope projects in Africa. A community has grown around Mama Hope and has conversations in the comment fields of social media platforms like Facebook. The organization shares *content* that focuses on the capabilities of the community and illustrates the central message that once communities receive resources, they can take care of themselves. These themes come alive in videos the organization has created and posted to YouTube that receive tens of thousands of views and are shared throughout the Internet to reach a wider audience. Mama Hope *collaborates* with other organizations in the Stop the Pity movement, expanding the support base for the campaign and broadening its exposure. Part of this collaboration entails cross promoting other organizations and sharing the materials they have developed and information on their events and projects through Mama Hope's Facebook and Twitter accounts. The connection that Mama Hope has made with its supporters inspires *collective action,* especially in the form of fundraising. The organization has found fundraising efforts with a time limit that allow people to have an instant impact to be most effective: for example, spreading the news on Twitter and Facebook requesting $2,000 for a water improvement project for International Water Week, asking people to give $20, and sending updates on the amount raised and how the money will be used. Integrating donations with other forms of social media has also worked well, so when people make donations to Mama Hope, the news of this donation is registered on their Facebook wall. Another form of action that Mama Hope encourages is for people to be critical observers of social marketing related to Africa and call out organizations that use pity and stereotypes in their materials. Social media has given Mama Hope a significant international presence and allowed their staff and operations to expand, from one person and one project in 2006 to eleven staff in the United States and Africa and ten projects in 2013, with a growing number of volunteers and new projects in the pipeline.

Activity: Using Social Media in Your Advocacy Project

Think about how you might use social media in your advocacy project by responding to this self-assessment:

1. How comfortable are you with using social media? What forms of social media do you currently use? If you are primarily using one or two platforms, explore other options mentioned in this chapter.

2. What forms of social media do you think your potential allies use? What about influential decision makers on your topic? If you are unsure, you can do a quick survey using free online programs like SurveyMonkey and SurveyGizmo.

3. What types of materials are you most likely to share from your advocacy project: text, photos, video, or audio?

4. What do you hope to achieve using social media? For example, are you seeking primarily to raise awareness or raise funds? Will you use social media for communication, collaboration, content, or collective action?

5. How much time and effort will you invest in social media? Consider creating a social media calendar (see Box 8.5) that will help create structure.

6. How will you track the impact of your social media work?

7. Will you have a central platform that will be the core location for your online activity? How can you use other forms of social media to drive people toward your core?

8. How often will you review your social media strategy and reassess the platforms you use and the messages you send? You might schedule a time to review your strategy on a regular basis, such as quarterly.

REFERENCES

Aaker, J., & Smith, A. (2010). *The dragonfly effect: Quick, effective, and powerful ways to use social media to drive social change.* San Francisco, CA: Jossey-Bass.

American Speech-Language-Hearing Association (n.d.). *Meeting with your members of Congress locally: Follow-up thank you letter.* Retrieved from http://www.asha.org/Advocacy/grassroots/thankyouLetter/

Black, A. P., & Baker, M. (2011). The impact of parent advocacy groups, the Internet, and social networking on rare diseases: The IDEA League and the IDEA League United Kingdom example. *Epilepsia, 52*(2), 102–104.

Fine, A. (2006). *Momentum: Igniting social change in the connected age.* San Francisco, CA: Jossey-Bass.

Kristof, N. (2012, February 4). After recess, change the world. *New York Times,* p. SR11. Retrieved from http://www.nytimes.com/2012/02/05/opinion/sunday/kristof-after-recess-change-the-world.html

Madden, P. (1995, September 5). Why parents: How parents. *British Journal of Learning Disabilities, 23*(3), 90–93.

Morozov, E. (2009). From slacktivism to activism. *Foreign Policy.* Retrieved from http://neteffect.foreignpolicy.com/posts/2009/09/05/from_slacktivism_to_activism?wpisrc=obinsite

Obar, J. A., Zube, P., & Lampe, C. (2012). Advocacy 2.0: An analysis of how advocacy groups in the United States perceive and use social media as tools for facilitating civic engagement and collective action. *Journal of Information Policy, 2,* 1–25.

Ogilvy Public Relations Worldwide, & Georgetown University's Center for Social Impact Communication (2011, November). *Dynamics of cause engagement.* Retrieved from http://www.slideshare.net/georgetowncsic/dynamics-of-cause-engagement-final-report

Trainor, A. (2010). Diverse approaches to parent advocacy during special education home school interactions. *Remedial and Special Education, 31,* 34–47.

Vocell, J. (2012, October 17). 5 social media metrics you should be monitoring. *Social Media Today.* Retrieved from http://socialmediatoday.com/jvocell/914271/5-social-media-metrics-you-should-be-monitoring

Wright, P. (1998). The art of writing letters. *Wrightslaw.* Retrieved from http://www.wrightslaw.com/advoc/articles/DRAFT_Letters.html

Wright, P. (2007). 12 Rules for writing great letters. *Wrightslaw.* Retrieved from http://www.wrightslaw.com/advoc/articles/12rules_letters.htm

CHAPTER 9

Step 6—Reinforcing Successful Advocacy Outcomes

The advocacy project concludes with Step 6 as advocates learn from their experiences and work to reinforce the outcomes they have achieved. After completing all of the previous steps, you may have reached a positive outcome. If that is the case, it is important to thank the decision makers who played a role in your advocacy success. This chapter explains that most decision makers wish to be thanked in a public manner that will help voters and colleagues to see them in the most positive light. Using the opportunity to thank the decision maker can provide an opportunity to secure a long-term partner in future advocacy efforts. Now is also the time to evaluate the advocacy project and assess the information you have been monitoring throughout the process. Evaluation enables the advocate to learn from experience and to modify and improve strategies for your current project as well as future endeavors. Good planning and forethought often lead to advocacy success. However, there are occasions when advocacy projects are unsuccessful. A case study of an unsuccessful child advocacy campaign is examined for lessons learned to inform future advocacy.

THE IMPORTANCE OF REINFORCING SUCCESSFUL ADVOCACY OUTCOMES

If your advocacy project has achieved its objectives and goals, congratulations! However, even after reaching success, your work as an advocate is not quite over. At this stage in your project, it is essential to maintain the positive will you have engendered and the relationships you have built with other advocates, gatekeepers, and decision makers. This will ensure that you can turn your first child advocacy victory into a lifetime of good work on behalf of children and families (as discussed in Chapter 10, "Where Do We Go From Here?").

If you have worked with others on your advocacy project, take time to celebrate your victory. Acknowledge the individual contributions of your team members and how your joint effort has led to success. This can be a time to share your evaluation findings (as discussed in the next section). You may also be ready to start planting the seeds for your next advocacy project by identifying what else needs to be done to fully achieve your advocacy goal or expand from your original focus to address other issues facing children and families. For example, you may win a legislative victory but need to monitor that legislation to make sure that it is implemented properly. Recall the policy process described in Chapter 4, in the section called Analyzing the Policy Context. The actual change you are seeking happens during the implementation phase, so continue to follow what happens to make sure that the policy is implemented as planned. Another scenario is a legislative victory for a policy that has a sunset clause. This means that the policy must be reconsidered and reauthorized after a certain interval (e.g., 10 years). See Box 9.1 for a discussion of an advocacy effort to sustain a piece of legislation with a sunset clause. If this is the case for your advocacy victory, you will need to plan a future advocacy project to assure the continued existence and success of the legislation.

BOX 9.1

San Francisco's Groundbreaking Children's Amendment

By Margaret Brodkin, Margaret Brodkin and Associates and former
Executive Director of Coleman Advocates for Children and Youth (United States)

How It Came to Be

Four years of advocacy work and coalition building to increase funding for children in the city budget of San Francisco preceded the creation and passage of the Children's Fund in 1991. The work was led by the city's major child advocacy organization, Coleman Advocates for Children and Youth. It was the frustration of year-to-year budget battles which spawned the idea of a Fiscal Bill of Rights for children—hard-wiring funding for children's services into the charter of the city. An amendment to the city charter creating a dedicated funding stream was proposed by the Children's Budget Coalition after 4 years of effort. All of the elected officials opposed the idea—saying that it was bad public policy and would tie their hands (of course that was the idea). Children's advocates, led by Coleman, proceeded to circumvent city hall and go directly to the voters—collecting 68,000 signatures, sufficient to have the measure placed on the ballot. When children pulling little red wagons entered city hall to submit the signatures, the politics of children in San Francisco changed forever. Suddenly almost every elected official chose to support the measure, and it passed by 54.5% of the vote.

What It Does

The Children's Fund sets aside 3% of the property tax revenues exclusively for children's services, specifically for child care and early education; recreation, cultural, and after-school programs; health services; training employment and job placement; youth empowerment and leadership development; youth violence prevention programs; youth tutoring and educational enrichment; and family and parent support services. In order to ensure that the Fund is not used to supplant existing services, the charter amendment creating the Fund requires the city to establish a Children's Baseline Budget, a calculation of city spending on kids prior to the Fund—and an amount which the city cannot reduce. The charter amendment creating the Fund also established a needs assessment and planning process for children's services.

Accomplishments

The Children's Fund has transformed children's services. It funds over 250 programs, serving almost 50% of the city's child population. The current Fund is close to $50 million annually. It has created a stable funding base and prevented cuts in locally funded services. It has also leveraged millions in other revenues for children's programs and empowered an entity in city government to be a voice and program generator for children—the Department of Children, Youth, and their Families. Most of the money goes to community-based agencies. The Fund has been an engine of innovation—leading to new models of service, new neighborhoods being served, and new target populations.

Keeping the Children's Fund Alive

The original Children's Fund was set to sunset 10 years after it passed. The reauthorization campaign, which was conducted in 2000, engaged all of the beneficiaries of the Fund, including an active voice for young people. The measure passed by 74%, 20 points higher than the first time around. By then, the Fund had been integrated into the city budget. Although the measure was put on the ballot by a unanimous vote of the board of supervisors (demonstrating a complete political turnabout from the initial measure), the campaign was again run through Coleman by a coalition of community groups.

The second Children's Fund measure was written to sunset after 15 years—in 2016. As that time approaches, community groups are again organizing a coalition to support the measure as well as to improve transparency, community input, and to expand services to under-served populations, such as transitional age youth. This time the folks in city hall are planning to rewrite the measure and lead the campaign themselves. This causes inevitable and familiar tensions between the advocates and the establishment. So here's the question: Is the fact that city officials now want to own the Children's Fund campaign a sign of institutionalization and political success? Or is it a potential co-optation of what was once a community-driven triumph?

Gatekeepers and decision makers, especially decision makers, need to and want to be thanked publicly. The impact of the thanks is to put them in the best possible light with their supervisor or with their district's voters. The authors call this "thank-you as a form of behavior modification." By thanking them in a positive and public manner, you can modify the behavior of these powerful figures to make them your allies for life, or at least until your next advocacy campaign. For micro advocacy, which often involves a decision maker who is an administrator or holds an unelected position, a thank-you may come in the form of a letter to that person's supervisor, praising the work of the decision maker. You can also

*Importance of relationships

share your positive experience with others in your school or community by word-of-mouth, enhancing the decision maker's reputation. With mezzo or macro advocacy, particularly involving policy advocacy with an elected decision maker, a strategy of public recognition involving the media is recommended.

A way to thank the decision maker publically, particularly an elected official, is through a recognition event. There are a few critical things needed to honor decision makers. First, thank the decision maker in a way that highlights his or her contribution to your campaign and positively depicts this person. You can do this by giving the decision maker a gift, such as an engraved plaque, that will be seen in his or her office and spark conversations for many months to come. Second, invite the media and follow up to make sure that representatives will be in attendance. If possible, involve broadcast and print media and even local citizens who are active through social media such as community blogs. Third, make sure the decision maker leaves your event understanding that your advocacy group is the best one he or she could work with to make change in the district.

This strategy of holding a decision maker recognition event was used for an advocacy campaign that resulted in the passage of legislation for a family stress center (described in Chapter 2 in the section titled Influencing Outcomes: Gatekeepers and Decision Makers). The group of advocates from the Childcare Council of Contra Costa County held an event for Senator Dan Boatwright, thanking him for tenaciously fighting to get the bill passed. The event was held at a public auditorium. The Senator was given a plaque by the advocates with photo opportunities for the media in attendance. In a follow-up interview after the event, the team leader for the advocacy project was interviewed by the largest newspaper in the county about the impact of the senator's work on his district. The advocate clearly stated that Senator Boatwright had improved conditions for children because the senator had championed legislation for Contra Costa County's new Family Stress Center that without his support would never have gone through. Weeks later, this advocate was walking the halls of the state legislature when someone came up behind him and captured him in a bear hug. As the advocate turned around, he saw Senator Boatwright standing there with a smile on his face. Senator Boatwright stated, "I hear that you've been saying good things about me in the district." A complimentary statement in the media is gold to an elected decision maker. This type of relationship building between advocate and decision maker can nurture a mutually beneficial connection that allows the advocate to continue to achieve advocacy successes and provides the decision maker with expertise and collaboration to develop legislation on behalf of children and families.

The importance of media when publicly thanking the decision maker cannot be overstated. Media is the prime way that elected decision makers are able to connect with their constituencies, so they greatly value positive coverage. A story once told by (the late) California state senator Nick Petris illustrates this. Senator Petris explained that he was invited to meetings or celebrations in his district by a wide variety of groups and could not attend all the events in a given year. Every year a powerful professional association invited him to their annual meeting with nearly 600 members in attendance. On the same day and time, he was always invited to an event at the local botanical gardens held by the rose society with an active membership of under 50 people. The rose society invited all of the local and one regional television station, and the event appeared every year on the 6:00 p.m., 10:00 p.m., and 11:00 p.m. television news. Senator Petris attended the rose society meeting every year, much to the chagrin of the large professional association. He even tried to get the association not to have its event on the same night as the rose society. This example illustrates the importance of media to politicians. You may have a group of 15 members as your advocacy coalition, but if you have access to print, broadcast, and social media, you can still deliver a powerful form of recognition and reinforcement to the decision maker and his or her gatekeeper.

MONITORING AND EVALUATION

As mentioned in Chapter 3 (in the section titled Developing Your Advocacy Plan), evaluation is an essential part of your advocacy work. While this more extended discussion of monitoring and evaluation is located here in Step 6, advocates are encouraged to think about these processes from the very beginning of their projects. *Monitoring* involves tracking the outputs of your work by assessing how your activities and materials are moving your project toward its objectives. *Evaluation* entails measuring the short- and medium-term outcomes (called interim outcomes) that are the changes resulting from your work and the impacts that are the concrete changes in people's lives due to your advocacy (Laney, 2003). In other words, "Monitoring . . . seeks to understand what is happening. Evaluation seeks to understand why what happened, happened" (BOND, n.d.). Consider who will use this information and how they will use it—the most important audience is the advocates themselves. Monitoring and evaluation are important for learning from your experience, changing your approach as needed, and ensuring accountability for your efforts to your stakeholders and funders (Harvard Family Research Project, 2009).

Evaluating advocacy bears some similarities to evaluating the outcomes of programs and services, but it also brings some distinct challenges. These challenges particularly hold for mezzo or macro advocacy efforts intended to bring about new policies or other forms of social change. One challenge is that achieving the intended policy or other social change cannot be the sole measure of success. Achieving changes of this nature can require decades as public opinion changes and political will shifts. As the case study at the end of this chapter describes, there can be short-term outcomes that are also important, such as influencing public perceptions on your advocacy topic. It is important to document these short- and medium-term successes in part to sustain the financial support of funders who require accountability and demonstrated results (DeVita, Montilla, Reid, & Fatiregun, 2004). Another challenge is that it can be difficult to attribute a success such as policy change to the efforts of a specific advocacy campaign (Baumgartner & Leech, 1998). How can advocates prove that their efforts caused the result rather than the work of other advocates or other competing explanations for the change? Advocates can use evaluation to demonstrate contribution to the outcome rather than claiming attribution of the change to their efforts alone. A third challenge is that advocacy takes place within a political and historical context that plays a major role in the potential for success. Strategies that work for one issue at a particular time may not transfer to another issue at another time. Advocacy campaigns that are successful dynamically respond to these conditions and change tactics as needed, complicating the evaluation process of determining what worked (Teles & Schmitt, 2011). Despite these challenges, there are strategies that can be used to monitor and evaluate your advocacy work.

Creating a logic model is a helpful way to plan your advocacy project (see discussion of logic models in the section called Developing Your Advocacy Plan in Chapter 3) as well as your monitoring and evaluation work. It is ideal to include the development of a logic model in your planning, but if that does not occur, it can be helpful to construct one prior to engaging in monitoring and evaluation (Whelan, 2008). A logic model shows the connections between the *inputs* or resources you have, the *activities* you will engage in, the *outputs* or products of your work, and the *short-term* and *medium-term outcomes* you hope to achieve (also sometimes called *proximal* and *distal outcomes*) that meet your target goal as well as the ultimate *impact* or real-world change you plan to accomplish. Hoefer (2011) calls this process of developing a logic model to guide your project *advocacy mapping* because it helps advocates understand where they are and where they plan to go. You can use the logic model template in this chapter (see Box 9.2) or construct your logic model using the Advocacy Progress Planner from the Aspen Institute, http://planning.continuous-progress.org/. This online tool will guide you through identifying goals and impacts, audiences (decision makers and gatekeepers), context, activities, inputs, and benchmarks to measure your progress.

BOX 9.2

Logic Model Template

| Inputs | Activities | Outputs | Outcomes | | Impacts |
			Short-Term	Medium-Term	

Use your logic model to monitor your outputs, also called *activity or tactic measures* (Harvard Family Research Project, 2009), which are counts of concrete activities, people, or events (see Box 9.3 for examples). Monitoring is ongoing, and the purpose is to identify where your plan is succeeding and where it needs to be changed. While evaluation focuses on achievements, monitoring is about understanding processes. When deciding how to track the outputs of your work, consider collecting information in these areas to inform your ongoing advocacy strategy:

- Internal issues: How are your advocacy team members interacting, and how well are your advocacy activities being implemented?
- External issues: What is happening in the political and social context of your advocacy project, and how might these events affect the results of your project?

- Collaborative issues: How is your team of advocates cooperating with other possible individuals and organizations that might be allies to meet your goal?
- Progress toward objectives: What kinds of changes have occurred that move you toward the objectives and goals of your advocacy project? (O'Flynn, 2009)

Track the key audiences that may affect the success of your advocacy, which may include decision makers, gatekeepers, allies, media, and the public. For example, if your target decision maker is an elected official, monitor his statements and gauge whether his rhetoric is moving closer to your position (BOND, n.d.). Your approach can be informal, such as keeping a log of your project activities and recording significant communications with decision makers and allies, minutes of meetings and events, and media coverage of your campaign. If you are using social media in your advocacy project (as discussed in Chapter 8, "Step 5—Conducting Strategic Follow-Up"), there are a number of metrics that you can use to track the impact of your messaging and materials. These include monitoring your email listserv growth; numbers of Twitter followers; number of friends on Facebook; and frequency that content is liked, commented upon, or shared (M+R Strategic Services & Nonprofit Technology Network, 2013). You can share this real-time information to keep your fellow advocates engaged and updated on the advocacy project (see the section in Chapter 8, titled Keeping the Advocates Engaged).

BOX 9.3

Examples of Advocacy Outputs, Interim Outcomes, and Impacts

Level of Advocacy	Outputs	Interim Outcomes	Impacts
Micro	• Number of letters written on behalf of the child • Number of meetings attended with key decision makers	• Improved capacity of the advocate, as demonstrated by increased knowledge of the issue and skills for advocacy • Increased decision maker knowledge, as demonstrated by greater awareness of the child's condition or needs	• Appropriate services for the target child, including easier access to services and higher quality services
Mezzo	• Number of events and attendance at community events	• Growth in constituency base, as measured by number of website visits or social media followers	

(Continued)

(Continued)

Level of Advocacy	Outputs	Interim Outcomes	Impacts
	• Number of meetings with decision makers	• Decision maker support, as measured by specific favorable actions	• Improved social and physical conditions for the target community or group of children, including better outcomes such as improved safety
Macro	• Number of allies and constituencies represented (e.g., business, nonprofits) • Number of meetings with policy makers and types of policy makers (e.g., key committee members)	• Increased visibility of the advocacy project, as measured by number and type of invitations to speak as experts • Increased political will on the issue, as measured by number of political officials who publicly support the advocacy project	• Improved services or systems for the target population, including more effective and available programs

Source: Adapted from Harvard Family Research Project (2009). A User's Guide to Advocacy Evaluation Planning. Retrieved from http://www.hfrp.org/evaluation/publications-resources/a-user-s-guide-to-advocacy-evaluation-planning

Measure achievement of interim outcomes and impacts with evaluation (see Box 9.3 for examples of advocacy interim outcomes and impacts). Evaluation typically takes place at a discreet point in time, either midway through or periodically throughout an advocacy project (called *formative* evaluation) or at the completion of the project (called *summative* evaluation). When it occurs along the way, evaluation can be used for course correction to change your advocacy plan, whereas evaluation that occurs at the end of a project can be used to learn lessons for future ones. As mentioned in Chapter 3, evaluation is *internal* when it is conducted by members of the advocacy team or *external* when conducted by someone outside the project like a volunteer or paid consultant. To develop your evaluation plan, refer back to your planning blueprint (Chapter 3). As stated in the planning blueprint, evaluation answers the following question: "Have the activities that have been carried out met their performance measures, which have gone to meet the objectives and desired outcomes?" Advocacy evaluations typically answer these questions:

- Were the original objectives achieved, and to what degree?
- How did the objectives change over the course of the project, and why?

- What were the impacts, if any, on advocacy targets (i.e., a specific child, group, or category of children)?
- Which specific strategies worked and which did not?
- What factors in the external environment contributed to success or failure? (O'Flynn, 2009)

In your evaluation, you ultimately want to learn whether your efforts have resulted in the desired change for children. But it is also important, particularly for formative evaluations, to measure the milestones along the way to ultimate impact. These interim outcomes can include building your coalition by recruiting new advocates and inspiring advocacy activities among your allies, gaining new champions by winning gatekeepers and decision makers over to your cause and encouraging action on their part, and promoting interest in your issue by increasing the percentage of your target audience that knows and cares about the topic (Harvard Family Research Project, 2009). Fine (2006) recommends that efforts to create social change, particularly those using social media, measure connectedness, meaningful participation, and use of information as means to documenting progress. *Connectedness* is about developing relationships with a broad base of support and engaging those supporters in two-way conversations in an effort to influence the way they think and behave with regard to the advocacy issue. *Meaningful participation* is about creating a variety of opportunities to participate in an advocacy effort and keeping allies engaged. *Use of information* is about assessing the quality of materials and whether the information is useful and inspires action. Choose measures that are most meaningful and useful for your campaign; it is better to be selective and track the data that can help your project rather than get overwhelmed with too much data (Harvard Family Research Project, 2009).

An advocacy evaluation can use the same research methods as described in Chapter 5, "Step 2—Research for Background and Impact" (see section called Primary Research). The research approach may be quantitative, to collect numerical data on your effectiveness, or qualitative, to understand the influence of your project through narrative information like stories and statements. Common methods used for advocacy evaluation include key stakeholder interviews that provide perspectives and feedback on your project, case studies that provide detailed descriptions of advocacy strategies and results, focus groups that gather opinions and ideas from important audiences, participant observation that gives the evaluator a perspective on the project by sitting in on meetings and events for firsthand experience, and public opinion polling that gauges the attitudes and knowledge of a constituency (Coffman & Reed, n.d.).

There are also methods that are specific to advocacy evaluation, including bellwether methodology, policy maker ratings, intense period debriefs, and systems mapping. *Bellwether methodology* is helpful for policy advocacy that seeks to change political will on an issue and can be used to determine whether certain advocacy messages have reached key audiences. Using this method, an external evaluator interviews influential figures, or bellwethers, related and unrelated to the advocacy issue (without informing the participants about the topic in advance so that their responses are authentic and spontaneous) to learn about where the issue is on the broad political agenda, how it is perceived,

ways to measure evaluation

and the likelihood of action. This evaluation approach can be used formatively so that an ongoing campaign can identify how its message is influencing key audiences and remedy gaps, or summatively, so that a completed project can learn how effective it was in spreading a message and increasing the profile of an issue. *Policymaker ratings* is a way of measuring decision makers' support on issues and can be conducted informally by the advocates themselves based on information they have collected through ongoing outreach and strategic follow-up (as discussed in Chapter 8, Step 5). A group of advocates independently assess a list of policy makers, using a specific rating scale identifying level of evidence (see Coffman & Reed, n.d., for scale) based on the following criteria: 1) policy maker level of support based on public behaviors and actions on the issue; 2) policy maker influence related to social position, knowledge, and reputation; and 3) the rater's level of confidence in the accuracy of ratings for the first two scales. The individual assessments are a starting point for a conversation to determine final ratings by group consensus, or the assessments can be pooled and averaged. This activity can be used to measure policy makers' positions on issues and how these change over time and can be repeated at various points of the campaign to inform outreach strategies. *Intense period debriefs* convene the team of advocates after a burst of intense activity occurs or a policy window opens (see description of policy windows in the section in Chapter 2, titled Timing and Strategic Considerations). An external evaluator conducts focus groups or individual interviews to discuss recent events and asks the advocates about 1) the context during the policy window, including public mood; 2) what happened within the campaign and how advocates responded to events; 3) perspectives on what was achieved or not achieved; and 4) how strategies might be adjusted in light of this experience. This form of evaluation provides real-time information and documents the behind-the-scenes story of the advocacy project. *Systems mapping* can be used by macro advocacy projects seeking systems change (see Chapter 2 for a definition of systems change) to visually diagram a system by identifying the parts and relationships expected to change, how they will change, and ways of measuring whether these changes have occurred. This process can be led by an external evaluator or the advocates themselves and is similar to the logic model approach described earlier but without assumptions of linear change and with greater emphasis on the complexity of relationships and components within a system. Development of a systems map can be informed by key stakeholder interviews or network analysis techniques that identify the nature and strength of relationships between individuals, groups, and institutions. This method can be used to clarify the expected process of change and guide data collection planning to document change (Coffman & Reed, n.d.).

Document your monitoring and evaluation in a user-friendly fashion. Rather than the stereotypical report that collects dust on a shelf, use your results to communicate dynamically with allies, champions, and funders as part of strategic follow-up (Step 5). Look for opportunities to disseminate your findings to a wide audience that includes the broader community. Sharing your findings "stimulates interest in further work; heartens those involved; impresses those being influenced; and forges new alliances" (Laney, 2003, p. 7). Ideally, monitoring and evaluation become part of a feedback loop that provides timely and relevant information to advocacy projects so that they can reconsider their strategies and become maximally effective.

Share findings from eval.

LEARNING FROM UNSUCCESSFUL ADVOCACY EFFORTS

There are times when even the best advocacy efforts go unrewarded. Failure to gain a decision maker's assistance or failure of that decision maker to gain support from those who can make change for children happens more often than not. However, there is certainly a critical mass of knowledge and skill that is built up through learning from the mistakes of past advocacy efforts. Advocacy is not for the faint of heart. As the watchword "I will not take no for an answer" (Chapter 2) suggests, the advocate must use willpower and resolve to keep moving forward. By examining unsuccessful efforts and reflecting on lessons learned, the advocate can prepare for future advocacy projects and better understand how to turn "nos" into "yeses."

After any advocacy campaign, even an unsuccessful one, take time to convene the people who have played an important role in the project. This can include the gatekeepers, decision makers, and fellow advocates. Rather than a pity party, have a party to celebrate new friends, new information gained, and new directions for future change. Bolster each other's spirits to encourage continued effort toward the desired change. Once you have brought the important players together, have a discussion about the advocacy approach and how it should be modified for the future. Just as if you had achieved the goal of the advocacy campaign, your project concludes by planning the next one. Engage in conversation about what went right or wrong. Your coalition can weigh in on whether to continue using the same basic approaches or make adjustments to your strategies that may promote success next time. If the failure you encountered involved not winning over a key decision maker, request a meeting with that person and ask how you might have approached things differently and possibly won support.

Advocates must be lifelong learners. Even a failure, when treated in the right manner, can constructively lead to a better, more well-coordinated and ultimately successful advocacy effort in the future. Willingness to maintain a commitment to make positive change for children and families is what, ultimately, will lead to the satisfaction of knowing that you, as a child advocate, have made a difference. The next section provides a case example of an unsuccessful effort to pass universal preschool in California and how advocates inside and outside that campaign have learned lessons from the experience that can be applied to other child advocacy efforts.

Case Study: Learning From an Unsuccessful Campaign for Universal Preschool in California

A coalition led by actor and film director Rob Reiner brought the issue of universal preschool before the voters of California in 2006 through Proposition 82, Preschool for All. The Preschool for All campaign submitted petitions with more than 1 million signatures, of which 716,000 were certified, far exceeding the 598,000 required to get on the ballot (Institute of Governmental Studies, 2006). The proposed legislation would have provided all 4-year-olds in the state with access to 1 year of free and voluntary part-day preschool. Services would have been offered for at least 3 hours a day, 180 days a year, with linkages (but not funding) to child care centers offering care for additional hours. Parents would have been offered a choice of programs with the requirements that preschools had to be available near students' homes and serve children with special needs, including non-English speakers. The program would have been administered by California's Superintendent of Public Instruction and implemented by County Offices of Education, which would select preschools (public or private) to provide the service. Providers would have had to meet certain requirements, including adherence to a statewide set of curriculum standards that would be designed to prepare children for academic content taught in kindergarten through third grades. Teachers in the Preschool for All program would, after a certain period of time, have been required to have a Bachelor's degree and receive a new early childhood credential. Full-time teachers (who taught the equivalent of two 3-hour sessions a day) would have been compensated at a rate similar to teachers in California's K–12 public education system. The program would have been funded through a 1.7% income tax increase for individuals making $400,000 a year or over or couples earning $800,000 a year or over, a funding source estimated to raise about $2 billion a year for a per-child program price of $6,000 per year (Legislative Analyst, 2006).

The groundwork for this advocacy campaign came earlier through the successful passage of Proposition 10, the California Children and Families Act, in 1998. As with Preschool for All, advocates including Reiner developed the initiative and collected the necessary signatures to put Proposition 10 on the California statewide ballot. This initiative created a new tobacco tax and dedicated the revenue to services for pregnant women, children under 5, and their families. Approximately $590 million is raised annually and doled out to counties proportional to their birthrate. County "Prop 10" or "First 5" Commissions develop strategic plans with community inputs and decide how to allocate funding. Funding is used for local health programs, early childhood education, and family support programs as well as public education on early childhood development and smoking cessation programs for pregnant women and parents of young children (First 5 California, n.d.). The initiative passed despite stiff opposition from the tobacco industry and survived a repeal attempt in 2000 through another ballot initiative (Bodenhorn & Kelch, 2001).

Building on this initial child advocacy success, a coalition formed to advance the issue of universal preschool in California. This coalition, led by Reiner, included labor organizations, business interests, advocacy groups, powerful politicians, and donors (Legislative Analyst, 2006). Groups like the California Police Chief's Association came out in favor of the policy and persuaded the Los Angeles and San Francisco chambers of commerce to support it as well, despite their typical antitax stance (Kirp & Stipek, 2006). The central message of the campaign was that preschool is essential for every child's future, so all children deserve access to high-quality early childhood education. A quotable quote from State Schools Chief Jack O'Connell expressed this by claiming universal preschool would be "the great equalizer" (Fuller, Bridges, & Pai, 2007, p. 185). Advocates supported their case by pointing to research from the Rand Corporation that suggested every dollar invested in preschool would save an estimated $2.62 of public spending through lower juvenile crime and high school drop-out rates (Karoly & Bigelow, 2005). They also highlighted the findings from other studies that showed children who complete high-quality preschool programs (with educated teachers) are more likely to read by third grade, graduate from high school, and go on to college. These points were made in public service television commercials sponsored by the Preschool for All campaign. In terms of the financing of the proposed policy, advocates made the argument that tax increases on the wealthiest state citizens would be the best way to pay for the program by establishing a new funding stream rather than relying on the state's overstretched general fund. They argued that the wealthy citizens affected by the tax increase wouldn't feel it, especially since it would be coming shortly after tax cuts by the federal government for this income bracket (Institute of Governmental Studies, 2006). The campaign ultimately raised and spent almost 4 times as much as the opposition with large donations from Hollywood celebrities and labor unions (Fuller, Bridges, & Pai, 2007).

The opposition to Proposition 82 included preschools (particularly Montessori preschools, represented by the California Montessori Council), church groups, taxpayer organizations, and a long list of other chambers of commerce (No on 82, 2006). They made several arguments against the proposition. One argument was that funding would subsidize families who already could and did pay for preschool and that the research advocates used to demonstrate the impact of early childhood education came from studies of poor children, not middle-class children. The Rand study, for example, based its findings regarding the return on preschool investments on the Chicago Child-Parent Centers (described in Chapter 2, Box 2.4) that served exclusively low-income African American children. Prominent decision maker and democratic leader of the state senate Don Perata withdrew his support, stating that the program "wouldn't improve access to those who need it most: poor, disadvantaged, and English learners" (Fuller, Bridges, & Pai, 2007, p. 176). Another argument stemmed from the plan for statewide standards, raising concerns that control of early childhood education would shift from parents and community preschools to government bureaucrats. Preschool directors and associations opposed the idea of having to align their classroom teaching to a single set of standards and feared the competition from providers offering a service for free if they did not participate (Fuller, Bridges, & Pai, 2007). Existing preschool providers also opposed the requirement that teachers have a bachelor's degree and be paid equivalent to K–12 teachers. They and other critics argued that the bachelor's requirement would homogenize the workforce, forcing bilingual and non-English-speaking providers out of the field, resulting in less culturally appropriate care for California's diverse child population (Jacobson, 2009). A public relations firm hired by the No on 82 campaign attempted to reframe the issue, not to be against universal preschool, but to say that this was not the right initiative at the right time. The counterarguments made three related points: 1) The state should fix K–12 education first, before turning to early childhood education; 2) The limited funds available for preschool should be used for a targeted program benefitting children in need, not all children; and 3) Proposition 82 would replace the current well-functioning preschool system with a bureaucracy modeled on the failing K–12 system (Bicker, Castillo, & Fairbanks Public Affairs Firm, 2006).

The opposition's messages began to gain traction as the Preschool for All campaign experienced a series of challenges and setbacks. First 5 California Commission, the statewide association of county commissions established by Proposition 10 and chaired by Rob Reiner, ran a series of ads about the benefits of preschool during the signature gathering process to get Proposition 82 qualified for the state ballot. This was perceived by many as using taxpayer funds to highlight ideas related to a voter initiative, a conflict of interest and ethical violation. First 5 California was also accused of having paid people working on the Preschool for All campaign, using public funds. Reiner resigned as chair of First 5 California in March, months before the vote on Proposition 82 on the June ballot (Institute of Governmental Studies, 2006). Governor Schwarzenegger came out against Proposition 82, arguing that the program would mostly benefit middle- and upper-class children already enrolled in preschool, and within a month of the vote, he proposed an alternative plan that would increase government funding for preschool programs serving low-income children. By a week before the election, 43 newspapers came out against the initiative, citing the opposition's points about lack of targeting to low-income children, bureaucratic takeover of community preschools, and other criticisms about the approach rather than the concept of preschool access. Voters rejected the proposition by a margin of 61% with exit interviews suggesting that moderates and democrats were represented among its detractors (Fuller, Bridges, & Pai, 2007).

While this campaign was unsuccessful, child advocates can learn many lessons from it regarding policy approaches, political interests of coalition members, and intermediate successes that may come with failure. Several critics have suggested the flaws of the campaign lay more with its strategy than its core purpose. The public has shown commitment to the concept of preschool, but the delivery is key. Though a universal approach promises broad access and thus a wider base of citizen support, the higher costs can bring up questions about providing benefits to those capable of paying for preschool (Rose, 2010). Another issue is the choice between a centralized state-run system run by experts and professionals versus a decentralized approach characterized by parental choice and community options. The Preschool for All campaign endorsed the former, which brings up concerns about standardizing curriculum, learning, and testing. This strategy was related to the players in the Preschool for All coalition, including K–12 educators interested in a policy approach that could relieve the pressure to raise test scores and labor unions interested in expanding their membership (and thereby membership revenue and political clout) to publicly employed preschool teachers (Fuller, Bridges, & Pai, 2007).

While the ultimate goal of the campaign was not achieved, it nevertheless resulted in positive changes. For example, the California Federation of Teachers (2006) *Early Educator* newsletter noted that the campaign created closer linkages among the individuals and organizations that backed the initiative, offered chances for organizations like the Federation of Teachers to get members appointed and elected to boards and commissions that draft early childhood education policy, and provided opportunities for advocates to become trained and experienced spokespeople on behalf of quality preschool education. The campaign also resulted in greater public awareness of the importance of preschool.

Despite the defeat, advocates for universal preschool in California are undeterred, and the campaign continues in a different form with a different strategy. Advocates working through organizations like Early Edge California (formerly Preschool California) continue to work with the legislature, though they have expressed reservations about attempting another state ballot initiative (DeFao, 2006). The Packard Foundation has remained a strong financial backer, spending more than $45 million in grants to support activities to promote education, advocacy, and outreach to political leaders and key constituents; research and policy proposals that make the case for expanding access to quality preschool; and community and systems building through model preschool programs in geopolitically significant areas (see Box 9.4 for a visual depiction of the Preschool for California's Children Strategy). A study by Harvard Family Research Project (2008) found the Foundation's work helped to sustain the momentum of the Proposition 82 campaign and has resulted in gains such as an increased number of key decision makers championing the issue.

BOX 9.4

Visual Depiction of the
Preschool for California's Children Strategy

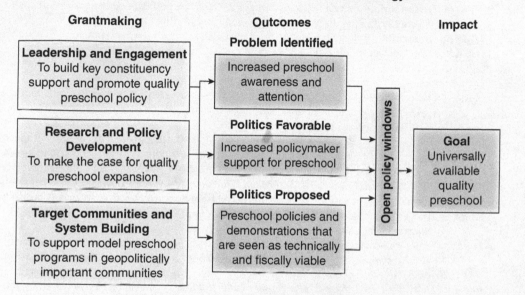

Source: Harvard Family Research Project (2008, September). Preschool for California's Children: Summary of 2003–2008 Evaluation Findings. Retrieved from http://www.packard.org/wp-content/uploads/2011/03/Preschool_Evaluation.pdf

Activity: Reinforcing a Successful Advocacy Outcome

How can you reinforce the advocacy outcome that you have achieved or hope to achieve? Consider your key stakeholders, including your allies and important gatekeepers and decision makers. How can you celebrate the efforts of your fellow advocates? How can you recognize the support of gatekeepers and decision makers who may have helped you achieve this success? Do a quick write where you spend 5 minutes brainstorming a list of possible events and activities to reinforce and celebrate a successful advocacy outcome.

REFERENCES

Baumgartner, F. R., & Leech, B. L. (1998). *Basic interests: The importance of groups in politics and in political science.* Princeton, NJ: Princeton University.

Bicker, Castillo, & Fairbanks Public Affairs Firm (2006). *No on Proposition 82–universal preschool initiative.* Retrieved from http://www.bcfpublicaffairs.com/page/case-studies/8&ajax=9

Bodenhorn, K. A., & Kelch, D. R. (2001). Implementation of California's Children and Families First Act of 1998. *The Future of Children, 11*(1) 151–157.

BOND (n.d.). Monitoring and evaluating advocacy. *BOND Guidance Notes Series 6.* Retrieved from http://www.innonet.org/client_docs/File/advocacy/bond_monitoring.htm

California Federation of Teachers (2006, July). *Early educator.* Retrieved from http://www.cft.org/uploads/ec/docs/ecenljuly2006.pdf

Coffman, J., & Reed, E. (n.d.). *Unique methods in advocacy evaluation.* Retrieved from http://www.innonet.org/resources/files/Unique_Methods_Brief.pdf

DeFao, J. (2006, June 8). Proposition 82/Preschool supporters aren't giving up on their quest. *San Francisco Chronicle.* Retrieved from http://www.sfgate.com/politics/article/PROPOSITION-82-Preschool-supporters-aren-t-2517638.php

DeVita, C. J., Montilla, M., Reid, B., & Fatiregun, O. (2004). *Organizational factors influencing advocacy for children.* Washington, DC: Center on Nonprofits and Philanthropy, The Urban Institute. Retrieved from http://www.urban.org/uploadedPDF/410993_Advocacy_for_Children.pdf

Fine, A. (2006). *Momentum: Igniting social change in the connected age.* San Francisco, CA: Jossey-Bass.

First 5 California (n.d.). *Proposition 10 Facts.* Retrieved from http://www.ccfc.ca.gov/press/prop.asp

Fuller, B., Bridges, M., & Pai, S. (2007). *Standardized childhood: The political and cultural struggle over early education.* Palo Alto, CA: Stanford University Press.

Harvard Family Research Project (2008, September). *Preschool for California's children: Summary of 2003–2008 evaluation findings.* Retrieved from http://www.packard.org/wp-content/uploads/2011/03/Preschool_Evaluation.pdf

Harvard Family Research Project (2009). *A user's guide to advocacy evaluation planning.* Retrieved from http://www.hfrp.org/evaluation/publications-resources/a-user-s-guide-to-advocacy-evaluation-planning

Hoefer, R. (2011). *Advocacy practice for social justice* (2nd ed.). Chicago, IL: Lyceum Books.

Institute of Governmental Studies (2006). *Proposition 82.* Retrieved from http://igs.berkeley.edu/library/elections/proposition-82

Jacobson, L. (2009, October). *On the cusp in California: How preK–3rd strategies could improve education in the Golden State.* New York, NY: New America Foundation. Retrieved from http://www.newamerica.net/files/On_The_Cusp_in_CA.pdf

Karoly, L. A., & Bigelow, J. H. (2005). *The economics of investing in universal preschool education in California.* Santa Monica, CA: The RAND Corporation. Retrieved from http://www.rand.org/content/dam/rand/pubs/monographs/2005/RAND_MG349.pdf

Kirp, D. L., & Stipek, D. (2006, June 1). On Proposition 82's call for universal preschool: Should the state educate 4-year-olds? PRO: Preschool is a smart investment. *San Francisco Chronicle.* Retrieved from http://www.sfgate.com/opinion/openforum/article/On-Proposition-82-s-call-for-universal-preschool-2517588.php

Laney, M. L. (2003). *Advocacy impact assessment guidelines.* Retrieved from http://www.innonet.org/resources/files/Advocacy_Impact_Assessment_Guidelines.pdf

Legislative Analyst (2006). *Analysis by the legislative analyst, Proposition 82.* Retrieved from http://primary2006.sos.ca.gov/voterguide/props/prop82/prop82_analysis.htm

M+R Strategic Services & Nonprofit Technology Network (2013). *2013 eNonprofit benchmarks study: An analysis of online messaging, fundraising, advocacy, social media, and mobile metrics for non-profit organizations.* Retrieved from http://www.e-benchmarksstudy.com/

No on 82 (2006). *We oppose Prop. 82: Coalition list as of 5/22/06.* Retrieved from http://digital.library.ucla.edu/websites/2006_997_165/pdf/coalition.pdf

O'Flynn, M. (2009, October). *Tracking progress in advocacy: Why and how to monitor and evaluate advocacy projects and programmes.* M&E Paper 4. International NGO Training and Research Centre. Retrieved from http://www.stoptb.org/assets/documents/global/awards/cfcs/Tracking-Progress-in-Advocacy-Why-and-How-to-Monitor-and-Evaluate-Advocacy-Projects-and-Programmes.pdf

Rose, E. (2010). *The promise of preschool: From Head Start to universal pre-kindergarten.* New York, NY: Oxford University Press.

Teles, S., & Schmitt, M. (2011, Summer). The elusive craft of evaluating advocacy. *Stanford Social Innovation Review.* Retrieved from http://www.ssireview.org/articles/entry/the_elusive_craft_of_evaluating_advocacy/

Whelan, J. (2008). *Advocacy evaluation: Review and opportunities.* Retrieved from http://www.innonet.org/resources/files/Whelan_Advocacy_Evaluation.pdf

CHAPTER 10

Where Do We Go From Here?

Child advocates do not stop at a single success—there is a lifetime of children's issues to champion. Once individuals that care about children get the advocacy bug, they are likely to remain active. This chapter considers how to sustain inspiration and develop a lifelong commitment to being an advocate for children. A case study on the World Forum for Early Care and Education provides an example of how a group of passionate advocates for children came together to start a worldwide movement for early childhood care and education. Readers are urged to explore child advocacy organizations that could be potential partners in an activity.

BECOMING A CHILD ADVOCATE FOR LIFE

What is your vision for children? Find a comfortable position, close your eyes, and relax so that you can imagine a new world that is fit for all children as you contemplate the following questions. What does the world, your country, and your community look like? What are children doing in this world? What do their environments look like? How do other children, parents, teachers, neighbors, and government officials treat them? How are their views responded to? Dream about this world and what it looks like and feels like. Take a moment to write out a description of this vision. How does it differ from current reality? What would be your three main priorities to create change in order to realize this vision?

World leaders, advocates for children, and children themselves also had a visioning process for children at the 2002 United Nations Special Session on Children. At the conclusion of this special session, 180 nations adopted its outcome document, "A World Fit for Children," as an agenda for the next decade. This document expressed commitment to change policy and dedicate new resources to promote healthy lives; provide quality education for all; protect children against abuse, exploitation, and violence; and combat HIV/AIDS (United Nations Children's Fund, 2002). Child delegates at the special session created a statement called "A World Fit for Us" (see Box 10.1). While not all of the intended goals were met over the last decade, the outcome document is nevertheless inspirational. As child advocates, we need a vision to guide our work. Let your vision for children continue to inspire your ongoing efforts to become a child advocate not just for one project, but for life.

BOX 10.1

A World Fit for Us

We are the world's children.

> We are the victims of exploitation and abuse.
>
> We are street children.
>
> We are the children of war.
>
> We are the victims and orphans of HIV/AIDS.
>
> We are denied good-quality education and health care.
>
> We are victims of political, economic, cultural, religious and environmental discrimination.
>
> We are children whose voices are not being heard: it is time we are taken into account.
>
> We want a world fit for children, because a world fit for us is a world fit for everyone.

In this world,

We see respect for the rights of the child:

- governments and adults having a real and effective commitment to the principle of children's rights and applying the Convention on the Rights of the Child to all children,
- safe, secure and healthy environments for children in families, communities, and nations.

We see an end to exploitation, abuse and violence:

- laws that protect children from exploitation and abuse being implemented and respected by all,
- centres and programmes that help to rebuild the lives of victimized children.

We see an end to war:

- world leaders resolving conflict through peaceful dialogue instead of by using force,
- child refugees and child victims of war protected in every way and having the same opportunities as all other children,
- disarmament, elimination of the arms trade and an end to the use of child soldiers.

We see the provision of health care:

- affordable and accessible life-saving drugs and treatment for all children,
- strong and accountable partnerships established among all to promote better health for children.

(Continued)

(Continued)

We see the eradication of HIV/AIDS:

- educational systems that include HIV prevention programmes,
- free testing and counselling centres,
- information about HIV/AIDS freely available to the public,
- orphans of AIDS and children living with HIV/AIDS cared for and enjoying the same opportunities as all other children.

We see the protection of the environment:

- conservation and rescue of natural resources,
- awareness of the need to live in environments that are healthy and favourable to our development,
- accessible surroundings for children with special needs.

We see an end to the vicious cycle of poverty:

- anti-poverty committees that bring about transparency in expenditure and give attention to the needs of all children,
- cancellation of the debt that impedes progress for children.

We see the provision of education:

- equal opportunities and access to quality education that is free and compulsory,
- school environments in which children feel happy about learning,
- education for life that goes beyond the academic and includes lessons in understanding, human rights, peace, acceptance and active citizenship.

We see the active participation of children:

- raised awareness and respect among people of all ages about every child's right to full and meaningful participation, in the spirit of the Convention on the Rights of the Child,
- children actively involved in decision-making at all levels and in planning, implementing, monitoring and evaluating all matters affecting the rights of the child.

We pledge an equal partnership in this fight for children's rights. And while we promise to support the actions you take on behalf of children, we also ask for your commitment and support in the actions we are taking—because the children of the world are misunderstood.

We are not the sources of problems; we are the resources that are needed to solve them.

We are not expenses; we are investments.

We are not just young people; we are people and citizens of this world.

Until others accept their responsibility to us, we will fight for our rights.

We have the will, the knowledge, the sensitivity and the dedication.

We promise that as adults we will defend children's rights with the same passion that we have now as children.

We promise to treat each other with dignity and respect.

We promise to be open and sensitive to our differences.

We are the children of the world, and despite our different backgrounds, we share a common reality.

We are united by our struggle to make the world a better place for all.

You call us the future, but we are also the present.

Source: United Nations Children's Fund (2002). *A world fit for children.* Retrieved from http://www.unicef.org/publications/files/A_World_Fit_Children.pdf

What would a lifetime of advocacy entail for you? Try another visioning exercise. Project yourself into the future, to the age of 90. Imagine that you are looking back over a rich and active life as a child advocate. What would be the focus of your advocacy? What would you have achieved during that time? Write a short bio of your many accomplishments. It is not easy to keep a lifelong commitment, which is why it can be helpful to actively take a vow and make a binding promise, much like a marriage vow. You are invited to take the pledge for children (see Box 10.2). Being a lifelong advocate for children is about making a constant commitment to champion children at the micro, mezzo, and macro levels as you observe their needs for advocacy. Taking a pledge can help cement this commitment as part of your identity.

BOX 10.2

A Pledge for Children

Because I acknowledge that

- all children are equally deserving of care and protection
- all children should be put first among government priorities
- all children should be cared for and kept safe
- all children should have access to medical care for prevention and treatment
- all children should be protected from violence and exploitation
- all children should be listened to and have their views taken into account
- all children deserve education
- all children should be protected from war

(Continued)

(Continued)

– all children should be protected from the disastrous consequences of extreme environmental change (e.g., drought, floods, and pollution)

– all children should have the financial and other resources they need to thrive

I [NAME] pledge to become a champion for children.

How can you keep the fire of your inspiration (as described in Chapter 1) burning and avoid letting it become burned out? Successful advocacy begins with a well-rested advocate. The general best practices of self-care apply to advocates. These include balancing your work and life, making time for personal relationships, taking good physical care of yourself through proper nutrition and exercise, and having some spiritual practice (religious or otherwise) that helps you connect with what is meaningful. It is important to actively set boundaries so that commitment to a cause does not overwhelm your life. Advocates who are constantly serving others can suffer from compassion fatigue as they deplete their reserves and lose their passion for creating change for children. As an inspirational statement paraphrased from Mother Teresa reminds us, "To keep the lamp burning, we have to keep putting oil in it" (Mother Teresa Center, 2010).

One way to sustain inspiration and avoid burnout is to keep a journal on your child advocacy activities. Through journaling, the writer records, examines, and learns from experience (Stevens & Cooper, 2009). This can give you a chance to contemplate your work, reflect on your own personal growth, and even bring a sense of humor to your challenges and setbacks. The process of writing can also help to unlock creativity by allowing for spontaneity and encouraging insight. Ultimately, journal writing can promote self-understanding by providing an opportunity to observe patterns in thinking and changes over time. This can promote reflective practice, a process of *reflection-on-action* that builds a habit of *reflection-in-action*, resulting in a skilled expertise that grows over time as understanding of the work becomes tacit, spontaneous, and automatic (Schön, 1983). See Box 10.3 for some methods of structuring a reflective journal.

BOX 10.3

Three Formats for Reflective Journal Writing

Head/Heart/Hands

Source: Welch, M. (1999). The ABCs of reflection: A template for students and instructors to implement written reflection in service-learning. *National Society of Experiential Education Quarterly, 25*(2), 1, 23–25.

a. HEAD: What have I learned intellectually from my experience?

b. HEART: What have I learned about myself emotionally?

c. HANDS: What have I learned about helping others? About the needs of my community? About the needs of my world? How does my learning inform my actions?

Three-Part Journal

Source: Bringle, R. G., & Hatcher, J. A. (1999). Reflection in service learning: Making meaning of experience. *Educational Horizons, 77,* 179–185.

a. DESCRIPTION: A narrative of events, experiences, situations, interactions, problems encountered, thoughts, and feelings.

b. ANALYSIS: How does the experience relate to your personal life (e.g., values, attitudes, philosophy) and the goals of your advocacy effort?

c. APPLICATION: What have you learned from the experience that you can use to act differently next time?

What? So What? Now What?

Source: Eyler, J., Giles, D. E., & Schmiede, A. (1996). *A practitioner's guide to reflection in service-learning: Student voices and reflections.* Nashville, TN: Vanderbilt University.

a. WHAT? Asks where have you been, what did you do, what happened, what did you experience, who else was involved, and what were the reactions and feelings brought up by the experience.

b. SO WHAT? Asks about the meaning and impact of the experience in terms of how it has changed you and how it has changed others.

c. NOW WHAT? Asks you to look to the future and consider where you go from here; what you do now; how this experience moves you toward your vision for the future; and what knowledge, resources, or skills you will need to move to the next step.

Another way to keep going is to find a community of fellow advocates. This can give you a sense of common purpose. Alone you can accomplish something, but with others, you can multiply your impact. In addition, a community can provide essential emotional support. These interactions provide a chance to share stories, reminisce about why you started this work in the first place, and reflect on your personal growth. The relationships you build can also make your work more rewarding (Loeb, 2010). As an advocate at the micro level, for a specific child, you can find support through ties with other advocates, such as support groups for parents of children with special needs. At the mezzo and macro levels, you can work with like-minded individuals and organizations to advance a shared cause. As Paul Loeb (2010) points out, "Working for social change in solitude is a contradiction in terms" (p. 312).

While we all have a role in changing the world for children, this need does not rest on the shoulders of any one individual. Advocates can feel burdened by a sense that they must do everything and fight every battle. But your cause would be better served by building local and national coalitions to create large-scale social change. The case study that follows describes the process of creating a worldwide community called the World Forum for Early Care and Education. The activity that follows encourages you to explore the websites of prominent child advocacy organizations to learn about how these organizations do their work and how you could partner with these organizations as a volunteer or through a coalition of organizations working for the same cause.

Case Study: How the World Forum on Early Care and Education Was Developed

By Bonnie and Roger Neugebauer, Founders,
World Forum on Early Care and Education (United States)

In 1998, at a meeting in a pub in Sydney, Australia, leaders of *Exchange Magazine* in the United States and Pademelon Press in Australia came up with the idea of the World Forum on Early Care and Education. The idea grew from our mutual conviction that the children of the world would benefit if early childhood professionals around the world shared perspectives, exchanged stories about their lives, and developed ongoing relationships.

Step one in accomplishing this vision was to send out our message far and wide. We contacted everyone we knew who did work in early care and education on a global basis. These connectors put us in touch with key leaders in nations on every continent. We then recruited these gatekeepers to spread the word in the early childhood communities in their countries about the World Forum. In May of 1999, over 500 early childhood professionals from 30 nations responding to this outreach gathered in Honolulu, Hawaii, to share their stories at the first ever World Forum on Early Care and Education.

Since that auspicious conversation in Sydney, over 4,000 individuals from nearly 100 nations have participated in activities of the World Forum Foundation. Our informal group of gatekeepers has evolved into a team of 90 national representatives who are the eyes, ears, and voices of the World Forum in their countries. In retrospect, what has made individuals around the world so willing to help build this community is that we were offering the opportunity to build connections with peers around the world—not selling a product, a philosophy, or a formula for success. People have resonated with this vision.

A gratifying endorsement of our success in creating a global early childhood community came recently from Maysoun Chehab, a World Forum community member from Lebanon, who said, "The World Forum is like one big family and each one of us is a part of that family" (Personal communication, June 15, 2013).

Activity: Explore Child Advocacy Organizations' Websites

The list that follows provides examples of prominent child advocacy organizations throughout the world. Explore the websites of these organizations to learn more about their missions and activities and how you might be able to partner with these organizations as a volunteer, or team up with the organizations as part of a coalition of organizations dedicated to the same cause. In addition to this list, conduct your own search for child advocacy organizations that relate to your topic of interest and geographical location.

The authors invite readers to connect with the International Child Resource Institute (ICRI) and its worldwide network of child advocates. You can share stories about your advocacy projects, pass on information useful for advocacy, ask questions of fellow advocates, and request trainings by the authors on the six steps. Visit www.icrichild.org and look for the advocacy tab, like ICRI on Facebook, join the ICRI group on LinkedIn, or send an email to info@icrichild.org. We welcome you as fellow advocates in the global quest to improve conditions for children, youth, and families!

Name of Organization	Mission Statement	Website
Children's Defense Fund	"The Children's Defense Fund Leave No Child Behind® mission is to ensure every child a *Healthy Start*, a *Head Start*, a *Fair Start*, a *Safe Start* and a *Moral Start* in life and successful passage to adulthood with the help of caring families and communities. CDF provides a strong, effective and independent voice for all the children of America who cannot vote, lobby or speak for themselves. We pay particular attention to the needs of poor and minority children and those with disabilities. CDF educates the nation about the needs of children and encourages preventive investments before they get sick, drop out of school, get into trouble or suffer family breakdown."	http://www.childrensdefense.org
Children Now	"Children Now's mission is to find common ground among influential opinion leaders, interest groups and policymakers, who together can develop and drive socially innovative, "win-win" approaches to helping all children achieve their full potential."	http://www.childrennow.org
Fight Crime, Invest in Kids	"Fight Crime: Invest in Kids takes a hard-nosed look at crime prevention strategies, informs the public and policymakers about those findings, and urges investment in programs proven effective by research. Our organization focuses on high quality early education programs, prevention of child abuse and neglect, after-school programs for children and teens, and interventions to get troubled kids back on track."	http://www.fightcrime.org

(Continued)

(Continued)

Name of Organization	Mission Statement	Website
International Child Resource Institute (ICRI)	"ICRI works to improve the lives of children and families around the world. We focus on early childhood care and education, children's rights, empowerment of women and girls, maternal/child health, and grassroots community development. ICRI's credo is "we only go where we are invited," and all of our programs advance local leadership and promote community collaboration. Since ICRI was founded in 1981, we have developed or operated over 300 programs in over 50 countries, all with the goal of empowering the village to raise the child."	www.icrichild.org
ICRI regional offices	• ICRI Africa (Kenya) • ICRI Ghana • Child Resource Institute Zimbabwe • ICRI Nepal • ICRI India • Malaysian Child Resource Institute (MCRI) • ICRI Chile • ICRI Europe (Sweden)	Overview: www .icrichild.org ICRI Africa: http:// icriafrica.org/ Malaysian Child Resource Institute: http://www.mcri .org.my/ ICRI Nepal: http:// icrinepal.org/
National Court Appointed Special Advocate Association (CASA)	"The mission of the National Court Appointed Special Advocate (CASA) Association, together with its state and local members, is to support and promote court-appointed volunteer advocacy so that every abused or neglected child can be safe, establish permanence and have the opportunity to thrive."	http://www .casaforchildren.org
Jane Goodall's Roots & Shoots	The mission of Roots and Shoots is "to foster respect and compassion for all living things, to promote understanding of all cultures and beliefs and to inspire each individual to take action to make the world a better place for people, animals and the environment. Our goals are global: • To implement positive change through active learning about, caring for and interacting with the environment	http:// rootsandshoots.org

Name of Organization	Mission Statement	Website
	• To demonstrate care and concern for all animals • To enhance understanding among individuals of different cultures, ethnic groups, religions, socio-economic levels and nations through our global communications network • To help young people develop self-respect, confidence in themselves and hope for the future Our philosophy is based on the belief that every individual matters, every individual has a role to play and every individual makes a difference. This core idea is at the root of Dr. Jane Goodall's philosophy."	
Save the Children	"Save the Children's mission is to inspire breakthroughs in the way the world treats children and to achieve immediate and lasting change in their lives. Our 2013–2015 strategic plan, Investing in Impact for Children, builds upon our historic foundation of serving children for nearly one hundred years as we invest in innovation to achieve real results for children now and in the future."	http://www.savethechildren.org
United Nations Children's Fund (UNICEF)	"UNICEF is mandated by the United Nations General Assembly to advocate for the protection of children's rights, to help meet their basic needs and to expand their opportunities to reach their full potential. UNICEF is guided by the Convention on the Rights of the Child and strives to establish children's rights as enduring ethical principles and international standards of behavior towards children. UNICEF insists that the survival, protection and development of children are universal development imperatives that are integral to human progress. UNICEF mobilizes political will and material resources to help countries, particularly developing countries, ensure a "first call for children" and to build their capacity to form appropriate policies and deliver services for children and their families.".	http://www.unicef.org

(Continued)

(Continued)

Name of Organization	Mission Statement	Website
Voices for America's Children	"Voices for America's Children is the nation's largest network of multi-issue child advocacy organizations. Our nonprofit, nonpartisan network spans almost every state, the District of Columbia and the U.S. Virgin Islands. We lead advocacy efforts at the community, state and federal levels to improve the lives of all children, especially those most vulnerable, and their families."	http://www.voices.org
World Forum Foundation	"The mission of the World Forum Foundation is to promote an on-going global exchange of ideas on the delivery of quality services for young children in diverse settings. This mission is accomplished through convening gatherings of early childhood professionals around the world and by promoting the continuing exchange of ideas among participants."	http://worldforum foundation.org

REFERENCES

Bringle, R. G., & Hatcher, J. A. (1999). Reflection in service learning: Making meaning of experience. *Educational Horizons, 77*, 179–185.

Eyler, J., Giles, D. E., & Schmiede, A. (1996). *A practitioner's guide to reflection in service-learning: Student voices and reflections.* Nashville, TN: Vanderbilt University.

Loeb, P. R. (2010). *Soul of a citizen: Living with conviction in challenging times.* New York, NY: St. Martin's Griffin.

Mother Teresa Center (2010). *The following quotes are significantly paraphrased versions or personal interpretations of statements Mother Teresa made; they are not her authentic words.* Retrieved from http://www.motherteresa.org/08_info/Quotesf.html#2

Schön, D. (1983). *The reflective practitioner: How professionals think in action.* London, UK: Temple Smith.

Stevens, D. D., & Cooper, J. E. (2009). *Journal keeping: How to use reflective writing for effective learning, teaching, professional insight, and positive change.* Sterling, VA: Stylus.

United Nations Children's Fund (2002). *A world fit for children.* Retrieved from http://www.unicef.org/publications/files/A_World_Fit_Children.pdf

Welch, M. (1999). The ABCs of reflection: A template for students and instructors to implement written reflection in service-learning. *National Society of Experiential Education Quarterly, 25*(2), 1, 23–25.

Index

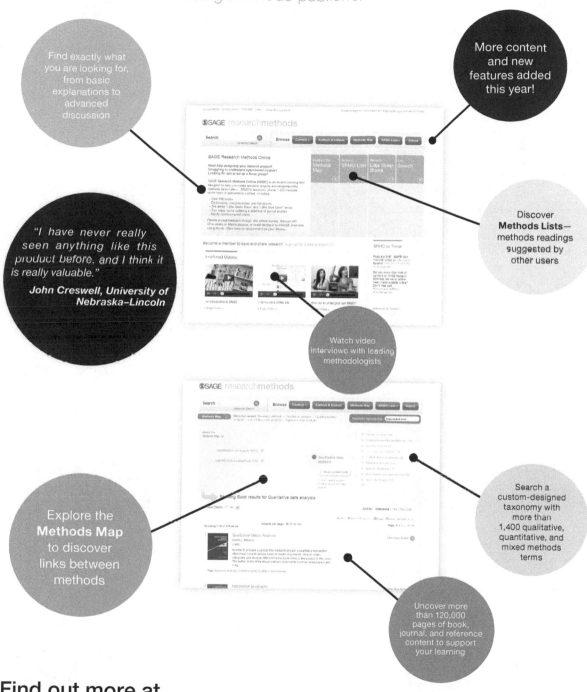

SAGE researchmethods

The essential online tool for researchers from the world's leading methods publisher

Find exactly what you are looking for, from basic explanations to advanced discussion

More content and new features added this year!

"I have never really seen anything like this product before, and I think it is really valuable."

John Creswell, University of Nebraska–Lincoln

Discover **Methods Lists**— methods readings suggested by other users

Watch video interviews with leading methodologists

Explore the **Methods Map** to discover links between methods

Search a custom-designed taxonomy with more than 1,400 qualitative, quantitative, and mixed methods terms

Uncover more than 120,000 pages of book, journal, and reference content to support your learning

Find out more at
www.sageresearchmethods.com

CPSIA information can be obtained
at www.ICGtesting.com
Printed in the USA
FFHW011620250119
50278448-55319FF